SURVIVE

STORIES OF CASTAWAYS
AND CANNIBALS

SURVIVE

STORIES OF CASTAWAYS AND CANNIBALS

EDITED BY NATE HARDCASTLE
ADRENALINE SERIES EDITOR CLINT WILLIS

Thunder's Mouth Press
New York

SURVIVE: STORIES OF CASTAWAYS AND CANNIBALS

Compilation copyright © 2001 by Clint Willis
Introductions copyright © 2001 by Nate Hardcastle

Adrenaline ® and the Adrenaline® logo are trademarks of
Avalon Publishing Group Incorporated, New York, NY.

An Adrenaline Book®

Published by
Thunder's Mouth Press
An Imprint of Avalon Publishing Group Incorporated
161 William Street, 16th floor
New York, NY 10038

A Balliett & Fitzgerald book

Book design: Sue Canavan

frontispiece photo: Survivors of Shipwreck at Sea in a Life Boat, Copyright
© 2001 Corbis

Library of Congress Control Number: 2001097339

ISBN: 1-56025-367-3

9 8 7 6 5 4 3 2 1

Printed in the United States of America
Distributed by Publishers Group West

For my parents.

contents

p h o t o g r a p h s

introduction

Most of us in the world's developed countries can get the things we really need—water, food, shelter. That's a good thing: Freedom from suffering is an end in itself.

That said, our lives sometimes seem to lack something comfort can't provide. Painter Tobias Schneebaum left a comfortable life in New York City for the Peruvian Amazon, where he joyfully endured days of wet tramping through the jungle in search of a tribe of people he thought might kill and eat him. He found the tribe and something more:

> I have become what I have always been and it has taken a life-
> time, all of my own life, to reach this point where it is as if I
> know finally that I am alive and that I am here, right now.

Many of the characters in this book are trying simply to stay alive. They don't have time to worry about the concerns that preoccupy most of us: power, achievement, sex. The very constraints of their circumstances create space that is necessary for some kinds of clarity.

Steven Callahan survived a 76-day odyssey across the Atlantic in a five-and-a-half-foot lifeboat, fighting off starvation by catching fish with a makeshift speargun. The ordeal was torturous, but also intensely spiritual. Here he is just after being rescued:

> . . . Sometimes the fabric of life is woven into such a fantastic pattern. I needed a miracle and my fish gave it to me. That and more. They've shown me that miracles swim and fly and walk, rain down and roll away all around me. I look around at life's magnificent arena . . . I have never felt so humble, nor so peaceful, free, and at ease.

Epiphanies like Callahan's aren't easy to reach. Survival stories are horrible more often then they are beautiful.

Cannibalism occurs in twelve of this book's sixteen selections. We find the idea of eating people revolting. Yet like most taboos it's also interesting; we're curious about it. We satisfy our curiosity by reading stories and imagining ourselves into them, wondering what we'd do.

We usually keep thoughts of cannibalism at a distance by laughing about them or by reminding ourselves that a particular story happened long ago or ended happily for the survivors. Some people maintain that distance by denying that cannibalism happens. Scholars and earlier readers have publicly questioned the veracity of six of this book's nine purportedly non-fiction selections featuring cannabalism.

The doubts seem justified in some cases: Pierre Viaud's 18th-century story about cannibalism after a shipwreck should be taken with a grain of salt (so to speak). Some of his assertions don't make much sense. Historians think his publisher took liberties with the text to boost sales—common practice in the eighteenth-century publishing business. Likewise, scholars have argued convincingly that Herman Melville's description of man-eaters in *Typee* is at least partly fiction. Then again, Tobias Schneebaum's account of eating a piece of a human heart rings curiously true—though it's impossible to say if the truth of his account is emotional or literal.

These stories are full of suffering. Louise Longo went sailing with her ex-husband, hoping to reconcile with him; a storm forced them into a lifeboat and he died soon afterward—and then things got much worse. Ernest Shackleton's support team in Antarctica in 1915 endured extreme hunger and brutal cold laying supplies for a leader who never came; three men died. The men, women and children of the Donner Party, snowbound in the Sierra Nevada mountains during the winter of 1846 and 1847, and the rugby players whose plane crashed in the Andes more than a century later mostly died or survived by eating their dead.

Such suffering may be hard to read about, but it engages us, offering glimpses of something essential. When the most basic needs become paramount, some people can achieve a kind of clarity. This clarity in turn can lead to acts of compassion and genuine courage.

Most of the accounts in this book exist because people endured their miserable circumstances: They survived. Their stories testify to human beings' ingenuity and strength in the face of pain or the prospect of death. Survivors like sailor Steven Callahan or rugby player Roberto Canessa or pioneer James Reed or Antarctic explorer Ernest Joyce have something to teach us. If nothing else, they remind me that while suffering is part of life, so is deliverance.

—*Nate Hardcastle*

from The Unknown Shore
by Patrick O'Brian

This passage from an early Patrick O'Brian (1914–2000) novel finds the crew of the Wager *shipwrecked off southern Chile. A native (a "cacique") who agrees to lead them to Spanish settlements soon departs to hunt seals, leaving his slave Manuel and promising to return. Six disgruntled seamen steal Manuel and the crew's barge, stranding Toby Barrow, Jack Byron and the rest of the crew.*

O n the other hand," said Tobias, "it is a comfort to reflect that we have nothing left to lose—that we are in the lowest possible condition—that nothing can be worse."

"No doubt," said Jack uneasily, "what you say is very moral, Toby, and uncommon philosophic; but I wish you would not make such damned unlucky remarks. I can think of half a dozen ways in which we could be worse off."

They were sitting in the lee of a rock, watching the great waves break upon the beach: their thunder made the whole air tremble, and the shattered spindrift wafted from the sea like smoke, for although the wind was quiet now the heavy swell that had set in from the west on the day the barge had gone was still running high, and the canoe far out at sea could only be seen at rare intervals.

"He will be making for the cove beyond the potatoes," said Jack, referring to the returning cacique. "The reef will protect him there. You may say what you please," he added, although Tobias had not spoken, "but that fellow is a wonderful seaman. He is a horrible creature—have never seen a nastier—but he does amazing things at sea."

"It will be difficult to explain everything to him. It will be harder still to persuade him to serve us. I wish I had paid more attention . . ." Tobias broke off, and mentally rehearsed the more-or-less Spanish phrases that he had composed for the occasion. His head was often light, now that they were hungry all day long with an extreme and painful hunger, even after they had eaten, and he could not always succeed in keeping the Spanish from turning into Latin. It was difficult to collect his ideas and it would be difficult to convey them, as well as dangerous.

His forebodings were justified. The cacique was convinced that they had murdered Manuel: he grew false and foxy, agreed to everything, spoke civilly and nodded and smirked, all with the sole idea of getting away, safe out of their hands. Like most stupid men, he was barely capable of listening and he had little idea of what had happened until, by a very pretty stroke of luck, Manuel himself walked in, in the middle of a tedious, futile negotiation. He had left the barge the first time it touched land, and in the intervening days he had walked back along the coast: he was born to the country, but the journey had marked him sore.

His arrival changed the face of things. It fortunately happened that the cacique numbered the most eager covetousness among his vices, and his eyes had often dwelt upon Jack's fowling-piece, a handsome weapon, silver-mounted and damascened: no Indian of his tribe had ever owned one, nor was there a single firearm among the infinitely superior settled Indians of Chiloe, to the north. For this and a few other things that they still had about them he undertook to conduct them as before. But, he said, after a pause, his canoe would not hold them all.

Tobias fell silent: the last time that he had heard this expression, the last time he had thought there is not room for all, was very strong in his mind. He leant his forehead on his hand; but after a moment he was forced from his thought of Marine Bay by the shouting of the cacique, furious that the interpretation should have stopped.

"What does he say?" cried Captain Cheap, shaking him by the shoulder.

Tobias listened again, and replied, "He says that it will be necessary to go two days' journey. There are some other Indians: they have more canoes and will take us all. He says that you and Mr Byron should go with him. He will leave his wife. The Indians will come here, and then everybody will go north together. He says that the canoes will be carried over the land, but when or how I do not understand."

Jack was used to most sea-going operations by this time, but paddling a canoe was new to him and he did not do it very well: he did not even paddle as well as a woman, and this increased the cacique's angry contempt for him. For the first few hours the Indian shrieked at him every few minutes, and throughout the day he threw handfuls of water at the back of Jack's head; and Jack, concentrating on the way he was to dig his paddle into the sea, murmured, "If I had you to myself for ten minutes with a rope's end, my friend . . ." He thought of the paddle as something he was thrusting into the cacique's vitals, and the canoe went along fast, if not gracefully.

Captain Cheap sat in the middle, by the pot of fire. His shoulder would have made him useless as a rower even if he had not had such notions of what was due to his rank, but the cacique did not resent this: he was impressed by what some would call the captain's unbelievable and monstrous selfishness, and favoured it. There seemed to be some sympathy or fellow-feeling between the two, and at the close of the first day he voluntarily gave the captain as good a piece of seal as he ate himself. Jack had a hunk of gristle on that occasion, but the next day he had nothing.

It was his birthday, as it happened, and he spent it from sunrise to sunset kneeling in the bows of the canoe, watching the send of the sea, paddling with the utmost attention and growing fainter and fainter with hunger and cold. The utmost attention was scarcely enough, in one not born to a canoe, for the thing was frail, sensitive, narrow and so easily overset that time and again a cross-wave's lapping nearly had them down: for those who had time to regard it philosophically it was an interesting craft, being made of five planks shaped with fire and oyster-shell scrapers, sewn together with long, tough creeper and caulked remarkably well with the pounded bark of the same creeper, a plant called supplejack; but, having no thwarts, it had to be propelled by men kneeling upright—a position that is intolerably painful after a little while to those whose limbs are not trained to it from childhood. Towards the end of the second day Jack began to wonder whether he could possibly last out another hour, another ten minutes. They passed through a shower of hail that to some degree refreshed or at least enlivened him, but when the light began to fade in the icy drizzle that followed the hail, he found that his courage was failing. The top of a wave came in, and they shouted out in fury behind him: he looked round the darkening sky with a haggard face, and it seemed to him that it would be very easy to die. They were out of sight of land. He had no idea any more of their direction and little memory of their purpose, and he would have thrown down his paddle if he had felt slightly less dislike for his companions. But you cannot behave shabbily before those whom you despise, and hatred alone kept him paddling, not ten minutes longer, but two interminable hours after the sun had gone down; after which time the cacique guided the canoe straight in from the offing into a bay where half a dozen wigwams stood.

The cacique took the captain up the beach from the landing-place and into one of the wigwams: Jack was left outside in the rain-filled darkness. The bitter cold invaded him now that he was no longer in continual movement: he stood there shivering for some time, automatically emptying the water out of his pocket—he had made himself a sail-cloth lining, in order never to lose anything valuable, such as a limpet or one of the little insipid half-potatoes, and it held water like a bucket.

There was a glow under the wall of the wigwam, the glow of a fire: he bent to go in, but then straightened up again. If he were to be thrust out, which was quite likely, it would be more than he could bear. Even in this extremity he would not submit to humiliation in front of Captain Cheap at the hands of the cacique and his friends.

There was a glow from the next wigwam, too, and he walked towards it, while the dogs that had been barking all this time redoubled their noise. He thought of the spears that the Indians always carried, of the perpetual ill-temper and brooding passion in which these unhappy people seemed to live; but all this amounted to less than his loathing of humiliation, and going down on his knees and hands he crawled into the tent.

Two women were sitting by the dying fire, dressed in feather cloaks; one was old and very ugly, the other young. They stared at him through the smoke in amazement, and when, with as polite a bow as the lowness of the wigwam would permit, he advanced towards the warmth, they hurried silently away, darting through the hole like rabbits.

"Well, it will be charming while it lasts," said Jack, huddling his frozen body to the little fire. A few minutes later there was a noise outside and he held himself tense; but it was only the women coming back, in great good humour now. They seemed thoroughly amused by something, and it occurred to Jack that the sight of a face with amusement on it rather than anxiety, hostility or wolfish starvation was almost as good as a meal. He sat easy again, rubbed his hands to show that he loved the fire, nodded and smiled; they also nodded and smiled, and addressed long observations to him, presumably of a humorous nature, for both laughed very heartily at the end. Presently the old lady fetched in some wood for the fire, and Jack, finding that his pride made no objection to his lowering himself before these kind souls, pointed earnestly to his mouth, and rubbed his stomach.

In the back of the wigwam there was a tumble of old pieces of bark, and after rummaging about among them and turning most of them over, the young woman, who appeared to be the housekeeper (and a most indifferent one), came up with a handsome gleaming fish, a kind of mullet, that must have weighed four pounds. She brought it to the fire, scraped the ashes aside, and grilled it, after her fashion. The smell of the fish was a painful delight; the delay while it was lightly scorched on either side was nearly intolerable; and when it came, passed on a piece of birch-bark, a lifetime's training in civility deserted him—he seized the fish without a word or a smile and ate it, head, fins and bone and skin. Only towards the very end did a returning glimmer of decency prompt him to express his obligation with nods and greasy smiles, and even to offer the dish, holding it out towards them (but not very far). They had watched him intently all the while he ate, and now they laughed, harangued him in a very cheerful manner, and laughed again.

The heat in the wigwam was now quite extraordinary: Jack was warm right through to his spine, his clothes were dry, and for the first time in months and months he did not feel hungry; he gazed at the Indian women as they squatted there in their feather cloaks, and smiled most affectionately upon them. They seemed to waver in the rosy light of the embers as his eyes closed of themselves. He swayed as he sat, and, three parts asleep, he assured them of his infinite good will.

The old woman arranged him a soft platform of birch twigs, and lying down he said, "My dear madam, I wish I had some token of my esteem to offer you—I wish . . ." But here a huge, mounting, irresistible sleep interrupted him, cut him off and bore him down.

When he woke up he found that they had covered him with their feather cloaks, light, and as warm as a bird's nest (though smelly). The old woman was tending the fire; the young one was talking quietly to some thin, sharp-looking, smooth dogs that had come in during the night. The dogs were painted with blue, dull red and ochre spots: Jack registered this fact, and at the same time became aware that he was prodigiously hungry, so hungry that he could not forbear telling the women about it at once. They seemed to find this perfectly natural—as natural as their having to go out into the wet and the cold with the spotted dogs to catch his breakfast. Presently they came back, streaming wet from head to foot but as cheerful as ever, and cooked him three more fishes, laughing as they dripped.

It is wonderful what a good night's rest will do, and a full belly. Jack walked about the wigwams in the morning, looking at them with the liveliest interest, whereas the day before he would not have turned his eyes to see a double-headed phoenix, had the phoenix not been edible.

The camp was full of women and children—no more than two men, and one of them lame—and Captain Cheap, on appearing with the cacique, said that, as he understood it, the men were to come back in two or three days: they were gone to make war or to say their prayers or something that he could not make out.

Jack would have been happier to hear that the men were all gone for ever, but as the day was almost pleasant, for once, with a little watery sun and no wind, he determined to enjoy himself as much as he could while he might. There was a stream running down to the shore, and here, by way of a particular indulgence, he washed his shirt and cleaned his grieko by thumping it with a stone, killing hundreds at a blow. Jack was not unduly fussy about dirt or vermin, but now he found it a wonderful relief not to have so many creatures crawling on him, and to be clean for once. If only Tobias had been there, equally well fed, Jack would have asked for little more.

While his shirt was drying, he took a turn upon the rocks above the stream, and from there he saw, to his dismay, that the women were dismantling the wigwams, unfastening the curled strips of bark and carrying them down to the canoes, which were now all at the water's edge. He ran for his shirt and hurried down after them. They were only going fishing for a day or two, said his two particular friends, who divined his anxiety: they pointed to a couple of untouched wigwams, where Captain Cheap and the cacique would stay, and he understood very well what they meant. But they seemed perfectly willing to take him with them, if he had a curiosity to see their fishing, and they gave him a paddle.

A dozen canoes worked out beyond the white water; there were children in many of them, little, naked, amphibious things that fell into the surf quite often during the preparations and the departure, and were either spooned out by their mothers with paddles or left to extricate themselves as best they might: children who could scarcely walk upright would come creeping out of the vicious roar and drag of a breaking wave with as much calmness as if they had been seals. And when the canoes had come out into the quiet swell beyond the reefs and the scattered islets the fishing began: the young woman (whose name, in the face of all probability, appeared to be Maudie) handed her feather cloak to Jack, took a basket between her teeth and slipped over the side. The spotted dogs watched over the low gunwale with their pricked ears brought to bear on the splash: the splash subsided, and time went by. Still it went by, and Jack looked anxiously at the old woman; she seemed quite unmoved, but more and more time passed, and it became increasingly obvious to Jack that no one could stay under that long. The first sign that the young woman might still be alive was a gentle thumping of the dogs' tails; they all brought their ears still more to bear, and a moment later a black head broke the surface. Maudie handed in the basket, filled now with sea-urchins, breathed hard for a few moments as she held on to the side, and then plunged to the bottom of the frigid sea.

This went on and on, while the old lady told Jack that she had been accustomed to staying down twice as long, in her youth, and to diving twice as deep; modern young people, she said, sought nothing but a life of ease and luxury. Jack said "Yes, ma'am," and "No, ma'am," and "Upon my word, ma'am, you do not say so?" at decent intervals and watched the sea-urchins pile up and walk slowly about on their purple prickles. At length the young woman climbed back in: her natural colour was brown, but with the cold she had gone a dismal purple, and her lips were bluish grey; she trembled violently, uncontrollably, and for some time she was too perished even to smile. The old woman chuckled tolerantly, slapped her with a paddle and they rowed off towards the east after the other canoes. In a quarter of an hour the young woman was quite recovered, and she talked away with never a pause until noon, when they all landed on a low, sheltered point, where the sea ran into various shallow creeks. Here they set up their wigwams. At one time Jack had esteemed himself reasonably good at withstanding the cold and the wet (he already had the nickname of Foulweather Jack in the Navy), but the young woman's performance had disabused him of this idea: and he had once thought himself tolerably handy, but now the old woman's expert erection of the wigwam set him right again. He tried to help, but it was no good: they gave him a couple of sea-urchins to keep him quiet and made him go and sit among the dogs: he had rarely felt humbler. Indeed, the dogs were far more useful than ever he could be, for presently the entire body, dogs and all, moved off to a sandy inlet; the dogs knew very well what was afoot, and when the women had all walked in about neck-deep, so that a line of them held a net across the narrowest part of the water, the dogs with one accord dived in at the far end—dived, like so many otters—and drove the fish that were in the creek towards the net. From time to time they came up, yapping, to breathe and to take their bearings, and, with extraordinary intelligence, they combined their efforts to beat the entire shoal into the extended net. It was an unusually numerous shoal, and it was an unusually fortunate day; they left barely a fish in this creek nor in the next, and before sunset they had taken as many as they could carry.

The Indians did not understand salting or smoking (perhaps neither would have answered in that sodden atmosphere), and they were obliged to eat everything within a day or two. It was a delightful interlude, a time of steady, unrestrained eating, and talking and laughing. Jack recited verse to his women; they seemed favourably impressed, and harangued him in their turn with what might have been a metrical composition, but was more probably a cooking receipt—the word for fish coming in again and again. He knew several Indian words by now, all of them to do with food: after a few months of starvation one begins to understand that one is primarily a walking stomach, and that the satisfaction of its needs is the great and fundamental pleasure of the world.

But it could not last. The skies clouded, and with them the faces of the women: the canoes were run out into the rising sea, and they had no sooner reached the bay where the cacique and the captain had remained, than the men of the tribe appeared in the offing. When the men landed, all gaiety left the encampment; the children and dogs retired to a certain distance and the women came forward with anxious, downcast expressions and dutiful greetings. Jack's two friends were the property of the chief, a burly savage who had painted his face navy-blue, although nature had made it repulsive enough in the first place: something the young woman said did not please her husband, who snatched her up in his arms and threw her down on the rocks; he threw her down again and again, but, not content with that, he beat her, snorting and gasping like a beast with the force of his blows.

If Jack had been a hero of easy fiction he would have knocked the fellow down; but being no more than a half-grown mortal, still weak with starvation and exposure, and unarmed in an armed camp of the chief's own relatives, he turned away, his heart filled with impotent hatred—hatred not only for the chief but for all bullying and domineering and for the whole brutish tradition whereby men, in order to show how manly they can be, affect to despise all pleasantness, kind merriment and civility, and concentrate upon being tough, as inhuman as possible, with the result that their lives are nasty, short and brutish, wholly selfish and devoid of joy; and not only their lives but the lives of all around them, particularly the weaker sort.

Now life resumed its former aspect, gloomy, unhappy and dangerous. After hours and hours of talk between the cacique and the blue chief it was decided that they should return, that the main body of Indians should follow them in a few days and that they should then all go away to the north together. In those parts of the world where it is as difficult to live in one place as it is in another people undertake voyages, even huge migrations, very easily: the cacique had no sooner said his last word to the blue chief than he walked down to his canoe, followed by the captain and Jack, and in half an hour they were out of sight.

It was a better voyage than the journey out; the wind was behind them and the sea was somewhat calmer; Jack, for one, was a good deal stronger, and he was handier with the paddle now. When they had been going for five hours a seal blew a little way ahead of them, rolling black under the wave: the Indian dropped his paddle, whipped up a spear and crouched as tense and glaring as a cat. He cried "Pa-pa-pa-pa," high and shrill, and the seal put up its head to look. In one sliding movement, incredibly fast, the Indian threw his spear: it pierced the seal's head from eye to eye. This was between twenty and thirty yards over a heaving, glancing sea, a fantastic piece of skill; but the cacique, paddling furiously and shrieking at Jack to grapple the seal at once, did not seem to think a great deal of it. It put him into a reasonably good humour, however, and when his family came down to the water to greet him he picked up the smallest child and tossed it into the air, laughing like a Christian.

In Jack's absence Tobias and the others had done very poorly. The cacique's wife was a woman entirely unlike Jack's friends, and she had given them no more than a few sea-urchins, and those bitterly grudged. Sea-urchins are delicious appetisers, but as they are almost all hollow, they cannot satisfy except in enormous quantities. Jack's fish, therefore—the fish that he had carried in his bosom, having no other container and being unable to trust his companions—was more welcome than can easily be expressed, although it was pink with the dye of his waistcoat and only just good enough to be eaten, even by the standards of extreme hunger.

"How I wish you had been there, Toby," said Jack. "It would have set you up for a week, the smell alone. No, I assure you," he said, turning his head away from the offered piece, "I ate very well before coming ashore. Gormandise while you may, for Heaven knows when we shall have a bellyful again."

This was sound enough, for in the days that passed before the other Indians joined them everybody went short of food, even the cacique. Like most people who live on the edge of starvation, the Indian and his family were capable of eating huge amounts at a sitting: they ate the whole of the seal, apart from a little that they gave to Captain Cheap, in a very short time, and then in spite of the unpropitious weather they took to the sea again.

It was upon his return from one of these fishing expeditions that the cacique gave an almost perfect exhibition of savagery and the cult of toughness carried to its logical extremity: he and his wife had one basket of urchins, no more, from a whole day's work, and on reaching the shore the cacique passed this basket to the smallest child, who, not having yet learnt caution, had come down to meet the canoe. The child slipped, let the basket fall in the surf, and the urchins were lost. The cacique leaped out, seized the child by an arm and a leg and hurled it with all his force against the naked rock.

The killing of this child was the most shocking thing that Jack had ever seen in a life not rare in terrible sights, and it left a weight of horror on his mind that would not go. It was scarcely alleviated by the coming of the other Indians, with the canoes that were to take them northwards and, for a time, his two kind women, with their cheerful faces. But even though they were there, within a few yards of the wretched wigwam that Mr Hamilton, Campbell and Tobias had botched together, they might almost have been in Asia, for the blue chief was as jealous as a Turk—the women were either at work on the sea or they were kept rigorously within. They nevertheless, and at the risk of their lives, contrived to pass some victuals out through the back of the tent to Jack—a boiled cormorant, a seal's head, two half-eaten flippers—and it was with strong regret that he and Tobias saw them go: several of the women were sent off, with most of the fishing dogs, some days before the main body began their journey.

This voyage was begun neither happily nor with any good omen. The whole movement seemed to be part of a tribal migration: these Indians, who were called Min-Taitao, were travelling upwards to their northern limits with the approach of mid-winter; they were not going on account of the *Wager*'s people, whom they regarded as nuisances, very much in the way, hangers-on who were too contemptibly soft to feed themselves, incompetent fools; and the taking of the white men was an irritating hindrance to their progress. They put them into separate canoes so that they would be less trouble, and on a lowering morning, with a strong west wind, they set out on a rising, angry sea and began to work along the coast towards the remote, miserably barren country of Marine Bay.

In time, and after drenching and freezing days at sea, they reached a place where, in a maze of sand-bars and subdivided channels, a river seeped into the head of a deep, wide bay. The barge had been here before, but they had taken no notice of the fresh water; it had not seemed practicable for the boat, and indeed it was not. The Indians unloaded the canoes, carried them over the sand and launched them again in a fresh-water lake, or wide swelling of the river. Paddling across this, they came to a stream with various branches; the branch they took grew narrower all day long, and far stronger. Towards the evening it seemed to Jack that this was to be a repetition of the appalling time when John Bosman died, and in fact it was so hard that even the comparatively well-fed Indians were drawn to the utmost of their endurance. They lay that night under the pouring rain in a naked swamp, without putting up their wigwams, because there was not a single pole to be found, and these Indians never carried poles with them but only the pieces of bark.

The next day resembled the first, but the day after that brought them far up into a dripping forest, where the river turned away to the east: in these three days they had nothing whatever to eat, except for some bitter yellowish roots. Here they hauled out, and in the morning the Indians took the canoes to pieces; it was simply done, by cutting the creeper that sewed the planks together, and in theory it was then simple to carry the canoes, thus divided into convenient loads, across the country until another river, flowing northwards, should take them in the right direction. But this was a wicked country, the deepest forest that they had ever seen, and the trees stood in ground so interspersed with bogs and half-hidden pools of mud that it was difficult to understand how so many could find enough firm ground to hold themselves upright. A great many did not, and were either supported, slanting, by their neighbours, or lay flat along, sometimes growing in that position, but more often dead; and these falling trees in their crash broke many others, and their stumps stood long after, often covered by undergrowth, jagged, splintered stumbling-blocks every few yards along the miles and miles of march. Everywhere there were wind-fallen branches, white and rotting, and in the windless bottom of the forest cold fungus stood dying under the winter frosts.

By this time Captain Cheap was growing very weak: Mr Hamilton was sadly reduced too, but he could still walk and manage his load, which was a plank. Captain Cheap could scarcely get along at all, however, even at the beginning of the day, and he was obliged to be helped by Tobias and Campbell, who also carried a full burden each. Jack, who was in the last canoe to be dismantled, had a putrid lump of seal wrapped in the captain's piece of canvas. It had been given to the captain by an Indian who did not think it worth carrying over the long portage, and the understanding was that it would be shared in the evening, when a fire would make it edible.

The canoe was very long in taking apart, because these Indians preferred to clear the holes of the caulking now rather than when they came to sew the planks together again—the more usual practice—and by the time it was ready the others were far ahead. The planks were delicate objects; a fall would break their perforated edges; and the Indians, having weighed Jack's load, added nothing to it, but set off after their companions, carrying the whole of the canoe.

"It is just as well," thought Jack, scrambling up a muddy slope behind them, "for I do not believe that I could carry so much as a paddle more." The canvas was an awkward burden, painfully heavy and apt to slide; he carried it on his neck and shoulders, with a line across his forehead, after the example of the Indians, because he needed both hands to get along and to keep up with them. They made their way through a long valley, which must have become dammed at its lower end within the last few years, for although the mud and swamp lay waist-deep in places, yet the broken stumps still stood in the firmer ground below. Jack had no shoes (he had eaten them long ago), and although his feet were quite hard they were not as hard as the Indians', and soon the blood was running under the black ooze that covered his legs.

Hour after hour they went through the forest, and the Indians, full of meat and born to the country, kept drawing ahead. Sometimes they were slipping away through close-packed saplings, which waved above them; sometimes he could hear them pushing through tall undergrowth; sometimes as he emerged at one edge of a yellow-scummed mire he would see them disappearing at the far side of it, the open black mud showing where they had passed. They had no intention of waiting for him. With ever-increasing anxiety he hurried after the Indians through the gloom; his legs would scarcely bear him, and the pace was killing: he dreaded losing them—dreaded it beyond words.

Now there was a long slough between tall trees; there was no trace of the Indians, no marks in the mud, but he could hear them in front of him, in the trees beyond the slough. A very tall beech had fallen, and it lay out across the surface of the standing water; his way probably lay along its trunk, he thought, and he hurried out along this natural bridge. Halfway over his feet slipped on rotten wood, the trunk gave a turn, and in a moment he was in the slough, struggling wildly, with his head under the surface, pressed down by his burden. There was no ground under his feet, and his clawing hands met only mud. With a tearing effort he wrenched his head back and, turning, snatched a breath of air; there was a branch within reach, and before it broke he managed to pull himself upright. He could not reach the trunk again, however, and he stood there for some moments, with only his head above the water and his feet in yielding mud. His weight was pressing him deeper: he was forced to move, and with a heavy, floundering, swimming motion he urged himself forward. The slough was shallower; the mud was only up to his chest. With each step it was less, and in ten minutes he was on solid ground on the far side.

But his strength was almost entirely gone and he scarcely had the energy to be glad of his escape. Indeed, *glad* was not a word to use in connection with him at all at that time. One can bear a great deal, but there is a limit to human endurance, and suddenly it seemed to Jack that he had reached his limit. He sat, bowed right down, and indulged in the weakness of despair. But in fact he had not reached the end of his powers, as he knew very well after a minute or two; and when he had collected himself a little the haunting fear of being left quite filled his mind again: he was carrying no part of the canoe, and there was no material reason why the Indians should wait for him.

"It is no good," he said aloud, looking at his burden: and with a vague notion that it would be wrong to leave it lying there on the ground, he stowed it neatly in the crutch of a tree. Even without it he could barely get along at first, but presently he came to a small, clear stream, running in the direction that he should go—or thought he should go—and here, when he had washed the fetid mud from his mouth and face, he felt better; a few minutes later he saw the traces of the Indians, and, knowing that he was on the right track, he hurried on, leaving blood at every step, but less wretched than before.

For a good hour and more he followed this stream, and then quite suddenly it flowed out into a vast lake, huge and grey, with the Cordilleras on the other side; and on its muddy shore there were the Indians, reassembling their canoes. The others sat at a little distance. They seemed to be completely done up, and for some time nobody said anything; they, knowing that the Indians were not yet ready, had felt no particular anxiety; and no one who had just made that march could be expected to care for anything but his own fatigue.

"Where is my canvas and the seal?" asked Captain Cheap at last.

Jack explained. He was exhausted, but he was not beyond the prick of shame, and the low-voiced, bitter, heartfelt reproaches that met his explanation pierced him.

"I would not have believed it in *you*, Byron. I had conceived you more of a man—a braver man."

"I would have carried the seal myself," said Mr Hamilton, "but I thought it was in the best hands. It was a poor thing to do. It was poorly done."

"After all this, we are to have nothing to eat, because you left it in the wood," said Campbell. "Another night with nothing to eat."

Jack rose painfully, and turned back into the forest. "I will come with you," said Tobias; and when they had gone some way up the stream he said, "You must let me look at your feet, Jack. They are in a bad way." They sat down, and he searched the cuts and scratches for splinters. "Tell me where you left the bundle," he said, drawing out a jagged piece of wood, "and I will fetch it: I am remarkably fresh."

"I never could tell you for sure, Toby," said Jack, with a sort of smile. "Go back now, there's a good fellow—it would oblige me most, upon my honour." But he made no protest when Tobias walked on with him, and it would have been useless if he had.

It took something more than an hour to reach the place where Jack had left the seal and the canvas: on the way they talked very little, and now that they sat down under the crutched tree they said little more, being too weary; but the feeling of companionship was there.

"That was where I fell in," said Jack, showing the slough. Tobias nodded. "If we can find a sound branch," said Jack, "we can sling the load between us."

"There is a puma on the other side," said Tobias. Jack made no reply; Tobias had pointed out two dull little birds on the way up and as there was one flying about now, making a noise like the yapping of a small, silly dog, Jack thought (as far as he could think at all, through the dullness of exhaustion) that that was what he meant.

"We must go," said Jack, "or it will be night before we get back."

"Allow me two minutes to walk to the other side." Tobias walked across the shallower mud, vanished into the bushes and then returned with a pleased look on his pale, thin face.

"I believe you would creep out of your grave to look at a flaming bird," said Jack. "Come, take an end."

"A puma is not a bird," said Tobias, after a hundred paces. "It is a kind of cat—felis concolor. You may see it soon: it is moving along with us, on the right."

The word *cat* brought nothing into Jack's mind but a fleeting image of a shabby, brownish-black little creature called Tib that disgraced the drawing-room at home, and he plodded on in silence. Every hundred yards or so they changed shoulders, and during the third change there was a coughing noise to their right, a series of coughs, huge, deep, throaty coughs, that culminated in a shattering roar, unimaginably loud.

"Not a bird, Jack, you see," said Tobias.

"How big?" cried Jack, vividly alive now, with terror coursing up and down his spine.

"The size of an indifferent lion," said Tobias. "You can see him if you bend and look under the yellow bush. He is tearing up the earth, and biting it."

"Can he climb?"

"Oh, admirably."

"Toby, what shall we do?"

"Why, unless you wish to go and look at him, we had better go on. It is getting late. But do not hurry so, Jack, nor make jerking movements. If he should come out, take no notice of him, or look at him kindly—do not provoke him. He is not a froward puma, I believe."

Naked fear is the keenest spur of all; in spite of Tobias' placid assurance, Jack was terrified, and his fright carried him down the long stream to the lake in such a state of nervous tension that he noticed neither his wounded feet nor his famished stomach. Fear enabled him to do what he could not have done unterrified, and it needed all Tobias' fortitude and all his remaining strength to keep up with him.

They came out into the open at the beginning of the twilight, as the rain started to fall. Many of the canoes were already on the water, and as they hurried down several more were launched: the cacique was chattering with impatience, holding the stern of the canoe with Captain Cheap in it. They carried the bundle to the water's edge; the captain and the cacique seized it and threw it in. There were three other Indians in the canoe.

"Wait," said Captain Cheap, waving them back, and the cacique interrupted with a flow of words. The remaining canoes were launched on either side of them, and the cacique's canoe floated out from the shore. The Indians began to paddle—all the canoes were paddling now, with the blades flashing and the water white behind.

Jack hailed: they both cried out together, and over the widening water came a confused, vague answer, half-heard and interrupted by the cacique. "You can wait . . . other Indians . . . no room . . . another canoe."

They stood there silent on the bank. No shouting would bring back the boats; and they watched them over the water until they disappeared in the darkness and the rain.

•••

"Toby," said Jack, turning towards the deserted shore with a ghastly attempt at lightness, when his aching eyes could no longer see anything on the lake, "you said that we could not be worse off when the barge left us. Don't you wish you had held your tongue now?"

"It was a thoughtless thing to say," replied Tobias in a steady voice. "It smacked of hubris—of insolent security." And after a few minutes he said, "Let us go down the shore, where the trees are thicker, and see whether we cannot find a little shelter. If we can sleep, we shall be able to think more clearly in the morning, what to do."

They wandered down the grey edge of the lake, and the sad waves came lapping in on the yielding mud; they looked for a tree with a thick enough trunk to give them a lee and tolerably even dry ground below it, but the darkness was coming on fast, and they could find nothing that protected them more than a very little. The roots of the tree which they had chosen (a kind of beech) would not allow them to lie down; they crouched, huddled together for warmth, in a half-sitting position, shivering with cold and hunger; nevertheless, they went to sleep—lapsed into a kind of stunned unconsciousness.

Jack awoke in the black night, cramped and twisted with hunger, still partly entangled with a vivid dream of those beautiful days in the women's wigwam, the smoky wigwam, the warmth and the fish sizzling on the pink embers: when he had gathered his wits for a few minutes he said, "Toby? Are you awake? Do you smell it? There is a smell of fire; I swear it."

The wind had died to a breeze that eddied along the edge of the forest, and from time to time it brought them a whiff of smoke. "Yes," said Tobias. "It is smoke." They set out towards it, often stopping like dogs to sniff: there was a little suffused light from the east, and the white frost helped them as they blundered through the trees. They had not gone far into the most sheltered part before they saw a wigwam, lit from within and smoking at the top: there were loud, harsh, furious voices inside.

"It sounds like one of their religious . . ." began Tobias.

"I don't care if they are raising the Devil," said Jack. "Wait for me here."

Tobias heard the noise redouble, and in a moment Jack returned. "They kicked me in the face as I tried to crawl in," he said, "but at least they know we are here."

A triangle of light appeared in the low entrance of the wigwam and an old woman peered out, beckoning. Going into an assembly of unknown savages, defenceless, on hands and knees, might very well be a matter for some hesitation, and it was a measure of their desperate state that they hurried in at once. There were several Indians, men and women; and on the ground near the fire lay a naked chief, as thin as a man could be, and he was plainly dying.

Jack and Toby sat silent, motionless and inconspicuous: the shouting went on—it seemed to be ritual, for sometimes two men shouted together, with the same words. At dawn the old woman took a piece of seal, and holding it stretched between her teeth and her left hand, sliced off pieces with a shell; she passed it raw to the Indians, but for Jack and Tobias she put it to the fire, spitting liquid blubber from a piece she chewed upon the slices until they were done. They did not understand the significance of this, nor of many other things; but they ate the seal.

Shortly after this three of the men, more brutal than any they had yet seen (their cheek-bones were slashed with parallel, raised scars, and their faces were scarcely human at all), went out, motioning Jack to go with them. Although they were not part of the tribe that had joined with the cacique, they too had carried their canoe over the watershed, and they now began putting it together. Tobias had picked up a certain amount of the Indians' language by this time, but he found, when they would answer him at all, that these people spoke a different dialect: few of the words were the same, but at least it was clear that they were going to the north—that much could be learned by pointing—and it was probable from their manner that the Indians expected them and had been told about them. But this was not sure: the Indians' lack of surprise might come from mere indifference. The only certainty was that these Indians, even more than the last, looked upon Jack and Tobias as nuisances, if not worse.

The lowest savages have little curiosity. There are some who are unmoved by things outside their comprehension—metal, cloth and ships do not interest the most primitive of all. The survivors of the *Wager* were of consequence only to the cacique, whose comprehension was comparatively enlarged and to whom their remaining possessions were of value. These Indians knew nothing of firearms, had no notion of connecting whiteness with power and wealth and disbelieved what the cacique told them. They thought the cacique a fool and his protégés a troop of effeminate, uninteresting buffoons.

And what is more, men with different-coloured skins have different smells: the Indians (whose scent was very keen, which made it worse) thought the white smell perfectly disgusting. The white colour, too, was loathsomely ugly, in their opinion—corpse-like, and probably produced by a discreditable disease which might very well be infectious. Still more important, it was obvious to the dullest Indian intelligence that many powerful gods hated these people. Why otherwise should they be so driven up and down, despised and wretched? And some of this hatred might be transferred to anyone who befriended them: their ill-luck might rub off. Lastly, it was clear to the Indians that these wretched people had no religious sense, no sense of piety; they knew nothing about the various beings who were to be appeased by ritual words and gestures; they did not even understand the simplest propitiation of the earth and sky. They were best ignored.

Some faint notion of all this had been seeping into Tobias' mind for a long while, and as they sat a little apart, watching the Indians at work (the Indians had angrily rejected Jack's help, and when he brought them a fine length of supplejack they threw it into the water), he told Jack of his suspicions.

"You may be right," said Jack, "particularly about the smell. I have always noticed how they hold their noses when we are by. I had thought it was the captain; but they do it still, I find."

The Indians were ready. They renewed the ridges of their tribal scars with ash, and they stood there, dull blue with cold, shifting the little square of fur they wore to cover their windward sides; their deep-sunk eyes were bloodshot and rimmed with scarlet from the night-long smoke in the wigwam, and they all seemed to be on the edge of a furious rage. An old woman came from the tent: she was a person of some distinction, it appeared, for they neither kicked nor struck her, and she wore an ample cloak made of vultures' skins with the sparse feathers still on. Jack and Tobias stood in the most anxious hesitation: angry shouts asked them why they did not get in, the fools? And, half-comprehending, they scrambled aboard.

All day long they paddled over the lake, and all day long the snowy Cordilleras retreated from them: in the evening they came to the out-flowing river that drained the lake northwards, a fast, white-flowing stream, and here the Indians put into the shore. They put up their wigwam, but they would not allow any blasphemous, smelly, unlucky lepers in it (who would?); nor would they feed them. Jack and Tobias understood the general purpose of their remarks—it could not have been mistaken—and withdrew to an overhanging rock, which, by a very happy chance, had a deep pile of dry drifted leaves under it for a bed, and, more than that, the leaves had protected the still-edible stalks of some plants of rhubarb. They slept so well here that the Indians were up before them—they saw to their horror that in another five minutes the canoe might have gone, leaving them in that desolation.

The night had been fair, but the day was as foul as could be: rain and snow from the north-west, a furious river to contend with, long, thundering cascades, whirlpools and spray that put out the pot of fire amidships. They hurtled down the river with destruction on either hand, at a terrifying, lurching speed that brought them to the sea that night. The Indians hauled up on a stony beach and vanished into the woods, no doubt to an encampment that they knew. It was too dark to look for any food, and as they dared not wander away from the canoe, Jack and Tobias lay by it, on the stones under the sheeting rain. At about three in the morning Jack made an attempt at joining the Indians by the fire that they had at last succeeded in lighting—it glowed through the trees—but this gave great offence, and they kicked and beat him away.

The dawn came, after a hideously protracted night, and the Indians put out into the northern sea. At last Jack and Tobias had come into the water that they had laboured for so long; but whether they alone of all the *Wager*'s crew they could not tell; nor could they tell where they were going now, whether they would rejoin their friends or whether, perhaps, they might be kept as slaves. At low water they came in to a rocky cove and landed to gather shellfish; it was an excellent place, and it was a very great relief indeed to Jack and Tobias. But they were so afraid of being marooned that they dared not stop to eat; they filled their pockets, Jack's hat and Tobias' nightcap—in a vile condition now—and as soon as they saw the Indians turn towards the canoe they ran for it. Jack made as elegant a bow as the circumstances would allow (he was standing on slippery rock) and presented the handsomest of the mussels they had found to the old woman. She looked amazed, but she took it, and when she had washed it a great many times she ate it.

They now headed straight out to sea, steering north-east with a moderate wind, and after a while Jack, putting his battered old hat beside him (it had once been a marine's), began to copy the Indians in front—between the long, powerful strokes they held the paddle in one hand and took a limpet with the other and ate it.

"Capital limpets, Toby," he said, over his shoulder, tossing the shell into the sea. But instead of a civil reply there was a shrieking Indian voice, screaming out in a terrible passion. In an instant the canoe was arock with violence. One Indian had Jack by the neckerchief, twisting it hard, another had him by the ankles, taking a grip to throw him overboard: Tobias hampered the rear man, and the old woman lashed about her with a spear, howling with fury. By some fantastic chance the canoe did not overset, and in a few moments the old woman quelled the tumult. She harangued them, and although they still looked very ugly, the men set to their paddling again, but not without turning from time to time to threaten Jack and to point to the bottom of the canoe. Jack, three-parts throttled and entirely at a loss, stared back at them stupidly.

"I conceive," whispered Tobias, "that they had rather you did not throw the shells into the sea." It was quite true: each Indian had a little pile of shells by him—a simple act of politeness towards Plotho, the limpet-god, obvious to a child of three.

"Damn your eyes," said Jack, loosening his neck-cloth and taking up his paddle, "I shall not eat anything until we are ashore and they cannot see me."

In the late afternoon, when the canoe came in with the land again and they steered for a little, sheltered, tree-grown island, the Indians, as soon as they had hauled out the canoe, picked up their limpet-shells and carried them carefully beyond the high-water mark; Tobias and Jack meekly did the same. This met with a certain surly approval, and when, a little later, Jack was seen with a bunch of purple berries, on the point of eating them, an Indian dashed them out of his hand, and by a pantomime of death in agony, showed that they were poisonous.

This, however, marked the highest point of their good relations with the Indians. This tribe, like all the others, had an elaborate code of religious behaviour that governed all their waking moments; they were continually propitiating a host of malignant or at least very short-tempered spirits, and their guests were as continually offending them. It did not look as though a human sacrifice to the outraged deities could be long delayed: in the meantime the Indians drove them very hard and gave them nothing whatsoever from the two seals they killed.

It was some relief, therefore, when, at the end of a day of infernal hunger and toil, the canoe rounded a headland and suddenly opened a little cove all lined with other canoes and dotted with men. They could see Mr Hamilton's red coat—pink rags now—at once, and this was obviously the meeting-place.

It was some relief, but not very much: they were too tired to feel any strong emotion. In this stormy, cold, wet, rocky world the chief idea was self-preservation, even among those born to it; among strangers there was little room for any other thought. Campbell and Captain Cheap were sitting wretchedly under the inadequate shelter of a streaming rock: neither side was particularly pleased by the encounter—nobody seemed pleased. They were, in fact, reduced to a state not far from the last indifference.

At this place the cacique had a very large canoe—how it came to be there no one asked or cared: they were as incurious as savages now—and as the Taitao Indians were at that time going no farther, except for one small canoe that would go some way on in a week's time, he intended embarking the whole party in it and pursuing his journey at once. Mr Hamilton, however, was a man in whom proper pride had outlasted starvation and exposure, and he would not consent to travel under the insolent rule of the cacique. He would take his chance in the Taitao canoe that would go next week, and he would make his own way after that, if he could; he hoped with all his heart that they would meet again, and he would pray for them each night, as he hoped they would pray for him. They left him, not alone, it is true, but among a tribe of brutish savages who scarcely came up to his shoulder as he stood there on the beach, an erect, soldierly figure in spite of his rags.

The big canoe was monstrously heavy: it was heavier than anything they had ever seen among the Indians, and it needed a strong crew, six or eight men at least; but all the crew it had was the cacique's slave, Jack, Tobias and Campbell. The captain could not work, and the cacique would not; he squatted there, with his hideous wife and the surviving child, chattering sometimes, and grinning. His unbelievable vanity seemed stronger even than his desire to stay alive, for he would not bear a hand when for want of it they were almost sure to be lost, in overgrown seas, tide-rips and the thousand dangers of coasting the worst shore in the world. Still he sat, like a huge monkey. Yet in general the weather was not so extreme as it had been when the barge made its attempt: the cold grew stronger every day, but the full gales were rarer, and it was just possible for four paddles to work the canoe up towards Chiloe.

Chiloe: the cacique often boasted of his relations with the Spaniards there, and asserted that he knew five, ten, fifty of the Chilotan Indians—could always walk into their houses, and they would give him sheep, potatoes, anything, they loved and esteemed him so. Nobody believed him; nobody took any notice of his flow of words, which alternated with hours of affected gravity, when he would not answer a question. He usually addressed himself to the captain, who spent most of his time in silence, lying in the bottom of the canoe, weaker and iller every day. Nobody believed him; and as the days dragged by, they scarcely believed in Chiloe any more. It seemed that life was to consist of this for ever, an unnumbered series of days in which they urged the lumbering canoe through miles and miles and endless miles of water, often angry, always cold—hard labour the whole day, while the inhuman cacique squatted prating there; and every evening the feverish search along the darkening shore for something to eat, anything, dead or alive, to take the extreme anguish from their hunger; and then the dreadful night, lying under what shelter they could find.

April merged into May, and in that month, as they crept through the tangle of islands in the south of the Chonos archipelago, the cacique twice killed more seals than he could carry; and therefore made a general distribution—at all other times the rowers fed themselves or went without.

In the horrible repetition of days throughout the month of May these were the only two occasions of relief: in June there were none. The snow came more often, and thicker; the captain was now wandering in his mind almost all day long; his legs were hideously swollen, as if with scurvy, but his body was desperately thin. He was shockingly verminous. He no longer knew their names—called Tobias Murdoch— "Murdoch, you villain: five hundred lashes,"—but he kept his sealmeat with unvarying caution, and when he slept it was with his head upon the seal: his hair and his long beard were matted with the blubber.

At about the day of the solstice, mid-winter's day itself, they found themselves on a cape in the most northern island of the hundreds they had passed in the archipelago: far away to the leeward there was the cacique's tribal home, a very squalid place, and to go from there to Chiloe, he said, they always came to this cape. The crossing was shortest from here, but even so it was a desperately long voyage for an open boat: the cacique looked at the roaring sea and crossed himself. He looked at it with horror and moaned and chattered for hours together.

It was impossible to say what determined him to set out, but it was quite certain that they had not gone a mile before he regretted it. But by then there was no remedy: the wind was strong behind them, and the canoe ran at a furious speed under a little, messy lug-sail made of bits of skin, blanket and the remains of the captain's canvas, sewn together with supplejack and suspended on a tripod of wigwam poles. Once they were out of the shelter of the cape the wind increased to such a pitch that they would have broached-to at the slightest attempt to alter their course; and shortly after this became evident, the bottom plank of the canoe split from stem to stern. The water rushed in, but the canoe did not fall apart; it held together by the fourteen stitches of quartered supplejack at each end, and, with all hands baling madly, it just kept afloat until Campbell managed to pass a twisted net about it and draw all taut with a tourniquet. This gave a certain amount of support, but it did little for the leak; with each rise and fall of the long canoe the split opened and the water from below joined the water that poured in over the side. The hardest baling could never get her clear, but so long as they never slackened for a moment the canoe would not sink. Hours and hours went by, and steadily the wind increased, driving the half-foundered boat on from wave to wave: at about four the sky darkened with a leaden darkness, and then the snow came hissing down on the sea—it fell so thick and fast that it settled on their shoulders as they worked, for ever baling with all their might, and often the canoe showed all white before the spray wiped it off again. The snow deadened the sea and the wind a little and this was fortunate for them, for it gave them fair warning of the thunderous surf right ahead in the darkness of the early night.

The cacique could swim like a seal: in his terror he set the canoe straight in for the shore through the breakers, trusting that he would survive, whatever happened. But Jack could not see it like that: disobeying orders for the first time, he plucked the cacique from his place, struck him into the bottom of the canoe, kicked him down and steered along the coast until they found smooth water behind a reef, so that they could run ashore safely on the snow-covered coast of Chiloe.

● ● ●

"Why, ma'am," said Jack, "if you insist, I must obey." He took another mutton-chop piping hot from the grill, and with a courteous inclination of his head engulfed it. "Campbell," he cried, above the hum of voices, "may I trouble you for the ale? Toby, do not keep the bread entirely to yourself, I beg. Bread," he repeated, with an unctuous tear running down his crimson visage, "bread, oh *how* I love it!"

They were seated at a table in a long, low-ceilinged room; Captain Cheap lay on a pile of sheepskins by the fire, dozing, with a half-emptied bowl of broth by his side; the room was filled with Chilotan Indians, men and women—clean, handsome creatures in embroidered ponchos, who gazed wonderingly at their guests, with expressions of compassion. The news of their arrival had spread by now, and a stream of newcomers came tapping at the door, each of the women bringing a pot, with mutton, pork, chicken, soup, fish, eggs—an uncountable treasure of food.

"Egg," said Tobias, leering in his uncouth way. "Egg. Ha, ha!"

Campbell said nothing, but struggled still with the remnants of a noble ham: the pleasure on his face was so acute as to be very near to excessive pain—for a nothing he would have wept. He ate and ate, staring straight before him at his bowl with bolting eyes.

Their first night in Chiloe had been terrible; they had come ashore in an entirely uninhabited, uninhabitable part—the usual rock, swamp and impenetrable forest—and at one time they thought that Captain Cheap had died in the cold. The next day, when at last they were able to get afloat, they paddled up the coast, ten weary miles and more, with the small hope they ever had fading fast with the evening and the certain prospect of another storm: and then, quite suddenly, on the far side of a rocky creek, there was a field.

It was an almost unbelievable sight, this most southerly field in the world, on the very edge of the barbarian wastes and under the same monstrous skies; but there it was, the unmistakable rectangle of civilisation, with the furrows showing where the snow had blown across them. Then there were houses, a little village with lights. The cacique, demanding his pay, the gun, crammed in the last charge of powder that they had and asked how to fire it. Campbell (a revengeful spirit) showed him how to rest the butt on his chin and bade him pull the trigger. The gun went off, the kick knocked out the cacique's four front teeth and hurled him into the bottom of the canoe, and at the noise men came running down to help them in—good-looking men, wearing top-hats, with their hair done up in neat buns behind, breeches, ponchos and woollen gaiter—and at last they were out of the canoe; they were done with the vile thing for ever, and they were led up into a real house and installed by a beautiful fire.

The cacique (who took his injuries very much for granted, and valued the gun rather more for its malignance) sank into an obsequious, cringing object, and his prating was done with for good: the Chilotans allowed him into the house only because he was, at least nominally, a Christian—but even so, he was not admitted beyond the outward porch.

The Chilotans had been converted by the Jesuits, that often-maligned Society, who had liberated them from the burden of ghosts and demons which oppressed their southern neighbors, and had taught them the nature of charity, the duty of kindness. Some of the later padres had been perhaps too busy in taking the Chilotans' gold away from them, but had they taken fifty times as much still the Chilotans were incomparably the gainers by the interchange, even if it were only their happiness in this world that was to be counted. They knew how to live like human beings: their spirit-haunted cousins to the south did not.

from Adrift: Seventy-Six Days Lost at Sea
by Steven Callahan

Steven Callahan (born 1952) set out in 1982 to sail across the Atlantic in his sloop Solo. The boat sank six days after leaving the Canary Islands. Callahan was stranded in Rubber Ducky, a five-and-a-half-foot inflatable life raft. He survived seventy-six days on the raft, constructing a solar still to make drinking water, catching fish with a jury-rigged speargun and navigating with a sextant made from three pencils.

April 8 Day 63

The sea runs by in its usual form, five-foot, maybe six-foot rollers ribboning westward. The wind is a steady twenty to twenty-five knots— lively but not dangerous. *Rubber Ducky* rises to each surge and softly falls again. I stand, wobbling, my brain stuffed with images of food and drowned by dreams of drink. They are all I can think about, that and the rolling waves that snap around me. I divide the horizon into six segments. I scan one segment while balancing as best I can. Then I carefully turn, get reacclimated, and scan the next. When it's stormy, I often have to await an ascent to a large peak before I can see very far, but in these conditions nearly every wave will do. A ship squats, five to eight miles off. She's heading west northwest; might come a little closer. I await the right moment and pull the pin. My last parachute flare pops, sizzles skyward, and bursts. It is not as bright as it would be at night, looks more like a star poking its head through the murky sky. Ship number seven shyly slinks away. Only three flares left, all hand-held. A ship will have to run me down before it sees me now. Reaching the islands is my only hope.

Hesitantly I chance the final destruction of my spear and manage to impale another dorado. Mechanically I cut it up, slice the thick fillets into strips, poke holes in the strips, and hang them. It seems barbaric. I don't want to kill any more. Please let me land soon. When I am gone, how will my fish feel? How will I feel without them?

Now that I have fresh fish, I won't have to work as hard for the next couple of days. It's a moment of respite, though I know that I will never be able to rest until the voyage ends. It's almost unbelievable to think of how much time I had to spare in *the old days*, back before my equipment was failing regularly and before I became half starved. Now each job takes longer and longer to accomplish. I continually wonder how much more a body can take. I don't consider suicide—not now, after all I have come through—but I can understand how others might see it as a reasonable option in these circumstances. For me it is always easier to struggle on. To give myself courage, I tell myself that my hell could be worse, that it might get worse and I must prepare for that. My body is certain to deteriorate further. I tell myself that I can handle it. Compared to what others have been through, I'm fortunate. I tell myself these things over and over, building up fortitude, but parts of my body feel as if they are in flames. The fire from the sores on my back, butt, and legs shrieks upward and the flames burst forth into my skull. In a moment my spirit is in ashes and tears well in my eyes. They are not enough to even dampen the conflagration.

Kneeling in front of the doorway, I can raise my wounds from the salty cushions. The sun beats down on my head, and I slump across the bow. Dorados are drawn to my protruding knees and wheel around the raft all day long. They know I am not hunting. The triggers too seem to know when I have my spear in hand. I drag my arm through the cool water, as clear as glass. As the dorados slither out from under me, our eyes are only a foot apart. I sweep my hand toward them. I have never seen them touch one another, though I suppose they sometimes do, yet they let me stroke their slippery bodies. As soon as my fingers touch down, the dorados flip away as if irritated, but they return time and again. They have me trained, you see—successful wildlife management. How easy it would be to let go and die, to undergo the transformation into other bits of the universe, to be eaten by fish, to become fish. A dorado slips out and I graze the feathery flip of her tail. The little flirt immediately returns. But I can't let go. People are my tribe. It should be easy to surrender to the dorados or the sea, but it is not.

I measure my latitude with my sextant. About eighteen degrees. How accurate is it? I know now I will never last another twenty days. If I am too far north, I am done for. If I could manage the wind, I would make it take me south.

April 10 Day 65
In the morning the dorados are gone. Several of a new type of trigger-fish appear. They are almost black, with bright blue spots, puckered mouths, and fins like chiffon collars rolling in a breeze. They look to me like oceanic starlets. I call them my little coquettes.

Two long fish torpedo under the raft. They are even faster than the old blue dorados, though they must be a type of dorado. They're smaller than the blue dorados—two and a half to three feet—and their skin is a mottled green and brown, like army camouflage. One of them looks badly damaged: raw, pink skin shows where most of the camouflage has fallen away in large sheaths. I think of it as having ichthyofaunic mange.

Tiny black fish, maybe an inch or two long, sweep along before the raft, contrasting sharply with the Atlantic's topaz blue. Their bodies wiggle as if made of soft rubber. *Ducky*'s slow forward progress creates small ripples, what could jokingly be called a bow wave. Just as porpoises ride the pressure waves that are created by a ship's bow rushing through the sea, so these tiny black fish swab little arcs just ahead of *Ducky*'s backwash. I try to scoop them up with my coffee can, but they are always too fast.

Since the long battle to repair *Ducky*'s bottom tube, I've been pretty wiped out, but I feel a little stronger this evening. For the first time in over a week, I return to my yoga routine, first spreading out my cushion and sleeping bag to cushion the dorados' blows. The hemorrhoids are puffed out again, and my hollow butt provides little protection. I sit up, bend one scrawny leg until my heel rests firmly in my crotch, and then touch my head to the knee of my straightened leg, while grasping the foot of that leg with both hands. I perfect a twisting exercise while hanging on to the handline. Then I lie on my stomach and lift my head as if doing a pushup, but I keep my legs and hips on the floor and bend my spine back into a wheel. I scoot forward, lie on my back, raise my legs over my head, and bring them around until my feet hit the floor behind me. My body weaves about like a stock of kelp swaying in the currents. I have not only sea legs but sea arms and a sea back, perhaps even a sea brain.

My head is struck hard. I wiggle my jaw to see if it is loose. The new camouflaged dorados are very powerful and aggressive. They bombard the raft all day long, ramming it with their bullet heads, slapping at it with their bullwhip tails, and blasting off with incredible speed. I leap to the entrance and grab the spear, but they are always long gone. Sometimes I glimpse their tails as they shoot off into the distance. Sometimes I see them racing by, several fathoms below. They never move calmly like the big blue dorados. They always move frantically, like they're hopped up on speed.

As the sun sets, I hear squeaking again and spy some big black porpoises, purposefully cutting their way to the west. They do not come close, but I feel touched by the graceful ease with which they glide through the Atlantic's swell.

The frigate birds, three of them now, are still frozen in position, riding the invisible waves of the sky high above the water. I'm impressed that their delicate long wings survive the power of the sea. They are often above me at first light, or they drift up from the west soon after. Another snowy tern shows up; it is unbelievable that this tiny bird migrates eleven thousand miles every year.

A dark gray bird swings back and forth, approaching from where the clouds go, slowly getting closer. It flies like a crow. I tell myself that it must come from land. More important, it is a flying lump of food. It nears. I duck behind the canopy. I can't see it, but I hear it fluttering at the entrance to my cave, contemplating entry. It flaps away. I wait. A shadow flickers on the canopy, grows, and a slight weight puts an imprint on the tent peak. Cautiously I bend forward and see the bird perched, looking aft, its feathers rustling in the wind and then falling back into place. I shoot out my arm. Instantaneously the bird's wings spread. My fingers close on its straw legs. It squawks and snaps its wings down to gain lift, wheels its head around, and madly pecks at my fist. I grab its back with my other hand, drag its claws free of the tent, pull it into my den. In one quick move I twist its head around. There is a silent snap.

The beautiful plumage is so pristine and well tended that I feel like a criminal disturbing it. I don't know what kind of bird this is. It has webbed feet, a long thin beak, and pointed wings spanning about two and a half feet. It is a sooty color all over, except for a round light gray cap on the top of its head. The skin is very tough and the feathers are stuck well into it. Robertson suggests that it's easier to skin a bird than pluck it, so I cut off the wings and head with my sheath knife and peel off the skin. The breast makes up most of what is edible, and that's not much of a meal. The meat is of a different texture than fish, but it tastes almost the same. Once they are dissected into organs, bones, and muscle, it is surprising how similar to one another are the fish of the sea, birds of the sky, and, I suppose, mammals of the land. Five silvery sardines are in its stomach. Caught near land? There's little to the wings except bones and feathers. They're quite beautiful. I don't want to throw them out, so I hang them from the middle of the arch tube.

By evening the bigger blue dorados return en masse, still lorded over by the emerald elders. Escorting us into our sixty-fifth night is an assemblage of about fifty. Every now and then one of the brown and green camouflaged dorados strikes like the blow from a sledgehammer, unleashing a squirt of adrenalin in me as I momentarily mistake the blow for a shark attack. I call the smaller brown and green dorados tigers. As if inspired by the tigers, one of the biggest male blue dorados frequently flips along the perimeter of the raft, giving it great whacks, smashing the water into foam, and pushing *Ducky* this way and that. I ignore it. In the morning I get my easiest catch yet. Within ten minutes and using only two shots, I have a fine female hauled aboard.

By nightfall the waves have reared up again and ricochet off of *Ducky's* stern. Each wave that breaks on the raft echoes through the tubes and sounds like a blast from a shotgun going off next to my ear. The wind catches the water catchment cape, snaps it up and down, rips its buttonholes wider, and tries to tear it away. During the night conditions become wilder. Watery fists knock *Ducky* back and forth. I huddle athwartships, getting as far forward as I dare in an effort to stay dry while also trying to keep the stern down. Although the front of the canopy gives a little better protection, dryness is still relative. The back of the canopy is little more than a stretched rag. Wave crests fall on it and drain through onto my face, stinging my eyes and pouring into my sleeping bag. I continually wipe the water off the floor and the canopy, but everything is soaked in no time.

April 12 Day 67

It is April 12, the date that marked the anniversary of my marriage such a very long time ago. Frisha's life as my wife was not easy. I'd take off on a delivery trip or a passage and leave her behind. Sometimes we wouldn't see each other for months. She thought that it was all a very risky business, despite my reassurances. Not long before I left the States on *Solo*, she told me that she thought I would eventually meet my maker at sea, but that it would not be during this voyage. I wonder how she feels about it now. I wonder if she was right. What is Frisha doing? She must believe that I am dead while she studies to bring life from the soil. One day, perhaps, long after I am drowned and consumed by fish, a fisherman may haul aboard a catch that will find its way to her table. She will take the head, tail, and bones and heap them upon her compost pile, mix them with the soil so green life will sprout. Nature knows no waste.

A flying fish crashes onto the canopy behind the solar still. I am losing my taste for fish, but any chance from dorado arouses my appetite. My guts feel like they have fallen right out of me. No amount of fish can fill my vacant stomach. I sit up, grab the flyer, and wonder if it is scared or if it accepts death like another swimming stroke.

Maintaining discipline becomes more difficult each day. My fearsome and fearful crew mutter mutinous misgivings within the fo'c's'le of my head. Their spokesman yells at me.

"Water, Captain! We need more water. Would you have us die here, so close to port? What is a pint or two? We'll soon be in port. We can surely spare a pint—"

"Shut up!" I order. "We don't know how close we are. Might have to last to the Bahamas. Now, get back to work."

"But, Captain—"

"You heard me. You've got to stay on ration."

They gather together, mumbling among themselves, greedily eyeing the bags of water dangling from *Ducky's* bulwarks. We are shabby, almost done for. Legs already collapsed. Torso barely holds head up. Empty as a tin drum. Only arms have any strength left. It is indeed pitiful. Perhaps the loss of a pint would not hurt. No, I must maintain order. "Back to work," I say. "You can make it."

Yet I feel swayed more and more by my body's demands, feel stretched so tight between my body, mind, and spirit that I might snap at any moment. The solar still has another hole in it, and the distillate is more often polluted with salt water. I can detect less and less often when it is reasonably unsalty. I may go mad at any time. Mutiny will mean the end. I know I am close to land. I must be. I must convince us all.

We've been over the continental shelf for four days. One of my small charts shows the shelf about 120 miles to the east of the West Indies. I should see the tall, green slopes of an island, if my sextant is correct. I should hit Antigua—ironically, my original destination. But who knows? I could be hundreds of miles off. This triangle of pencils may be a foolish bit of junk. The chart could be grossly inaccurate. I spend endless hours scanning the horizon for a cloud shape that does not move, searching the sky for a long wisp of cloud that might suggest human flight. Nothing. I feel like a watch slowly winding down, a Timex thrown out of an airplane just once too often. I've overestimated my speed, or perhaps I'm drifting diagonally across the shelf. If there was only some way to measure the current. I'm assuming that I'm within two hundred miles of my calculated position, but if I've been off by as little as five miles a day, I could be four hundred miles away from where I hope I am—another eight or even fifteen days. "Water, Captain. Please? Water." Tick, tick, slower and slower. When will it stop? Can I wind it up until the end of the month without breaking the spring?

The next afternoon's sun is scorching. The solar still keeps passing out and looks as if it may not last much longer. By mid-bake-off I can feel myself begin to panic and shiver.

"More water, Captain. We must have more."

"No! No! Well, maybe. No! You can't have any. Not a drop."

The heat pours down. My flesh feels as if it is turning to desert sand. I cannot sit upright without having trouble focusing. Everything is foggy.

"Please, Captain. Water. Now, before it's too late."

"O.K. The tainted water. You can drink as much of it as you want. But the clear water remains. One pint of it a day. That's the limit. It's the limit until we see aircraft or land. Agreed?"

I hesitate. "Yes, all right."

A sludge of orange particles sits in the bottom of the plastic tube in which the wretched canopy water rests. I triple layer my T-shirt and strain the water through it into a tin again and again. The result is a pint of cloudy liquid. It is bitter. I can just keep it down.

My thirst becomes stronger. Within an hour I must drink more. In another hour more still. Soon the bitter pint is gone. It is as if my whole body has turned to ash. I must drink even more.

"No. Can't. No more until tomorrow."

"But we must. You've poisoned us now and we must."

"Stop it!" I must keep command. But my eyes are wild, my limbs shaking in an effort to hold back the panic.

My torso screams out. "Take it!" Limbs reach out for a sack of water.

"No!" I scramble to my knees, almost in tears. I get to my feet and look aft for a moment. I can't stand forever but for now the breeze cools me off.

There, in the sky—a jet! Not just a contrail or the faintest hint of a jet, but a silver-bodied bird streaking to Brazil! Quick, man, the EPIRB! Battery is probably shot. Well, the light's on at least and he can't be more than ten miles away. I'll leave it on for twelve hours. The jet looks small. It may not be a commercial flight. Regardless, it couldn't have come at a better time. We must be close. I fulfill my promise. I hand out a pint of clean, sweet water. Everybody relaxes.

A gooselike bird resembling a gannet flies over. It has even-colored brown plumage, except for dark rings around its eyes. Yesterday a jaeger winged by. It was not supposed to be there. Should I inform these birds that they are beyond their prescribed ranges? New fish, new birds, different water color, no Sargasso. It all adds up. This voyage *will* end soon. I stare intensely at the horizon until my eyes water.

The Miami Coast Guard is contacted by a ship off Puerto Rico that has sighted a small white boat, dismasted and adrift. The Coast Guard requests that the ship board the vessel. Negative. The boat is already lost to sight. The ship will not return. Description? White, twenty feet long, no markings, no one on board.

Solo was beige. She had a wide dark blue stripe all around the topsides and dark blue cabin sides. Her name was painted across her transom. A fourteen-inch-high number 57 was plastered on each side and on her deck.

Somehow the two boats are taken to be the same. Officially, "*Napoleon Solo* has been located with no one on board." In California, a ham operator picks up the message from the Long Beach Coast Guard and begins to notify those who have been keeping their ears open. Messages flock out. *Solo* is no longer missing.

My brother demands more information. Was the life raft on board? Was any other equipment visible? Were there any signs of possible piracy? What was the wreck's position? He wants to go check it out himself. The New York Coast Guard knows nothing of the matter. It proves impossible to get any information at all from them. Something funny seems to be going on. While my arm trails through the water stroking my doggies, my mother envisions me murdered by pirates or rotting in some fascist prison cell.

Indeed, something funny is going on. The Coast Guard begins to issue statements. At first they say that the message that *Solo* has been located must be a bogus one made by a ham operator without a license. Then they hint that it may have been sent by the Callahans themselves in order to stir up some action.

Slowly and meticulously, my family trace the message through the ham net to Germany and then to California, and then from Long Beach to Miami through the holes in the Coast Guard net. The truth has escaped. Still, the false message is being carried on the seafarer's net and is received by a friend of mine in Bermuda. The New York Coast Guard instructs the Callahans that if they want the message canceled, they will have to arrange it themselves. Finally it is done.

By this time my family have done everything they can to calculate my approximate position and get a search going. They have tried in vain to get the armed forces to fly over the areas of high probability during their routine patrols and maneuvers. They have also failed in attempts to gain the use of spy satellites that have the acuity to photograph trash cans from space. Not only is the target not specific in this case, but the area to be searched is at least 200 miles across, or 31,400 square miles. If each photo covered 900 square feet, or 30 feet on a side, it would take over a billion photos to check out the area. In every direction in which my family have turned to get a physical search under way, they have found a roadblock.

There is little else for them to do but to continue writing to politicians and maintain private contact with shipping companies. Although most people now feel I must have perished long ago, my parents decide that only if I don't show in six months will they consider the matter laid to rest. My brother Ed readies himself to return to his family in Hawaii. It is now just a waiting game for us all.

Finally, on April 20, the Coast Guard decides to rebroadcast for another week the message that *Solo* is overdue.

April 16 Day 71

The past few days have passed ever so slowly and I have been growing progressively more dim and depressed. We should have reached the islands days ago. We couldn't have passed between them, could we? No, they are too close together. I'd have seen at least one. And the birds still come at me from the west. When do I use the EPIRB for the last time? Even with the short range it must now have, the massive daytime Caribbean air traffic will hear the signal. But I must wait until I see land or can last no longer.

I am beginning to doubt everything—my position, my senses, my life itself. Maybe I am Prometheus, cursed to have my liver torn out each day and have it grow back each night. Maybe I am the Flying Dutchman, doomed to sail the seas forever and never rest again, to watch my own body rot and my equipment deteriorate. I am in an infinite vortex of horror, whirling deeper and deeper. Thinking of what I will do when it is all over is a bad joke. It will never be over. It is worse than death. If I were to search the most heinous parts of my mind to create a vision of a real hell, this would be the scene, exactly.

The last solar still has completely blown, just like the one before. The bottom cloth has rotted and ripped away. I have a full stock of water, but it will go quickly. Rainfall is my only well now.

April 18 Day 73

I continue to take note of the positive signs of approaching landfall. The tiger dorados have gone. A five- or ten-pound mottled brown fish, a tripletail, has lumbered around *Rubber Ducky* for two days. I've tried to hit it, but I've been impatient. I hurried the shots and only managed to poke it twice, driving it away. There have been more sooty birds in the sky, and the frigates continue to reel about overhead. I've grabbed two snowy terns, which landed for a short rest and received a permanent sleep. I've seen another ship, but at night and very far off. Somehow all of these changes do little for my continued depression. I am the Dutchman. I arise still feeling asleep. There is no time for relaxation, only time for stress. Work harder. Do more. Must it last forever?

I strike my fishing pose yet again. My aching arms grasp the few ounces of plastic and aluminum, the butter knife tied on like a caveman's stone point, but indubitably less effective. Now I can hold the pose only for a minute or so, no longer. The dorados brush against my knees as I push all of my weight down on one knee, then the other. They turn their sides to me as if wanting to show off the target area, and they swing out to the left and right or flip around deep below. Occasionally they wiggle their heads so near the surface that the water welters up. Perhaps one will rise and speak to me like the flounder in the fairy tale. Often I wait a microsecond too long, and the few square inches of bull's eye melt away into the dark water, which is just starting to brighten as the sun rises. This time I strike home, the battle rages, and I win again. The emerald elders court behind the lines like generals who are smart enough not to join in the melee any more.

Clouds race across my world, gray and smeared, too light for a heavy burst of rain, but the light sprinkles and misty air, combined with wave spray stirred up by the wind, prevent my fish from drying properly. Temporarily though, the stock of food allows me to concentrate my energy on designing new water-catchment systems. The first is simple. I stretch plastic from the cut-up still along the shaft of the spear gun. I can hold it out, away from the sheltering canopy, pulling a corner with my mouth. Next I set the blown still on the bow. I punch it into a flat, round plate and curl up the edges like a deep-dish pizza pie. Even in light showers, I can see that the two devices work. A fine mist collects into drops, that streak into dribbles, that run into wrinkled, plastic valleys, where I can slurp them up. I must move quickly to tend to each system and collect water before it's polluted by waves or the canopy. I am far enough west that the clouds are beginning to collect, and occasionally I see a "black cow," as some sailors call squally cumulus, grazing far off, its rain streaking to earth.

I stick with the routine that I've followed for two and a half months. At night I take a look around each time I awaken. Every half hour during the day, I stand and carefully peruse the horizon in all directions. I have done this more than two thousand times now. Instinctively I know how the waves roll, when one will duck and weave to give a clear view for another hundred yards or half a mile. This noon a freighter streams up from astern, a bit to the north of us. The hand flares are nearly invisible in the daylight, so I choose an orange smoke flare and pop it. The dense orange genie spreads its arms out and flies off downwind just above the water. Within a hundred feet it has been blown into a haze thinner than the smoke of a crowded pub. The ship cuts up the Atlantic a couple of miles abeam and smoothly steams off to the west. She *must* be headed to an island port.

April 19 Day 74

I work all the rest of the day and all of the morning of April 19 to create an elaborate water collection device. Using the aluminum tubing from the radar reflector and my last dead solar still, I make *Rubber Ducky* a bonnet that I secure to the summit of the canopy arch tube. The half circle of aluminum tubing keeps the face of the bonnet open and facing aft. A bridle adjusts the angle of the face, which I keep nearly vertical, and the wind blows the bonnet forward like a bag. I fit a drain and tubing that I can run inside to fill up containers while I tend to the other water collectors.

For hours I watch white, fluffy cumulus rise up from the horizon and slowly pass. Sometimes they band together and form dense herds running in long lines. Those that have grazed over the Atlantic long enough grow thick and muscular, rearing up to great billowing heights, churning violently, their underbellies flat and black. When they can hold no more, their rain thunders down in black streaks that lash the sea. I chew upon dried sticks of dorado awaiting the test of my new tools.

But it seems that the paths of the squalls are bound to differ from mine. Sometimes a long line of clouds passes close by. I watch the wispy edges swirl above me and feel a few drops or a momentary sprinkle coming down. It's just enough to show me that my new water collection gear is very effective. I'm convinced that I'll collect several pints, maybe even a gallon, if I can just get directly in the path of a single heavy shower. It's one thing to have a tool and quite another to be in a position to use it. My eyes wander from the horizon to the sky. I'm so tired of always awaiting something.

April 20 Day 75
Seventy-five days—April 20. With the drizzle and the salt spray, my dorado sticks have grown pasty rather than drying. I'm astonished that the dried sticks from one of the first dorados that I caught still seem to be fine. Only a slight whitish haze covers the deep amber, woody interior.

For an hour in late afternoon, I watch a drove of clouds run up from the east. I can tell that they're traveling a little to the south of my course. As they else rise up and charge onward, I ready myself, swallowing frequently, though there is no saliva to swallow. I try to wish them into running me down, but they ignore me and begin to sweep by about a mile away, clattering and flashing with lightning. Four separate heavy columns of rain pour down, so dense that they eclipse the blue sky behind. I watch tons of pure water flowing down like aerial waterfalls. If only I could be just a mile from where I am. No sips, no single mouthfuls, but an overflow of water I could guzzle. If only *Ducky* could sail instead of waddle. I have missed. My collection devices are bone dry and flutter in the wind....

The evening skies of my seventy-fifth day are smudged with clouds migrating westward. A drizzle falls, barely more than a fog, but any amount of saltless moisture causes me to jump into action. For two hours I swing my plastic buckets through the air, collecting a pint and a half. My catchment systems *will* do the trick.

As long as the waves are not too large, I do not worry about capsizing, so I curl up and sleep against the bow. These days it takes so long to choke out the pain and fall asleep. When I do, it is only an hour or less before a sharp stab from a wound or sore awakens me.

I arise to survey the black waters, which occasionally flash with phosphorescent lines from a breaking wave or the flight of a fish. A soft glow looms just to the south of dead ahead. And there, just to the north, is another. A fishing fleet? They do not move. My God, these are no ships! It is the nighttime halo of land that I detect! Standing, I glimpse a flip of light from the side. A lighthouse beam, just over the horizon, sweeps a wide bar of light like a club beating out a rhythm— flash, pause, flash-flash, rest; flash, pause, flash-flash. It *is* land. "Land!" I shout. "Land ho!" I'm dancing up and down, flinging my arms about, as if hugging an invisible campanion. I can't believe it!

This calls for a real celebration! Break out the drinks! In big, healthy swallows, I down two pints. I swagger and feel as lightheaded as if it were pure alcohol. I look out time and again to confirm that this is no illusion. I pinch myself. Ouch! Yes, and I have gotten the water to my lips and down my throat, which I've never been able to do in a dream. No, it isn't any dream. Oh real, how real! I bounce about like an idiot. I'm having quite a time.

O.K., now, calm down. You aren't home yet. What lighthouse is that? Antigua doesn't make sense. Are you north or south? *Ducky* is aimed down the empty corridor between the two glows that I see. When I get closer maybe I can paddle some, or maybe I can strap the paddles onto *Ducky*'s tubes to act like centerboards. Even if I can't hit land, the EPIRB will surely bring help. When the sun rises I'll flick the switch one last time.

I can hardly sleep but manage to drop off for a half hour now and again. Each time I awaken, I look out to confirm that this isn't the ultimate elaborate dream. Another glow begins to emerge dead ahead. Morning, I hope, will reveal the rim of an island down low on the horizon, close enough to reach before nightfall. A landing in daylight will be dangerous enough. If I reach the island tomorrow night . . . Well, one thing at a time. Rest now.

• • •

April 21 Day 76

Dawn of the seventy-sixth day arrives. I can't believe the rich panorama that meets my eyes. It is full of green. After months of little other than blue sky, blue fish, and blue sea, the brilliant, verdant green is overwhelming. It is not just the rim of one island that is ahead, as I had expected. To the south a mountainous island as lush as Eden juts out of the sea and reaches up toward the clouds. To the north is another island with a high peak. Directly ahead is a flat-topped isle—no vague outline, but in full living color. I'm five to ten miles out and headed right for the center. The northern half is composed of vertical cliffs against which the Atlantic smashes to foam. To the south the land slopes down to a long beach above which a few white buildings perch, probably houses.

Close as I am, I'm not safe yet. A landing is bound to be treacherous. If I hit the northern shore, I run the risk of being crushed against the sharp coral cliffs. To the south I'll have to rake across wide reefs before I hit the beach. Even if I get that far without being ripped to ribbons, I doubt I'll be able to walk or even crawl to get help. One way or the other, this voyage will end today, probably by late afternoon.

I flip on the EPIRB, and for the first time I break out the medical kit. As with all of my supplies, I have been saving it until I absolutely needed it. I take out some cream, smear it all over my sores, and fashion a diaper from the triangular bandage. I'll try to coerce *Ducky* to sail around the south side of the island, so I don't have to land through the breakers on the windward side. If *Ducky* refuses, I'll go for the beach. I'll need all the protection I can get. I'll wrap the foam cushion around my torso, which will keep me afloat and serve as a buffer against the coral. I'll cut off *Rubber Ducky*'s canopy, so that I won't get trapped inside and so I can wrap my legs and arms with the fabric.

I'll try to keep *Ducky* upright and ride her in, though the bottom tube will certainly be torn to bits. Everything must be orderly and secure. I rummage around, throwing out pieces of junk that I won't need and making room in my bags for the first aid kit and the other necessities. I gnaw on a couple of fish sticks, but they taste like lumps of tallow. I can survive with no more food. My doggies nudge at me. Yes, my friends, I will soon leave you. On what separate paths will we travel? I pitch the remaining rancid fish sticks and save only a few of the dried amber ones as souvenirs. Ah, yes, another pint of water to fortify myself for the landing.

As each wave passes, I hear something new. RRrrr . . . RRrrr . . . It grows louder. An engine! I leap to my knees. Coming from the island, a couple of hundred yards away, a sharp white bow, flared out at the rail, pitches forward against a wave and then crashes down with a splash. The boat climbs and falls, getting closer and closer. It's small, maybe twenty feet, and is made of roughhewn wood painted white, with a green stripe around the gunwale. Three incredulous dark faces peer toward me. Jumping to my feet, I wave to them and yell, "Hello!" They wave back. This time I have definitely been seen. I am saved! I can't believe it, just can't believe . . . Nearly over. No reef crossing, no anxious awaiting of an airplane. Two of the men are golden mahogany in color, and the third is black. The one at the helm wears a floppy straw hat with a wide brim that flaps up and down. His T-shirt flags out behind him as he rounds his boat ahead of me and slides to a halt. The three of them are about my age and seem perplexed as they loudly babble to one another in a strange tongue. It's been almost three months since I've heard another human voice.

"*Hablar español?*" I yell.

"No, no!" What is it that they say?

"*Parlez-vous français?*" I can't make out their reply. They all talk at the same time. I motion to the islands. "What islands?"

"Aahh." They seem to get it. "Guadeloupe, Guadeloupe." French. But is sure isn't like any French I've ever heard. It's Creole, I learn later, a rapid-fire, pidgin French. In a few minutes I figure out that the blackest of them is speaking English, with a Calypso beat and heavy Caribbean accent. I'd probably have trouble comprehending another New Englander at this point, but I begin to put it all together.

We sit in our tiny boats, rising and falling on the waves, only yards apart. For several moments we stop talking and stare at one another, not knowing quite what to say. Finally they ask me, "Whatch you doing, man? Whatch you want?"

"I'm on the sea for seventy-six days." They turn to each other, chattering away loudly. Perhaps they think I embarked from Europe in *Rubber Ducky III* as a stunt. "Do you have any fruit?" I ask.

"No, we have nothing like that with us." As if confused and not knowing what they should do, the ebony one asks instead, "You want to go to the island now?"

Yes, oh, definitely yes, I think, but I say nothing immediately. Their boat rolls toward me and then away, empty of fish. The present, the past, and the immediate future suddenly seem to fit together in some inexplicable way. I know that my struggle is over. The door to my escape has been fortuitously flung open by these fishermen. They are offering me the greatest gift possible: life itself. I feel as if I have struggled with a most demanding puzzle, and after fumbling for the key piece for a long time, it has fallen into my fingers. For the first time in two and a half months, my feelings, body, and mind are of one piece.

The frigates hover high above, drawn to me by my dorados and the flying fish on which they both feed. These fishermen saw the birds, knew there were fish here, and came to find them. They found me; but not me *instead* of their fish, me *and* their fish. Dorados. They have sustained me and have been my friends. They nearly killed me, too, and now they are my salvation. I am delivered to the hands of fishermen, my brothers of the sea. They rely on her just as I have. Their hooks, barbs, and bludgeons are similar to my own. Their clothing is as simple. Perhaps their lives are as poor. The puzzle is nearly finished. It is time to fit the last piece.

"No, I'm O.K. I have plenty of water. I can wait. You fish. Fish!" I yell as if reaching a revelation. "Plenty of fish, big fish, best fish in the sea!" They look at each other, talking. I urge them. "Plenty of fish here, you *must* fish!"

One bends over the engine and gives the line a yank. The boat leaps forward. They bait six-inch hooks with silvery fish that look like flyers without big wings. Several lines are tossed overboard, and in a moment, amidst tangled Creole yells and flailing arms, the engine is cut. One of them gives a heave, and a huge dorado jumps through the air in a wide arc and lands with a thud in the bottom of the boat. They roar off again, and before they've gone two hundred yards they stop and yank two more fat fish aboard. Their yelling never stops. Their cacophonous Creole becomes more jumbled and wild, as if short-circuiting from the overload of energy in the fishing frenzy. Repeatedly they open the throttle and the boat leaps forward. They bail frantically, cast out hooks, give their lines a jerk, and stop. The stern wave rushes up, lifts and pats the boat's rear. More fish are hauled from the sea.

I calmly open my water tins. Five pints of my hoarded wealth flow down my throat. I watch the dorados below me, calmly swimming about. Yes, we part here, my friends. You do not seem betrayed. Perhaps you do not mind enriching these poor men. They will never again see a catch the likes of you. What secrets do you know that I cannot even guess?

I wonder why I chanced to pack my spear gun in my emergency bag, why *Solo* stayed afloat just long enough for me to get my equipment. Why, when I had trouble hunting, did the dorado come closer? Why did they make it increasingly easier for me as I and my weapon became more broken and weak, until in the end they lay on their sides right under my point? Why have they provided me just enough food to hang on for eighteen hundred nautical miles? I know that they are only fish, and I am only a man. We do what we must and only what Nature allows us to do in this life. Yet sometimes the fabric of life is woven into such a fantastic pattern. I needed a miracle and my fish gave it to me. That and more. They've shown me that miracles swim and fly and walk, rain down and roll away all around me. I look around at life's magnificent arena. The dorados seem almost to be leaping into the fishermen's arms. I have never felt so humble, nor so peaceful, free, and at ease.

Tiny letters on the boat's quarters spell out her name, *Clemence*. She roars off one way and then the other, circling around *Rubber Ducky*, around and around. The men are pulling in a fish a minute. They swing by every so often to see if I'm all right. I wave to them. They come very close, and one of them holds out a bundle of brown paper as *Clemence* glides by. I unwrap the gift and behold a great prize: a mound of chipped coconut cemented together with raw brown sugar and capped with a dot of red sugar. Red! Even simple colors take on a miraculous significance.

"*Coco sucré*," one yells as they roar off again to continue the hunt. My smile—God, it's so strange to smile—feels wrapped right around my head. Sugar and fruit at the same time. I peel off a shard of coconut and lay it upon my watering tongue. I carefully chip away at the *coco sucré* like a sculptor working on a piece of granite, but I eat it all, every last bit of it.

Slowly the dorados below thin out. The fishermen are slowing down. A doggie comes by every so often as if to say farewell before shooting off after the hook. The sun is getting high, and I am very weary. Stop fishing now. Let's go in. Within a half hour, I am draped over the bow, trying to stay cool and conscious. Finally the massacre is over. It is time for my voyage to end.

from The Rivers Ran East
by Leonard Clark

Leonard Clark (1908–1957) in 1946 went to the Peruvian Amazon with an ancient map and a Peruvian guide named Jorge. His destination: thhe legendary El Dorado. The men bought several natives, or mansos, out of slavery from a shaman named Iye Marangui (the brother of the snake), who sported a flayed human skin. A rebel slave named José joined their expedition, which then entered a part of the Tambo River where natives killed white men on sight.

With night approaching fast, and an unknown river ahead, it was imperative that we find a spot that was defensible. After many days of taking chances with the Indians and losing much of our apprehension, and our good rest at Padre Antony's, we decided to risk a fire. After all, the Indians must know of our being on the river, and though we were not starving, we were certainly hungry. Finally we headed in for a landing. We beached our rafts on a curving sandbar, shaped like a boar's tusk, some quarter of a mile in length on the right side. It was covered by a great flock of pink spoonbill flamingoes, so tame they didn't fly but merely walked off a hundred yards or so.

A small herd of *cotos,* a large reddish monkey with a long tail and a terrific guttural roar, gamboled over the beach. I felt safe on this beach, as it looked defensible. With nothing to eat but the worms, I took a chance and stalked the *cotos,* and taking careful aim with the Colt, shot one of the four-foot-high bachelors, whose absence could best be spared by the herd. The *coto* howlers live in pairs in what are called *bancos,* usually the fork of a tree, and are seldom seen in herds on the ground.

After cleaning the monkey and singeing off its hair, we spitted the grotesquely boyish carcass over a dry smokeless fire made of the fine fuel, *capirona.* We found its haunch delicious. The four *mansos* ate the partly digested contents of the stomach, puzzled that Jorge and I should pass up this delicacy which was considered by them to be the choicest of all.

We had located our campground just in time. Indians were, as we had suspected, obviously everywhere about, as we saw from their code signs: stones placed in various ways; marks on twigs thrust into the sand; grass knotted in such and such a way. This last code was especially intriguing. The ancient Incas, unlike the Mayas, had no recognizable system of writing. But for all that they sent messages and kept records in code by knotting strings or clusters of fibers. The system has never been deciphered, but it is possible that the Campas hold the key to the lost language.

We had just finished eating when José pointed over the tree tops across the river, and cried:

"Signal smokes!"

Indian scouts must have immediately marked us down, for two fires were being lit on the top of the Gran Pajonal not five hundred yards away. The flames mounted high, belching columns of black smoke.

On that north side we were fairly well protected by the deep moat of the Tambo, a hundred and fifty yards across, and flowing swiftly at this point. Few Indians would dare attempt swimming it. At the far end of the *playa* stretched a roaring staircase of waves which would prevent any war party from coming upstream. At our back, along the edge of the *playa,* was a row of *bombonaje* palms. These palms stood some two hundred feet back from the river, with white sand all the way between. If anyone tried to cross this open space in the night, he would be seen. In short, we had chosen wisely, for we realized now that had we continued we would have drowned.

After eating the monkey we were still hungry, and so we tackled the palm worms. But even so, since it had been a hard day, we wanted more food for the six of us. As the Indians had marked us down, there was no point in not hunting again. The *playa* was obviously a favorite stamping ground for wildlife, as indicated by the skeins of tracks left in the sand. The ones with the enormous claw tracks with a heavy line furrowing down the middle, were crocodile. Others were the cracks of *milne*, the new bear; tapir (a pachyderm belonging to the rhinoceros family); coatimundi, a raccoon-like bear; wild pigs; red deer; ocelot; *ronsoco* (capybara). Also the giant *tamandua* anteater, a toothless monstrosity measuring a yard at the shoulders and covered with long hair striped in black and white, and having a very long thin head. There were jaguar and puma tracks. On the edge of the *playa*, alongside the jungle, was a *cocha* so filled with crocodiles that not a yard of water was free of them; there must have been thousands.

While one of the *mansos* stood guard in the edge of the jungle, we rested, lying in the clean granite and quartz sand. The signal smokes had ceased. After the moon came up we prepared to hunt, for come what may, we would need food in the days to come. Animals will lie up in the cooler parts of the jungle by day, but like to come into the open under cover of night. One of the *mansos* began whistling on a crocodile tooth, producing short plaintive sounds, and presently he was answered by a herd of *ronsocos*. We knew these strange beasts were good to eat. They are pig-sized, with a red coat and webbed feet, an amphibious rodent, whose flesh was devoured by the Campas with relish. This Perené *ronsoco is* a variation of the lower Amazon's capybara, which has been variously described as "sheeplike," "piglike," "guineapig-like," "rabbitlike." I was very anxious to inspect one at close range.

I cautiously crept off into the darkness, crawling along on my belly, a few inches at a time, peering into the darkness along the edge of the sand bank as I did not want to crawl into a nest of crocodiles. I had an awful fright when a long, black snake came out of its coil only a few feet from my face and slithered off into the river.

The little sounds of whistling from the *ronsocos* came closer, answering my own decoy—for I had borrowed the Indian's crocodile tooth—and finally, not fifty feet away, I made out seven shadowy shapes. Aiming very carefully, I fired, dropping the foremost. With squeals of terror, the others plunged into the river and swam across to the other side. I retrieved the dead *ronsoco*, and found that it weighed about 125 pounds. Dragging it back to the campfire I saw that none of the other descriptions really fitted it. Actually, the animal is an over-grown member of the cavy family, to which the tiny and very valuable chinchilla belongs. We skinned it, and saved the fat for our Campa stone lamp, given us by Padre Antony.

It was now ten o'clock. A half-moon shed its greenish-yellow light over the white *playa*. Suddenly—and with no warning whatever—a feather-shafted spear, whirring oddly, came out of the darkness and, slid, like a sharp knife into butter, right through the side of one of the *mansos*. The wide, bloody blade stuck out of his back. With a grunt, he pitched forward on his face into the fire. In a flash, Jorge kicked a heap of sand over the coals, twisted around in a sitting position, the shotgun flashing to his shoulder. But out of the darkness rimming the edge of the white-trunked jungle came no horde of angry *bravos*, only the usual night racket of the insects.

Caught in the open, our Indian guard probably dead somewhere at the foot of the palms across the *playa*, we were obviously within range of the spear thrower. I couldn't believe the Indians on the Gran Pajonal had been able to cross the river and get on our flank. It seemed more likely that only a few strays were out there among the trees. I began dig-ging a hole in the sand with my hands. There was no point in charging an unseen target, with the chances of receiving a spear through the chest. The others soon caught on, and in five minutes we lay in the bot-toms of five pits. Peering over the top of mine, I carefully studied—foot by foot—the dark fringe of rustling palms. But not a man-made move-ment or a suspicious sound came out of the shadowed jungle.

Now men react in different ways when confronted by extreme danger, and by death. I once saw a professional soldier—a colonel—who had been dropped by parachute behind the Japanese Army lines in China to inspect my command, actually wet his pants in front of all my guerrillas engaged in attacking an enemy post. Jorge, a very different sort, a hunter and jungle man who lived constantly with death, was laughing very quietly and grimly.

"What's so funny?" I asked, though I knew there was nothing humorous about that grim laugh.

"Well, my friend, I can't pin it down to any particular thing. I merely find I am laughing."

I turned to José alongside, gazing slit-eyed into the jungle. "Can you make me *shirondantse* (laugh)?" I asked. Curiously, there is no such idea as a "joke" comprehensible to the Campa mind. Life to the Campa is too terrible, too real. Nor have I ever seen a Campa laugh or smile, unless, perhaps, you do so first, then he will follow your example thinking it is polite and mannerly. José, however, was used to the queer ways of the *Huriapache* by now.

"*Si, patróne*," he answered guilelessly, not taking his eyes from the jungle.

"Do so," I suggested.

"*Si, patróne*. But it is difficult. Perhaps this will do—who knows? A Campa *bravo* near Sutsiki once constructed a bamboo monkey cage." José glanced from the jungle across to see if I were listening. Satisfied that I was, he moved his eyes back to the wall of trees. "*Patróne*—this man used to sit inside the cage so that the monkeys could come and laugh. . . ."

All this time we were waiting for death to come out of that tangle of jungle across the way, hearing only the ringing of the insects, seeing nothing. . . .

Finally I answered: "Why? And what would a Campa know about a cage for a monkey?"

"But, *patróne*! He wished to call the spirit of the monkey to him, and capture it in the cage."

"What's so funny about that?"

About this time Jorge was chuckling. "The two of you are very amusing," he pointed out. "I will explain what José means. . . ."

For a moment he hesitated, for the air was full of crocodile roars—though whether Indian signals or from the disturbed reptiles in the *cocha*, we had no way of knowing. Then Jorge began speaking. He was engaged rather unsuccessfully in this business of explanation, when for no reason at all I burst out laughing.

"What's so funny?" enquired Jorge, a trifle hurt.

But there was no time to explain. All I could do was hiss—"Sssst!" and point toward the bush. For out of its shadows and between the palm trunks, were coming an army of cat-footed savages . . . walking in a strange crouch and well spaced apart, not charging, but walking—advancing slowly and silent as death itself, straight toward us.

For a moment I was too stunned to act. Then Jorge threw the shotgun to his shoulder, drew a quick bead on a six-foot warrior in an enormous headdress, and pulled the trigger. The shotgun blasted the stillness, kicked back, and the headdress flew through the air. But not a single warrior of all those skulking behind wavered. There was not a sound out of any of them—no war whoops—nothing. They didn't miss a step, but kept coming in that odd tense crouch, silent as shadows, skulking across the *playa* in full sight under the moon, skulking with inhuman certainty of their prey and straight at us.

"*Sangre de Cristo!*" spat out the Peruvian, reloading.

I knew my original estimate of the *playa*'s defensibility had been wrong. The Indians had somehow crossed the river. We were in a jam. Jorge—with narrowed eye, the shotgun's stock seated hard against his jaw—was grimly swinging its barrel along the front rank of the advancing *bravos*. He seemed undecided on a target. Finally, when the gun's front sight stopped midway through the arc, I knew he had singled out for his last remaining charge of buckshot an enormous, predatory-looking Campa brave. The Indian was well out in front, wearing a basket crown with a white feather rising from the back of its narrow corona. This time the gun was not aimed at feathers, but at a man's belly.

"Hold your fire!" I ordered him. I struck down the gun, which roared out, plowing a furrow across the *playa* up to the Indian's feet. "It will do no good."

"These devils will burn us at the stake!" he cried out angrily.

With no other choice but to lie in the ooze of those deathtrap holes until the unwavering Indians came up and stuck their spears into our backs, I got up in full sight and started toward them as casually as I could. They were only fifty feet away and plainly visible in the moonlight, over a hundred warriors fanned out over the *playa* with others still slinking out of the somber shadows behind.

They were hard-faced, naked except for purplish-red loincloths and claw-and-tooth necklaces, hideously painted. Fully armed with battle-axes, blowguns, spears, bows and arrows, two of them actually carried nets. They came to an abrupt halt. The closest savages drew back their right arms, but did not throw their saw-edged spears, apparently awaiting a signal from the white-feathered chief.

"Ho! *Indios*!" I called out, holding my hands palm upward to show they were empty of weapons. I walked slowly forward, came to a stop in front of the tall Indian who was standing well out in front of the others. I recognized him instantly . . .

"Iye Marangui!" I exclaimed with involuntary surprise. This was the witchdoctor we had watched that night in his house near Sutsiki.

The grim face remained absolutely wooden, a complete deadpan, but he opened his maw of a mouth and grunted:

"*Taimroki Matse!*" (White Witch!)

I checked an impulse to extend my hand and shake his own, for this practice is abhorred by Campas who, like certain Moslems, do not wish to contaminate themselves. Instead, I spat at his feet, and pointing at the moon bellowed that its light was good for hunting, that the spirits were subservient to him on such a night, and that we, like all men, must prepare to join Pawa soon.

The customary formalities of greeting over, I turned on my heel and walked back to the pits. Jorge and the two Indians were uncovering the fire and building it into a huge bonfire of flames. The horde of silent

Indians followed me across the *playa*, gathered in a tight ring around the blaze. Jorge and I, together with José and the 'Opata man, were caught in the center. Iye Marangui stepped in with us and squatting on his heels began a thunderous oration, which from time to time José had to piece out and interpret for me. Apparently the *manso* they had speared at the fire was a "bad" Indian, an evil-eye who had been condemned to die but who had escaped to 'Opata.

When the witchman had broken off his tirade, I asked him a question:

"Where is my guard?"

The witchdoctor pressed a great thumb against the side of his throat and grunted significantly. I knew they had killed him.

I continued: "It is a great distance from your house to this *playa*. How long did it take you?"

"Suns!" he grunted, holding up three fingers, meaning three days.

We then knew that there were secret war trails through what was believed to be a pathless tangle of jungle, trails on which a Campa brave can run fifty miles in a single day. That they had come in three days seemed incredible, but there they were.

I knew that a powerful sorcerer of Iye Marangui's stature had not run a hundred and fifty miles merely to see that a sentence of death was carried out on an Indian he had declared *bruja*. I sensed that our fate was in his hands, but I knew better than to question him directly as to why he had intercepted us, for the Campas are intensely indirect during any form of conversation.

With a wild singsong series of sounds interspersed with grunts, he gave a command to an Indian standing just behind. This Indian instantly leapt forward and held out a very large and cumbersome bag—a cased *coto* monkey skin, with the shaggy brown hair still clinging to it.

Iye Marangui untied a buckskin cord at its neck, and began drawing out various objects: little packets in bark cloth, small skin bags, carved green jadeite stones in the form of frogs (symbol of the Rain God), bundles of feathers and other items. He started painting his heavy-jowled, flat face. He used *achiote,* the bright orange-red paint mixed (in his case) with snake oil, rubbing it all over his head, shoulders and arms. From a tiny sack he took a cobalt black paint and smeared it carefully on his forehead, finishing with a single glaring Brahmin-like white spot between the eyes. He removed his white feather *paquitsa* (headdress), and put on instead, over his own long thick hair a grim anaconda's head, rigidly mounted so that its mouth was hinged open as if striking. Poorly tanned, it emitted an incredibly vile stink, unusual for even an anaconda skin. The snake skin, a mottled black and brown, which was attached at the back to the headpiece, was about twenty-four feet long and a yard wide, and this Iye Marangui carefully coiled around his great body.

A spotted jaguar skin was spread on the sand for him, and on this the sorcerer sat crosslegged. The mounting flames of the fire played over him and the ghastly greenish glare from the moon picked out highlights in the paint. Jorge pointed out that the snake's eyes were probably diamonds. The stage for jungle sorcery, red magic, was set. . . .

Iye Marangui began swaying back and forth, his eyes closed. Sweat broke out in beads on his devilish face, for the night was sweltering. All at once he cried out in a discordant chant, which must have continued for several minutes, for suddenly I realized clouds had blotted out the moon and a smashing deluge of rain was falling on us. But not an Indian stirred, though like cats they hate rain. The downpour soon passed, the moon returned, and only a monotonous drip came from the dank jungle beyond, and the drone of the returning insect hordes.

Suddenly the sorcerer's flint-edged eyes flew open, and the chanting stopped. "I, the Brother of the Serpent, will dream!" he bellowed in a deep voice.

He then set about a self-imposed hypnosis. Certainly in the *playa's* shadows moved the shade of an old Frenchman named Dr. Franz Mesmer. After a few minutes the *brujo* seemed to have become a disembodied automaton swaying before the fire, into which he stared unblinkingly. The trance was induced quickly, partly through the eardrums, by the intricate sound pattern of a tom-tom beaten by one of the Indians. This was aided by the conventional system of a reflection from some bright object on the retina of the eye, in this case a large quartz crystal held in his fingers. Thus began his savage séance with the jungle gods.

All at once, without warning, the Brother of the Dancing Anacondas began screaming in a tiny voice—the opposite of his usual bellowing tones. José started whispering hurriedly in my ear, sometimes lapsing into Campa: "He is talking to the *catsiburere,* an *itasolenga* (spirit), a malignant man-dwarf, which in adulthood stands only three feet high. It has the hands of a man, also a man's head with white hair. One of its feet is clubbed, and short. Its skin is white. From its shoulders grow red hair and the wings of the white king vulture. It is the worst monster of the jungle. When a man is confronted by the *catsiburere* he becomes paralyzed with fright, and the dwarf falls upon him, and breaks all his bones. It has the strength of a thousand devils, it is *antanukire* (fierce, fiendish), and it eats of the flesh of its victims until the belly touches the ground and the wings and body are dripping with blood."

José was obviously becoming frightened. All about us were the straining faces of the savages, their hard, narrow eyes staring in fascination at the face of the witchman.

The *brujo's* thin, feeble voice picked up a note of whining, and I nudged José. He turned toward me and began speaking in a very frightened voice: "The *brujo* says—'Man (*champari*) has come from the stars (*enpoguiro*) . . . and to the silent (*pimagerette*) stars, he will return at death. . . .' "

The *brujo,* that two-hundred-pound hunk of bone and muscle, who had not flinched at the prospect of death from a shotgun, began sobbing and crying out plaintively as if the coils of the anaconda skin were crushing him. Presently his voice rose to a terrific pitch—shrill childish tones of anguish, and he began scratching at his painted chest with talon fingernails, drawing blood. Tears dripped from his eyes. Then Iye Marangui pitched forward on his face. He was shaking violently from head to foot. He raised his head with a jerk, got unsteadily to his feet.

He was still wrapped in the snakeskin and he tossed his demon's head this way and that, as if to clear his brain of sleep, hissing all the while. His eyes flew open. His face became ravenous, contorted with a cataleptic insanity, alternately twisting from grotesque expressions of fierceness to those of fawning. One instant he was a snake striking out at us; the next he was a feeding tiger roaring on all fours; then a vampire darting here and there, swooping about the fire, sucking at his own arm.

Here was unbridled art, or sheer madness. He seemed suddenly symbolic of the Campas' *andakangare* (a difficult word—perhaps a mixture of terror and danger), something supernatural. Then in a peak of fury he began running around the circle of Indians, who seemed to be frozen with fright, smelling at each in turn. Abruptly he broke off and leapt toward Jorge and me as we sat near the fire with José and our 'Opata Indian; all the while stomping in a thumping dance around us, smelling at each in turn. Abruptly he broke off and stopped in front of Padre Antony's man, pointing at him with the large crystal still clutched in one hand, hissing, and screaming crazily "*Notqui! Notqui!*"

Now *notqui* merely means "eye," but he was not referring to any ordinary kind of eye, for two warriors sprang forth and dragged the poor *manso* out of our midst, and throwing him hard to the ground with a terrific slam, held him struggling on his back near the fire. There was something malignant, merciless, urgent in their manner. The witchman grabbed up a firebrand, and after the others had brutally forced their victim's mouth open with the butt of a heavy spear, he plunged the burning limb with its flames into the *manso's* mouth, and by screwing it around, forced it straight down into the throat.

The back of Jorge's hard fist appeared from nowhere and knocked me solidly in the chest as I tried to rise, my hand already under my shirt and closed over the .45's grip. "Sit still, you fool! Do you want us all stretched out and killed like that? *Las bestias!*"

José said, "This is the killing of the *catsiburere.*"

The most terrible cries of anguish came from our poor friend undergoing that awful torture. His legs flew about, twisting this way and that, in what must have been an incredible agony of pain. The smell of burning flesh filled the air. Finally, after a time, a long time, he was still and quiet—thank God the man was dead. The witch rose to his feet a bit weary from his exertions, tossing the firebrand carelessly on the fire. He was satisfied, in fact he shone with virtue—hadn't the devil been driven out of a *catsiburere* who was living in the guise of a man?

"Ah! *Está bien!*" cried Jorge. "Now what!"

Somehow I must extricate myself from this predicament, and the two loyal *camaradas* who still remained alive with me, and the best method for doing so was to be sympathetic toward the savages' beliefs. To be sympathetic I must first understand them. This was going to be difficult, for the Campas, swayed by Iye Marangui, were proving anything but "simple primitives," and were dominated now by ghosts and malignant spirits, not mere fancies to them, but real living phenomena.

Ancient primitive, intuitive man—who today still lives on in the vivid mind of the Campas—had learned how to produce visions; even in recent historical times the Greek Delphic oracle and the primitive Christian saints resorted to them for warnings, prophecy, advice, comfort.

And so the Campa too can produce actual visions which appear before his eyes; day and night, he sees phantoms all about him—trees bend down and speak, snakes turn into human figures before his very eye, flowers melt into crocodiles. A man at Sutsiki had one night leapt out of his bed, straight from deep sleep, and run off into the jungle. Half an hour later he returned with a wild hog slung over his shoulder, which had walked into a trap set with a bamboo spring armed with a spear. When questioned, the Indian replied that he had gotten there just in time, as the pig had nearly wriggled off the spear. When I asked how he knew the pig had been trapped just at that moment, he stared at me in amazement, finally replying: "In my dreams I saw the spear strike the pig in the shoulder!" But now Iye Marangui was demonstrating how the Campa savage differs from all other methods known to priesthood and to science, in inducing such ecstatic visions. And it was a most astonishing thing.

The Campa witchman gets through the various phases of privation, isolation, fasting, and intense contemplation, with the deliberate use of a powerful drug called *camorampi* (Spanish, *soga de muerto*), literally, in Campa, "Soul Vine." The Jívaros use it, and they call it *natema;* other tribes call it *haya huasca;* it is some sort of unidentified jungle vine which is boiled with *cowa* leaves.

If after drinking the powerful drug, a man should see (visualize) a red parrot, its skeleton visible through the feathers (as under X-rays) and obviously made from solid gold—the sibyl *brujo* will explain, while in a trance, that the man's "friend," a "spirit," has warned him that his house will be burned by enemies and his women and children sold for *kishongare* (gold). The *brujo* warns the man to prepare for war—and being of a warrior race, he knows that he should attack first. His nearest neighbor is Parare, the Wolf; that's the guilty one. Kill him!

Preparations are then made to kill the Wolf. First, the priest, using one of the several types of telepathic communication which they claim to possess, sends out a dream (the translation is "spirit") to do battle with the "protective spirits" hovering around the Wolf. The *brujo* fashions a spear of wood and poisons it, and into this mundane object he dreams a spirit; next he launches the spear into the air toward the *paugotse* (house) of the enemy of his client. Having thus destroyed the Wolf's "spirit helpers," his client can safely destroy the body of the Wolf itself. The former dreamer then lies in ambush, as only a Campa can, and easily kills his enemy. The head is taken, or a scalp of hair; its spirit is now transferred through devious magical processes to that of the taker of the head.

As for the body of the dead man, Campas will bury it in the nearest river or *cocha*, though more often they burn the bodies. A witchman, however, is buried in the earth, together with his broken witch-cult objects, for to burn him would cause the sun to go out.

The Peruvian calls the *bravo* Indian treacherous, a subhuman object fit only for destruction. It should be understood that the Indian is not treacherous, in the sense implied, but is only carrying out his convictions that he is doing right. Doing "right" seems to be a universal instinct; but what constitutes right, and what constitutes wrong, differs with society and what it considers best for the majority. The Campas, feeling no obligation to the tribe, kill each other whenever an individual's interests seem threatened, and this is called "good."

Again, when an angry Campa goes in desperation to the witchman to get an interpretation of his dream, the following may develop: The warrior explains what he has dreamed that a certain man gave him a present. But when he happily goes next morning to the man's house to claim his present, he learns to his chagrin that the scoundrel denies remembering ever making the gift. And so the Indian who had had the dream goes away angry, feeling cheated. In this case, the sorcerer advises him to kill the welcher for his obvious crime of dishonesty, and at the same time to transfer the spirit of the departed to his own train of "helpers" in payment of the debt.

Iye Marangui that night on the *playa* asked me, the White Witch, how I would have settled the affair of the last dream above stated, a case which he had disposed of that day. I suggested hanging the head in a tree and letting the vultures dispose of it. At first he was astonished, but after reflecting smiled craftily, admitting it to be an excellent suggestion. He pointed out for all to hear, that the vultures would eat the gift head, and having annexed the soul to themselves, would be friendly to the head-taker, and one day return to claim the body of the head-taker when he too eventually died. Out of gratitude they would bear his own spirit into the air toward the Sun, Source of Creation!

Still cloaked in the snakeskin, Iye Marangui—enveloped in an air of terrible sincerity—now prepared a great mystical ritual. He seated himself on the jaguar skin. An Indian brought him a flat basket with a small lid on it. The witch removed the lid and thrusting in his black claw of a hand, dragged forth a coiling grayish black snake some three feet in length. I flinched, for it was one of the *alfaningas*, as yet unclassified, and one of the most deadly of Amazon reptiles. He took the snake in one hand, while with the other the Indian held a polished disk of *curi* (Spanish gold), five inches in diameter.

At a sulky howl from the *brujo*, a wall-eyed Indian elbowed his way through the crowd and entered the inner circle around the fire, carrying a small earthen bowl painted a dull rusty red.

"It is the *camorampi*," whispered José.

The *brujo* now put down the wriggling snake and the golden disk. He grasped the bowl in both hands and drank its contents. As he did so, the lethal *alfaninga* crawled slowly over the sand toward me, and then slid across my bare hand and into my lap. I could feel my entire spine tingle as the flat, lead-gray head raised to mine, the tiny black beady eyes fixed coldly on mine, and the whitish pink forked tongue darted in and out only a few inches from my mouth, getting my vibrations. Humans, as I have mentioned, undoubtedly betray fear on coming into contact with a snake, and snakes are receptive to it, and are frightened in turn. The snake was cold, but cast off a faint musklike odor. The *brujo*'s flinty eyes locked with mine, and he seemed both surprised and pleased. I would do. I was indeed a witchman.

He loudly finished gulping down the last of the draught, picked up the disk and, leaning forward, grasped the snake at its middle and placed it between his teeth. Instantly, angrily, it struck at his face— again and again—its fangs spurting twin streams of yellow venom. Then he removed the snake from his mouth. The two objects—the golden disk and the snake—he continued to hold throughout the ensuing ceremony of ritualistic magic, which was to last for two eternal, tensely torrid, mosquito-hellish hours.

The helper scampered out of our presence to join the crowd, all of whom were keyed to a high pitch of excitement and apparently frightened. The Anaconda Brother, this black-and-red painted savage, this witch savant could perform wonders equal to those of scientists—as Jorge and I knew from remembering what had happened in his own house. Now he explained that he had drunk the *camorampi*, the wonderful Soul Vine. This drug—unknown to science—was very like opium, apparently, in the De Quincy–like dreams it would presently bring on. José explained that it would compose the witch's earthly shell in a state identical to death *(kamingari)*, so that his mind, encased only in its essence *(pinarotse)*, or envelope of spirit, should move freely into the fateful future. Mind, explained by José as "lightning particles," would eventually return to the "dead" body on the *playa*, and so again become alive *(ayantare)*. Thus the body could be used again and again, in the service of the gods as the "clay" instrument, or totem, for conveying to the Indians, the true *(kiaria)* intelligence, which the freed mind had gathered beyond time and space.

Jorge stared fascinated, for he knew we were witnessing a most remarkable event in sorcery, something that no Peruvian ethnologist had seen before. In fact, no stranger had ever learned anything of the secret Campa religion. The Puna, perhaps the most intelligent outsider in contact with them, had sneeringly told us—the ignorant newcomers—that *"Los Campas"* had none, they merely worshipped devils. But now, for some strange reason known only to himself, Iye Marangui calmly explained that before he could look into the future, his spirit must first travel to the high spirit places. Thinking me a *brujo* like himself, he wished to exchange ideas. At least that was what I wanted to believe. Had I known what was in his twisted mind, I should never have had the nerve to observe the facts, much less jot them in my notebook.

A sacred snakeskin drum began pounding—rising and falling with monotony. José bent close, saying in a low half-whispering voice that the patron Campa devil Kamari was being called by the *brujo*. Kamari was a dark shade who walked in the jungle *(antami)* or slept in the *nija*, the deep waters of rivers and lagoons, or even lived among the clouds. Like the *brujo* whose servant he was, the God Kamari could enter anything, everywhere, and at will. He could turn into a jaguar and cause it to pounce on a man. He could creep like the anaconda, hide like the tapir, or run like the deer. That is the true reason why these four animals are never eaten as food. Kamari was malignant. Normally he appeared as a manlike creature, with a large birdlike beaked nose, much like that of the Sun God Ra, whom the ancient Egyptians believed to be the ancestor of their Pharaohs.

To create an impasse and so nullify the evil efforts of Kamari, the witchman must also seek the aid of Pahua (pronounced with a Quechuan inflection as Pawa at Sutsiki), the "Man of Gold," who lived in the middle of Ureatsere, the Sun. As José whispered on, the *brujo* correlated his ceremony and symbolically began worshipping before a new small fire which an Indian had built on a hastily erected stone dais. José explained it typified Ureatsere. Yuca, the god-given Campa staff of life was then fed to this symbol of the Sun. And to the flames were added copal. The actual fire, *pumaare,* was kindled from special sacred wood called *enshato,* which had been soaked in the "hot blood of the sun" and in the "hot blood of man killed in sacrifice." Blood, the Campas believe, is that fluid substance which links all living matter; the blood of the animal is that also of man. Even the juices of plants, the saps of trees, is blood in a different form only. Strangely enough, this is the present belief of science.

The gleaming, sweat-dripping, black-and-red-painted *abendaningare* rose from his tiger skin, and symbolically glided snakelike around the "Sun," keeping time to the gently patted tom-tom, while all the Indians chanted in a high wailing chorus and incense and food sacrifice were consumed in the votive flames. Thus having appeased Pahua, and having asked the Sun God's aid against Kamari, who typifies the "Spirit of Evil," the witch proceeded to worship Pachukuma.

This third deity in the complicated Campa pantheon (which includes Gods and Goddesses of Earth, Water—or Rain, Air, Fire, Space), was a sort of diabolical knight-errant ghost who acted as a Hermes-like messenger, or liaison, between mankind and Pahua. Both Pahua and Pachukuma were formed in the image of man, explained José, adding, "even as Christ and Lucifer," as if to explain his belief in both religions.

Letting this sink in, he continued his explanation: All about over the *playa,* the mystical Anaconda was crawling, wending its way around and through us, sliding up through the tree tops and out into the sky. "*Patróne*—that's why everyone is crying out and pointing all about and up toward the moon. They say they see it!"

And so the way was being cleared for looking into the future, a future explained as being predestined and fatalistic, a future in which man's free will played no part. The Brother of the Dancing Anacondas squatted again on his jaguar pelt, and symbolically recognized "death," by rubbing his white-spotted forehead against a human skull clutched in the vise of his knees. In both hands he held aloft to the moon the squirming *alfaninga*, and the golden disk. After questioning the fascinated José, I took the snake to symbolize "shadow wisdom," and the disk to be "man's control of the sun and the moon, for it reflects the rays of both, symbolically linking earth to these celestial bodies."

As the sibyl *brujo* struggled against the spirit of Kamari, he cried out as in a nightmare, rocking around on his hip sockets in a circle, holding aloft the symbolic snake and the shining disk. The food sacrifice sizzled out, burnt black, even as did Moses' offering in the wilderness. It might have been a human Inca sacrifice, instead of merely a vegetable one, for sometimes captives or condemned "third-eyes" (evileye) are burned and children fed to an anaconda.

The drug began telling: the *brujo* was apparently falling asleep, for his head was nodding. His features kept a rigid dignity for he was *listening*, said José, to the wind god sweeping through the "worlds" (stars). He began writhing in grotesque antics, dancing violently from the hips in ecstasy now, as a *jergón* snake sways before a fright-paralyzed bird. José believed the witch to be gazing into the golden face of Pahua. After half an hour of this swaying back and forth with a sort of grinding yogi movement, his black and red arms rigidly held aloft, still clutching the snake and the disk, he began a most terrifying dirge.

The minutes flew past; suddenly Iye Marangui dropped both snake and disk on the sand, and awoke from his sleep, shaking. José said he was not outwardly conscious, but in communication with the gods. The sorcerer spoke very slowly. His voice rumbled in a deep cadaverous bellow which echoed most unnaturally in that thick sound-cushioning jungle air—perhaps reminiscent of that other Indian's ventriloquistic voice we had heard during our first day in the jungle.

It had an unaccountable quality, such as might have been caused by a human voice echoing from the far end of a long hall of stupendous height. This is what José said in as free a translation as it is possible for me to render:

"*Looo* (uttered in a long drawn-out voice) . . . I, the *abendaningare*, a *hatingare* (traveler) have seized the sacred Anaconda, which in a thunder clap bears me instantly to a mountain top on Cachiri (the Moon)."

A long silence followed. Would he go on? Every eye in the grim-faced circle seemed to be asking that question. And then again came the great echoing voice—and again whispered José:

"*Looo* . . . Pahua is directing me to face Quipatse (Earth). *Looo*, the Earth is red in *tampea* (the air), like the Sun in tiger-mating time. A cloud covers Earth. Pahua sends Pachukuma off on an Anaconda, and he strikes it aside from the sky (*inquite*), that I, the *abendaningare*, may view all. *Looo*, I see *cuengare* (a fearful, or dangerous scene) of *champare* (men)! They, friends *(shanitka)* and enemies *(huairi)*, burn together and strange flames of hell *(kiaratse)*, rise among them all; *unila* (earth-quakes) and *empoguiro* (comets), fall from the skies all black! Thunder and lightning fall amongst them, like particles from the Sun. . . ."

This was followed by a deep silence, shattered by the Indians breaking out in a terrible wailing, each straining to watch the witch's face. Then:

"*Looo*, Pahua—that Shower of Gold, is appearing on a mountain nearby. Pahua sends me on the back of my Anaconda, to the center of creation—the Campa nation!"

The *brujo* awoke. Had he been to the earth's satellite, as José and the others believed? Or was his mind a well-ordered house of autosuggestion? The witch was obviously bursting with hauteur and pride, though his dark eyes reflected a tense fear, and his great hands shook.

"Of course, since we don't know the answer, we may as well put it all down to indigestion," said Jorge.

That broke the spell, and we found ourselves once again back on the *playa*, and faced with the desperate problem of getting away. But the possibilities did not look bright. The Indians were engaged in a terrific pow-wow among themselves. Iye Marangui peeled out of his anaconda skin, and hustling into a red *uma*, gruffly bade us follow him. Already the others were grabbing up our mosquito nets and ponchos, and various things scattered about.

"We are *esclavos*," groaned Jorge, getting to his feet. "Remember what happened to Rodriquiz, the prospector? I warned you none has ever escaped alive from the Gran Pajonal . . . nor shall we."

José, who had been cocking an ear toward the babble of the crowd around the fire, turned to me and whispered tensely: "It is worse than that. They say Iye Marangui wants to eat your heart, to add your knowledge to his own."

"Then that's the explanation for their cannibalism . . ." I finished for him. "The Incas, Aztecs, and Mayas offered human hearts to the Man in the Sun, none other than the Campas' Man of Gold. And the astronomer-priests ate the hearts afterwards. The ancient Bird-Snake culture actually still lives in these jungles."

Jorge and José both stared in amazement, while Jorge finally sputtered: "Are all yanquis mad? But come, my friends, *vaya con Dios*—go with God."

Not knowing where we were going—or why—or what would happen to us, we were shoved along and prodded with spears to the far end of the *playa*. Apparently the Indians were headed east, downriver. But then we were driven left into a rocky jumble, the beginning of the *mal-paso*, a roaring defile filled from side to side for 200 yards with the swift-flowing black and white waters of the Tambo. Into this deafening torrent the horde of a hundred warriors unhesitatingly plunged to their chins. A few carefully strung out behind a guide, who held aloft a firebrand snatched at the last moment from our fire.

Obviously the Campas knew of a secret ford for crossing. Though the river raged around us, tugging madly, for we three were flung in bodily and nearly drowned, we slowly waded across the slippery rocks lining the ford—a submerged dyke or reef—and emerged dripping on the opposite bank. Soon the party began stringing out and creeping along the face of a white salt cliff rising just beyond.

The moon was hanging low in the heavens now, but our way was bright enough once we climbed clear of the jungle's top. I followed close on the heels of a mule-legged *bravo*, with enormous red-painted feet and great toes splayed out for gripping the narrow, precarious path. Apparently this yard-wide shelf was caused by a steeply slanting fault, its surface was covered with loose stones and salt which had weathered away from above. Once on a bend, the fault narrowed to a foot. I was forced to place my shoulders against the wall, and trying not to look down hundreds of feet upon the jungle below, worked my way slowly around to safety.

Sweating and puffing for lack of breath, we struggled for a thousand feet up to the top of the plateau. Earlier we had seen signal fires from the same plateau, and now saw, bending away before us to the north, an endless tangle of palms and trees—the heart of the central tableland of the forbidden Gran Pajonal! The Indians began trotting down a narrow trail into the tangle. We were driven on after them, but after an hour, Jorge and I could no longer keep up, and the column slowed to a swift walk. From time to time I was tripped up by vines in the darker places, but was instantly prodded on with a spear in the hands of a grinning fiend following close.

We had gone all of ten miles from the edge of the rim, when daylight came, and some time after, Jorge, José and I were marched swiftly into a village of five houses, swarming with silent women and children. We were shoved into a hut on the far side. We lay on the earthen floor breathing hard, absolutely done in. I noticed that there were no windows, and the air was stifling. Overhead on heavy beams rose a V-shaped old grass-thatched roof, filled with vermin. Greenish spiders began coming down on long strands. Several red millipedes were crawling over the ground and so we finally got up and sat on a log lying near the wall opposite the doorway, and stared about us.

Logs were being brought to the open doorway and fixed upright in the ground, and bound with thick vines of *tamishi*. All around the hut the Indians were crowding and peering through the cracks between the logs, jeering and spitting at us. At midday a woman's hand pushed a small wooden trough through a gap under one of the logs. José cried out for water, but only jeers answered him.

"Captives of the cannibals . . ." groaned Jorge, as he got up and crossed the floor. He picked up the trough, smelled at it in disgust, and examined the contents. He held up one of the sour-smelling things in it, a cluster of rotted berries, a plum-sized fruit covered with scales. He bit into one, spitting out the scales and a yellow pulp. "Oily—tastes like acid. Probably that's what they fattened Rodriquiz on."

José remarked forlornly that they were fruit from the *mirity* palm, and added that when the pits, which looked somewhat like red golf balls, were baked and pulverized, the Indian women use them as abortives.

"Another medicine for science," said Jorge. I saw that his darkly tanned face was deeply lined and grim. He was not only tired in a physical sense, but even his mind reflected the ever-mounting tension of worry over the uncertainty of our situation. Unobserved by me before, this tiredness must have been accumulating for days, and only now showed in the spiritless eyes and the hard lines around the mouth. His hair (like my own, I realized) was long and tangled. And likewise his pants and shirt were dirty and even torn.

Hungry, we ate some of the pulp, and soon the floor was littered with the red pits. Vermin started coming in, especially a swarm of tiny pink ants that bit like fire. Jorge called them *pucacuras*, and warned against letting one bite anywhere near the eyes, for the acid in the stingers would cause painful and usually permanent blindness.

I heard some giggles from the other side of the wall just behind our log perch, which was elevated a foot on short posts. I glanced down just in time to spot a thick black snake wriggling along between my feet. I raised my shoe with a yell, which brought more giggles.

"It's all right," spoke up Jorge after a quick glance. "A *mussurama*—it won't hurt you. That one eats snakes."

A few feet away the *mussurama* coiled up in a hole filled with ashes and dust, its head raised a little, staring at us and darting out its tongue, but otherwise offering no harm.

"Why did they put it in here?" I wondered aloud.

José spoke up: "*Patróne*, it is only to see if we can be frightened. The children did it."

"The little bastards" I thought, but said: "Playful little devils, aren't they?"

Jorge said gloomily: "Perhaps it would be better for us if it was venomous."

All day we stayed in that sweltering dungeon, the dirt floor a filthy mess from old food and yuca expectorated about. With night we still remained miserable for they brought no light. Since those peering through the cracks couldn't see now, I began scouting around—while wondering where that damned snake was—trying to find a way out. The base of one of the logs proved to be pithy with rot, but when I drove a hard sliver into it, I found the core solid as a rock. The walls were of the metal-like *moena* wood. There was no use trying to break through. Mosquitoes flew in through the cracks and settled on us in clouds. It was the most awful night I had ever known. There was no sleep for Jorge or me, though José dozed off from time to time.

Next morning we heard the Indians outside in the village. But the only thing we saw of our captors was a woman's brown, scrawny hand at the crack under the wall, a hand quickly withdrawn, for Jorge slammed a rock at it. For breakfast we had more of the *mirity* oil berries. It began to look as if Jorge were right.

To relieve our tension I began questioning José about the Campas.

"Where shall I start?" he enquired.

"Start with the women," I suggested, "they can't possibly be as devilish as the men."

He started at random, and what he had to say wasn't very heartening. The women often mutilate the fallen after battle. It is due to their nagging that most of the killing is done—to obtain slaves and so lessen their own work. No woman wanted a man who could not kill another and protect her. As for the wives, he continued, on seeing me frown, they are reasonably faithful to the split-cane couch, but if one should prove otherwise, the husband whips her before his clan to "clean his face." In the case of the husband's stepping out, his spouse— or collective wives—whip the poor misunderstood miscreant along with the "other woman." Some wives will place the juices of the terrible *floripondo* plant in the husband's food; the poison attacks the brain tissues, turning him into a zombie-like slave, who comes and goes at her direction, a witless thing that she beats before all the other women.

"This," said José, "is *pashueitingare* (shame), avenged."

My interest aroused, and wishing for some single spark of human kindness, I asked about love, and learned that "love" is not necessarily a psychic state evolved by civilized man. The savage also marries for "love," which he calls *nitasutane*, because "he likes to be in 'love' throughout his life." To this blissful somnolent state, so desired by the more impractical male, his first wife apparently does not object, since all secondary wives are under her iron rule. José believed that the love impulse is very strong among these virile Campas. One morning just before Jorge and I had arrived at Stone's, a "wild" woman was found hanging by her neck from a tree limb. On inquiry, the intelligent José learned that the woman's husband had died while serving as a laborer, and "loving" him, she had committed *tongashare* (suicide), and so followed him to the Sun. Suicide is very common, and is usually committed by the taking of poison. Having exploded the modern theory of man's newly acquired capacity for "love" I felt satisfied for the moment, but not José, who was wound up.

The loving Campa *bravo* must ask the woman for permission to marry her, and not ask her father. Should she bite his nose and perhaps playfully bang him over the head with a club, it means she is interested in an offer. The wedding ceremony to the Sun God is enlivened by *chicha* and a shindig, songs and a little casual fighting with war clubs, rites to the minor gods and propitiation to the devils; and then follows the building of the new house with the aid, usually, of the happy bridegroom's brothers or clansmen. The *Matse* (Old Witches or Old Grandmothers), instruct the bride in her love life to come. Their tools, persisted José with great interest, are wooden carvings depicting the various positions available to the sex act, not unlike those—I gathered—seen in the murals of Pompeii. If possible the ingenious Campa seems to have outstripped civilization in devising a few new ones on his own, bringing the tribal total up to some forty. As he described some of these Jorge and I could not help wondering where sex leaves off and acrobatics begin.

Campa divorce is practiced with no ceremony other than the husband trading his wife off for a spear, a house, or a feather headdress he might fancy. If it is the wife who wants the separation, she is a wise woman who picks a better clubman than her ex-husband, for he is very apt to hunt her down and brain her. In any case the matter is settled between husband and wife.

"How about the men?" I asked.

José told us that each man fashions his own bows and arrows, his tools and canoe, burns the jungle for his garden patch, makes the cloth and most of the ornaments, these last being sacred.

Campa blowguns, or *tepi*, are bartered from the Chama tribe on the Ucayali. These guns are nine feet long. They have a slender, tapering tube of split *chonta* fitted with a mouthpiece of hollow bone. This mouthpiece is cemented with pitch and gum, while the tube itself is bandaged with fiber, polished black or dull brown. The bend of the bore is so finely drilled that it allows for the slightest drop due to weight. He warned us that the *tepi* can shoot with deadly accuracy at 100 feet, and hit a large target such as a man at a range of from 200 to 300 feet. The darts are ten inches long and contained in a section of bamboo. A type of curare poison, called *moca* among the Chamas, is also bartered for. It is prepared by the Chama witchmen, *cucucunas*. Other poison for darts and arrows may be the venom of snakes. While most upper Amazon tribes are familiar with some form of curare, the Campas are not. Chama *moca* is so virulent that a mere flesh wound will kill a lion, bear or tapir, though all these larger animals must be tracked down after being shot with a *tepi*.

Moca is undoubtedly a therapeutic agent similar to insulin. *Moca,* curiously, "relaxes" to the point of death, explained José, who had seen men die of it. The amazing thing is that the Campas themselves have an antidote. This is a quick application of rock salt applied to the wound after it has been slashed open with a knife, together with oral dosages of salt water. This is not too dissimilar from our own intravenous injection of salt solution for plague. If this is not done quickly, *moca* can cause nerve paralysis, limpness, nausea, asphyxiation, heart stoppage and death. Normally the Campas do not use the *tepi* in war against members of their own tribe, as a *bravo* can pluck out the ten-inch dart, make slashes parallel with the veins, and treat the wound with salt. Thus, not only *moca,* but snake-venom-tipped arrows are used solely on strangers, as Campas also have cures for the two main types of snake bite—and inject both antivenoms when in doubt.

When raiding, the Campas ferret out a village or a hunting camp or clanhouse, arriving at their target just before dawn. The psychological element aimed at is surprise. If the tactic and the carnage are successful, all the males will be killed, the skulls of the wounded bashed in. The women, babies and children are taken captive and later sold as slaves to the *patrónes.* (Few are the adult male Campas who have not killed at least once.)

If any of the Indians in the village have escaped the slaughter, they invariably rendezvous in the jungle and counterattack the raiders, attempting *asarmatandingare* (revenge), and to recover the slaves, and perhaps grab off a few of their own. Sometimes the counterattack is staged in the jungle after the raiders have split up their party and are returning to their own homes, but usually a few days are allowed to lapse as the enemy's guard is then relaxed, and also there is time to prepare ghost-spears and other magical rites.

These rites are conducted with musical instruments, *tamboros* (drums) and *sungares* (flutes). A dance, the *jubesherie* is held; the dancers wear belts of little jingling shells. Ornaments worn by the *bravos* are strictly defined as badges of distinction and grading, being taboo for all except those who qualify. Bracelets are of ivory, cloth, colored fibers, teeth, claws, animal and reptile skins, feathers, wood or beads, for the Campas believe that if metal is worn, the flesh will rot. After the dance the warriors start off for the manhunt.

José warned that should we be able to escape, we must beware of the trails. Traps and snares, *nofate*, are abundant and make both game and man trails exceedingly dangerous for strangers. The man-traps are called *samerense*. Deep holes are often placed in trails and runways, embedded with rows of sharp bamboo stakes, designed to impale strange *bravos* out raiding in the Gran Pajonal. Any explorer who should leave the Perené, the Tambo, or any of these western rivers, should be warned that moving inland without a local guide entails considerable risk.

José pointed out that three *caucheros* trying to get into the lower Tambo, and cruise for "weak rubber" trees, were victims of traps. Two of them fell into man-traps and were killed by poison. The third was captured after being taken out of a trap, and secured to a post driven into an anthill. The insects ate him alive. The skeleton was placed in the *caucheros'* canoe and floated downriver a few miles into Atalaya, as a warning for other Peruvians to stay off the river.

"All this is certainly fascinating," I pointed out, "but for the life of me, I can't see a ray of hope in it for us."

"*Patróne!*" José cried out in despair. "There is no hope. You see what they did to our three 'Opata friends on the *playa*. These Indians will tear our hearts out, and Iye Marangui and other witches will eat them. The people will eat our bodies. Believe me!"

"The damned cannibals!" whispered Jorge in English; then in Spanish to José, "The next thing you will be telling us they will feed us that *floripondo*."

"They will! They will!" cried José, quite beside himself. "They can amuse themselves longer with us when we are under the spell of this drug. A man does not die easily once he has drunk *floripondo*."

"We must get out of here!" The Peruvian spoke with such violence I was sure he would bring the guards down upon us.

With nightfall we were weak from hunger, for nothing since

morning had been shoved through the hole, and though we cried out for water, none had been brought.

Three hours passed in total darkness on that second night, when I was suddenly aware that José was hunting around. When I idly asked him what he was up to, he didn't answer, but after a while joined us on the log. I struck one of the last precious matches. (I still had four in my oiled-silk map case which of course had been in the money belt under my shirt and not taken from me as had the .45.) José had found the *mussurama* and crushed it under his bare feet, and was biting the black hide off, and actually eating the meat along the spine. Jorge and I were sick at the sight, but José appeared not to notice. As a Campa he was not doing anything unnatural to his instincts.

We listened through the cracks and when the village had settled down, and our two guards outside the door were quiet, I boosted Jorge up to the ceiling on my shoulders. It was pitch dark, but he managed to feel his way into the rafters at the back of the hut and soon dry grass was coming down upon my head. I knew he was making a hole through the thatched roof in the corner.

"Pssst!" came from above. "Reach up your hands."

I lost no time in complying, and a moment later found myself dangling in mid-air, and presently pulled up to the rafter on which Jorge was standing. Then together we reached down and José was hauled up, though when his knee thumped against the log it made a loud noise and my heart nearly stopped. The stars were shining through a small hole just overhead. Crouching on the rafter, we waited ten minutes, then José began climbing through the gap. His legs disappeared, and from the rustling in the thatch we knew he was lying on the roof, *outside*.

All at once the blood began running cold in my veins. One of the guards at the door was getting up. We could hear him talking with the other one. Suddenly the *thump-thump-thump* of his great feet could be heard on the ground. He was coming counterclockwise around the hut. There was no way to warn José outside, and we felt that all was up.

The guard made the last turn just under our corner. The next sound we heard was a soft grunt. Jorge pushed his shoulders through the hole and I followed. Immediately we saw that José had heard the guard, and when he was passing beneath, had jumped straight down, apparently striking him on the head with his great hard feet. José already had the man's spear in his hands and was thirty feet away at the edge of the forest. We leapt down to the ground, only twelve feet below, ran across the dangerous open space, and found ourselves crouching with José in the shadow of a small tree.

José whispered something, but I didn't understand him. Jorge hissed in my ear that we must take off our shoes. We dare not make a noise. This we did, and when I stepped out of mine and put my feet down on the bare ground, I stepped into a nest of fire-ants.

My feet throbbing and half-paralyzed, Jorge and I started out after José who was moving as only a Campa can—silent as a black *coralito* (coral snake). He knew our shortcomings, however, and moved very slowly, holding limbs aside for us which we could not see, for the slightest noise would draw the remaining guard. Any second now he might find his friend at the back of the hut. At last we were far enough away so that we could risk moving faster. We had not gone two hundred feet, however, before a scream went up behind us.

I wanted to run, blindly—do anything to hurry. But José clamped his hand, which was hard as a vise, on my shoulder. "Do not move, *patróne*—" he whispered.

We waited motionless for a very long time, all the while the yelling Indians streamed apparently out of the longhouses and gathered behind the hut, only a stone's throw away.

"You go," suddenly whispered José, pointing into the depths of the jungle. "Hurry!"

Jorge and I moved out as fast as we could under cover of the Indians' racket, though actually at a very slow fumbling walk, due to our bare feet and also that we could hardly see in the jungle of air-roots and vines. Ten minutes must have passed before I realized that José was not with us. "Where is José?" I asked Jorge in a whisper of alarm.

"I don't know. Hurry. Make not the slightest noise. The Indians are quiet—*listening*."

"But, we can't go without him! Besides—we would be lost."

"For God's sake—hurry!"

And so we went on and on, until we came to a small opening in the tangle where a single ray of light shot down from the star-filled sky. All at once I smelled something that struck terror at my heart. An Indian was near, and only a yard away. . . .

I felt around with my bare feet for a rock, and finding one I picked it up.

"It is I, *patróne*."

"Jose! How did you ever find us?"

Ignoring the question (for we probably had sounded like a herd of wild boars, even with our bare feet), he said, "We were being followed. I returned and killed the man."

His hand grasped mine and guided it along the flat blade of the spear; it was wet and sticky.

"Knowing a Campa is with you, they dare not follow until daylight," he whispered with grim satisfaction. "Come!"

We kept at José's broad humped back as he forced a way through the jungle, always with unerring instinct picking the best and more open places through the mass of clutching vegetation. Once we struck a trail, but he would not let us take it, warning of traps. "Besides, scouts will already be watching all the trails."

An hour later through a gap in the trees I saw, after getting my bearings on the Southern Cross, that the Indian was taking us on a line into the southeast, not south where our rafts were lying on the *playa*. Without those rafts we were in as bad a position as a shipwrecked sailor on a desert island. The Indian said we must abandon them, that warriors would start for the *playa* immediately on finding we had escaped. He hoped to intersect the Tambo far below the *mal-paso*, but first we had to reach the edge of the plateau.

"Hurry—*patróne*! There is no time to talk."

For five hours José took us slowly through that awful jungle thicket. Twice the Indian warned that he could smell a snake, and both times we had carefully to circle the spot. Walking with bare feet, we were anything but easy in our minds.

Finally, at dawn, and in full view, as there was no cover, we stood on the bare rim of the Cerro de la Sal. A thousand feet below roared the Tambo. Here the Indian left us hiding in a grove of palms and scouted west along the brink. Half an hour later he returned. He had been unable to find a way down. Next, he tried the eastern direction—and this time brought us along with him, for we must either find a way or be lost. The Campas would be well out on our tracks by now.

Expecting their yells behind us at any instant we limped along on torn feet, hurrying up as fast as we could, with José stopping often for us to catch up. Finally in desperation, though reluctantly, he brought forth our shoes from inside his shirt. He had picked them up though Indians had been everywhere. Gratefully we put them on and then, though we left easy-to-see tracks and made a terrific racket, we really moved out now, running behind him. At last José found a way off the plateau. It was down a steep rockslide that partly filled the head of a narrow canyon which cleaved the *cerro*. Taking care not to break our legs, we started down, sliding through rock screes and clinging to tree roots and lianas, until finally after half an hour we found ourselves at the bottom of the Cerro de la Sal.

Running as best we could through the jungle we lined out for the river, and three hundred yards beyond the cliff came upon its bank—a rocky, sandy stretch. José plunged unhesitatingly into the deep water. We dived in after him. Swimming hard, we finally succeeded in getting across after being carried downstream some four hundred yards. The Indian would not permit us to climb out on the far bank, but instead, started wading shoulder-deep along the muddy edge of the river. Once he pointed out an immense stingray, lying on the bottom. We splashed after José for a quarter of a mile until he turned right and crawled out of the water to enter a patch of bamboo.

"Rest!" he gasped, and then calming down explained that he must return to the river and make seeable tracks upriver from the point where we had reached the opposite bank. This would throw the trackers off, and above all delay them—for he swore that in addition to their dogs the Campas themselves could hunt by scent. The heat from

the sun would eventually burn off the telltale scent, but in the meanwhile he must act! When the Indian left, I crawled back to the river and
eliminated our tracks by tossing dry sand around.

All day Jorge and I lay low in that thicket, and had finally given up
José, thinking that he must have fallen into an ambush, or been run to
the ground. But with nightfall he came crawling in stark naked through
the bamboo. He called out in a low voice first, for he knew we would
arm ourselves with clubs and he might otherwise be brained on
entering our hole.

"Braves are hunting everywhere," he warned, "be very quiet."

Animal and bird calls were all around, on both sides of the river,
and these he whispered were signals. Also, during the late afternoon,
tracks inside the thicket indicated that a warrior had passed within
only fifty feet of us. José went on to explain that he had back-tracked
through the water and crossed the river over to the cliff side, and then
turned upriver along the bank making a few vague impressions where
the trackers would find them, pretending we had waded toward the
balsas and done it rather awkwardly. That would throw them off for a
while, for they would search the trees and every foot of ground for a
mile around the rafts.

All night we lay up. Though we now had water it was our second day
without real food other than the worms and *ronsoco*. I was weak and
nauseated, but after vomiting felt much better.

When Jorge and I awakened at dawn, José had vanished. We kept a
careful watch, not speaking, and by midmorning I heard just the
slightest rustling sound behind me, and on turning quickly, saw José
standing in an opening between the bamboos only four feet away. It
gave me a terrible start. Grinning, he whispered,

"Four warriors I have killed. I have a raft hidden just below."

He had found two paddles on the raft and he also had weapons
slung about him, a bow and several arrows in a lion's-tail quiver, a
spear, a blowgun and its bamboo section of darts. From his shoulder
hung a skin bag with several objects in it such as feathers, a bracelet,
and a bamboo tube of *achiote*. Every Indian carries such a bag (mea-

suring eighteen inches long and a foot wide), and in it is not only his make-up kit but all sorts of odds and ends such as flint and steel, medicines, arrowheads and charms. In one hand he clutched by its tail a fair-sized monkey—the *huapo*.

"*Carne!*" hoarsely whispered Jorge.

José soon had the skin off the monkey, which together with the head and guts, he immediately buried in the ground, fearing vultures would come and reveal our hiding place. He was soon handing Jorge and me small pieces of meat cut with his newly acquired Campa knife.

"You must chew it well!" He would not let us eat too much of the raw meat, and withheld it after a few mouthfuls.

Pointing up at several crow-sized birds with black bodies and red heads darting back and forth overhead and chattering madly, José scowled: "We stay here today. And if those soldier-birds do not reveal us—tonight we move."

The Indian picked up his blowgun and fitted a thin, brownish dart together with a twist of cotton, into its mouthpiece breech. *Pffff!* went the dart, and one of the birds came tumbling down. When José crawled slowly out of the hole, his eyes narrowed and twisting up at the jabbering flock, I felt that it would not be long before all of the meat hunting soldier-birds would be lying dead about that thicket of bamboos.

Jorge was stretched out on his side, listening intently to a persistent Indian signal—the cat mew of a fishing hawk. I couldn't help grinning, for I knew what this son of the conquistadores thought of the shirt Indians.

"You know—" he said soberly in a very low voice, his ear still cocked toward the river bank, "that José is a good man . . . our good friend too."

It was long past midnight before the last Indian signals echoing off the high salt cliffs on the far side of the river ceased. This final one was the persistent gobbling of a cock-turkey, a *piuri*, repeatedly summoning the hunting savages to him. It would have passed as a real turkey, except that these birds seldom gobble after sundown, at which time they go to roost in the higher limbs.

Even then we dared not move out. Crouching in the thicket we listened attentively to every sound that came from the trees and especially from the river: monkey chatters, the splash of fish—all were now judged genuine. But José seemed to be waiting for something, and when an hour had passed, I suddenly realized what it was when he glanced up into the sky: clouds were covering the heavens and the stars, a complete darkness creeping over the jungle.

Very quietly now we crawled through the bamboos, squirming along on our bellies, until we reached the river's south shore. José snaked into the water and we followed, taking great care not to raise the slightest ripple, for the surface was shiny with minute phosphorescent life. We feared the Indians more than the denizens of the deep. Twenty feet offshore we were in water up to our chins, and immediately started floating out toward the channel. From the middle of the river as we were being carried along, we could make out various objects, tall trees lining the low banks, and flotsam islands of hyacinth floating alongside. Despite the mosquitoes and the danger from snakes and crocodiles, we swam into one of these, a free island some half-acre in extent. To keep afloat, we need only spread our arms over the mass of the high bulbous stems.

We must have drifted downriver for two hours when José broke away from the hyacinth, swimming with only the barest ripple ahead of him, toward the left bank. Jorge and I were right behind, propelling ourselves along as cautiously as he. Reaching shallow water, the Indian waded silently into a *cocha* beyond the line of the trees.

Crouched in the river, Jorge and I waited for twenty long minutes, and then the Indian appeared pushing a narrow balsa raft ahead of him. By this time the rods of our eyes were so well adjusted to the darkness that we could see very plainly. We slid aboard and were once more adrift on the river. I seemed to be counting the inches linking us like a chain back to that bamboo thicket. Though rain was presently falling, and it was still dark, a flock of *yungaruru* pheasants began calling in their peculiar two-toned song, a very high note and a very low one—thus we realized that dawn was not far off.

Soon after, sand began flowing in the river, hissing under the raft, a sure indication that swift water was ahead. We dared not beach and risk an overland reconnaissance and so continued blindly on. A hot, rain-filled wind began blowing in gusts upriver, cavorting the raft this way and that. By energetically plying the two paddles we ran a 500-yard stretch of resounding white water, shooting through a winding slot of stone walls. At the bottom we extricated ourselves from a whirlpool, and once more glided silently on. I couldn't help it, I kept staring back over my shoulder.

There was more light on the river and we would certainly be visible to any Indian watching this stretch. The loyal José took the bamboo tube of *achiote* out of his skin bag—part of his swag—and handed it to me: "Take off your clothes, *patróne*."

Though fever-laden *culex* mosquitoes were swarming over the bright yellow surface of the river, I lost no time in complying. Jorge followed my example. We helped each other smear on the red paint, especially on our backs. Feathers were tied in our hair, which was long, and from the far banks we must have looked like three *bravos*. Delighted with our Indian appearance, José got out a pair of snake bracelets from the bag and slipped them on my arms. Our precious clothes and shoes and my money belt were hidden away in Jose's skin bag.

Several Indians swept into view, watching us intently from a high bank on the right side, but not a signal came from them as we drifted by. Birds began flying back and forth across the river, starting their day songs; but like many birds of these jungles they never finished their songs but usually stopped on some impossible and maddening note. Gaudy wild chickens such as the *gavilán* and the *trompetero*, were perched in the trees, the roosters beginning to crow. Still marching on our left, well back from the tangled bank, rose the sheer cliffs of the Gran Pajonal, soft white, streaked now with thick veins of orange.

A black thundercloud rolled up from behind and kept pace with us. The *pit-pit-pit* of the rain studded the tawny surface of the river. Sudden explosions and crackling electric fire broke the cloud asunder and after a violent tropical deluge, the sun shone copper in a pale blue sky; daylight had come. Though apprehensive, I saw that we were getting into lower country, for wide sandbars began replacing those of gravel. Stones still continued to clink musically as they bumped along the river's bed. These were well-rounded stones which would be ground down to sand and eventually, in the Lower Amazon basin, be pulverized to mud. That morning I was reminded that the earth turned through space (for the stars wheeled past overhead), that the mountains were washing into plains as in aeons past, and that we were part of the immense microstructure of this spinning ball of iron and nickel, mud and stone and water.

Once, in the Jungle
by Daniel Zalewski

What would eating human flesh be like? New York painter Tobias Schneebaum found out first-hand in 1956. Daniel Zalewski interviewed him in 2001 for the New York Times Magazine.

Tobias Schneebaum did not want to go back. For one thing, he feared that his old friends might be dead. It had been nearly a half-century, after all, since the Manhattan-born painter abandoned his easel, hitchhiked south to Peru, walked headlong into the Amazon jungle and went native with an isolated Indian tribe. For another, Schneebaum knew that the fantasy that had long ago propelled him into the forest—a desire to live somewhere untouched by Western culture—was becoming impossible to fulfill. "I worried that they weren't going to be naked anymore," he says wistfully of the Arakmbut people he lived with for seven months in 1956. "I thought, I don't want to see them clothed."

For someone who romanticizes Stone Age life as ardently as Schneebaum, the prospect of seeing his beloved Arakmbut wrenched into the modern world was indeed depressing. Schneebaum, who is now 80, lives in a tiny West Village apartment that is a shrine to his fascination with all things primitive. His walls are covered with masks, carved wooden shields and framed photographs of indigenous people he has met over a lifetime of remote travel. Dozens of plants complete the urban-jungle ambience.

Although Schneebaum was wary of sullying his exotic memories of Peru, there was a deeper reason he resisted the pleas of a pair of film-makers who kept begging him—an old man who'd had three hip replacements—to retrace his remarkable Amazon adventure. "I didn't want to think about the one bad thing that happened," he says in a frail but melodious voice. "For a time, I apparently cried out in my sleep. I had nightmares."

But the filmmakers, David and Laurie Gwen Shapiro, who are siblings, kept pushing him to go. Schneebaum finally relented. In June 1999, he traveled into the jungle one last time. The resulting documentary, *Keep the River on Your Right*, opens this Friday. As the film makes clear, the journey would be one of the hardest trips of Schneebaum's life. For he wasn't just going to revisit his quixotic attempt to shed his Western skin. He was going to relive the day he became a cannibal.

It was July, or maybe August, 1956. Schneebaum wasn't sure anymore. He'd been living in the jungle for so long.

He laid his paint-covered body down on a rock and stared up at the Amazon moon. The rock was one of many stone slabs jutting above the surface of the shallow, slow-moving river. Although he was in the middle of nowhere, he was not alone. On nearby rocks slept friends from the Arakmbut tribe. As the water gently flowed around them, his companions dozed off. But Schneebaum was too upset to sleep.

The day had begun routinely. In the morning, a group of men with spears gathered. It was time to look for food. Schneebaum was hopeless at hunting, and he constantly slipped on the muddy forest floor. But his pratfalls amused his companions. And so, as he had done many times before, Schneebaum tagged along.

It had been months since he first encountered some naked Arakmbut while walking along a tributary of the Madre de Dios River. In greeting, he took off his own clothes. The Arakmbut marveled at the tan lines on Schneebaum's body and returned his smiles with laughter. They took the tall stranger home. He was a baby Tarzan who just happened to be 34 years old.

The Arakmbut treated him well. They taught him words from their language and otherwise communicated through gesture. They shared their food with him and decorated his body in red pigments. At night in their communal hut, the Arakmbut men welcomed him into a warm body pile. These entanglements often turned amorous, to Schneebaum's delight. As he would later write, he had at last found a place where people "would accept me, teach me how to live without a feeling of aloneness, teach me love and allow for my sexuality."

With Schneebaum in tow, the hunting party ventured deep into the forest. Usually the group stayed close to the settlement; this time, however, they trekked all day. It was close to dusk when the Arakmbut began slowing down, almost to a creep. The men stopped just outside a small clearing. Through the trees, Schneebaum spied a small hut. He could hear the voices of men inside. Outside, bronze-colored women were cooking.

Suddenly, the Arakmbut charged, shouting and brandishing their spears. Schneebaum thought of running away, but he realized he was too far into the forest. Knowing what was happening, but not wanting to look, he leaned his trembling body against the hut and waited for the raid to be over.

The dead numbered around six. When Schneebaum finally glimpsed the corpses, he went off by himself to vomit. But he returned to the group. He discovered that some of the Arakmbut had begun dismembering their victims and wrapping body parts in leaves. Others rounded up women and children, who after some initial resistance appeared to accept their new roles as captives. The expanded party returned to the forest. Schneebaum carried one of the packages.

Not long after, his companions stopped and lighted a fire. The mood was triumphant, with plenty of laughter. The group began singing and dancing. At first he refused to join in, but he was pressed. He found himself caught up in the whirl.

A few of the leafy packages were unwrapped, and their contents were placed directly into the flames. After a while, meat was removed from the fire. Portions were passed around, one by one, to each member of the group. Eventually, a piece was placed in Schneebaum's hands.

He put the human flesh in his mouth and ate it.

After the feast, the hunting party and the captives continued homeward for a while, finally stopping for the night in a cool, open-air spot. Lying there in the middle of the river, Schneebaum decided that it was time to get out of the jungle. As much as he tried, he couldn't help viewing what had just happened through Western eyes. He and the Arakmbut were not one after all.

"That night, for the first time," Schneebaum says sadly, "I thought, What am I doing here?" He stares out his apartment window, which overlooks the Hudson River. "I had thought I was going to stay there forever." He is sitting in a small metal chair, munching idly on some mushroom pizza. "I thought it was the perfect place for me as long as they continued to give me food. I missed my old life at times, my friends and so on. But in Peru, those people were truly free. They had nothing holding them back."

This vision of liberation is clearly what attracted Schneebaum to the jungle in the first place. "It was a different time then, the 50's," he says. "It was hard. It wasn't easy to be yourself if you were gay. In the forest, I could be who I wanted to be."

But why did he want to be an Arakmbut? The anthropologist Clifford Geertz once wrote of his profession: "We are not, or at least I am not, seeking either to become natives (a compromised word in any case) or to mimic them. Only romantics or spies would seem to find point in that." Schneebaum falls squarely into the romantic camp. "I'm not an anthropologist, and I didn't go to Peru to gather information," he says with mild distaste. "I wanted to meet people and have a good time. I never thought about if I was exploiting anybody. I was doing something that thrilled me, and that was the only thing on my mind."

Schneebaum suffers from Parkinson's, which sometimes causes his face—dominated by a charmingly oversize nose—to turn masklike. But he lights up when asked about his days with the Arakmbut. "To have made the first contact with an indigenous group of people—one that was naked—was the most exciting thing that ever happened in my life," he says. "I ached with pleasure." He speaks of the "delicious" roast tapir he was given to eat, and jokes about almost gagging on the Arakmbut's home brew, a drink made from cassava fermented with spit. He motions to his closet, where an enormous wooden bow from Peru rests next to a mop and broom. "I never did learn how to use those things," he says, laughing.

The raid, however, taught Schneebaum the limits of his sylvan fantasy. Although he went into the jungle to escape the oppressive mores of Western culture, he has struggled ever since with the fact that he broke one of its biggest taboos.

In 1969, he tried to deal with what happened by writing a heavily embroidered memoir about his Peru adventure. He called it *Keep the River on the Right*, a nod to his improvised path through the jungle. (In addition to temporal changes and literary flourishes, the book disguised the Arakmbut's identity, calling them the Akarama.) Although the book devoted only a few pages to cannibalism, it brought him a fleeting fame that both pleased and dismayed him. Some people were amazed by his story. Others were repulsed.

How could he have eaten human flesh? "I didn't want to be the typical tourist who would run away from anything that was interesting," he says. His tone suddenly turns more grave. "I wouldn't say they forced me, but they wanted me to do it, to become part of the group. So I'm glad I did it. On the other hand, I'm terribly upset that I did it. And that's as honest as I can be." He pauses, then adds: "The killing horrified me more than the cannibalism. They were already dead, after all." Yet even if what happened to Schneebaum is merely a bizarre object lesson in the perils of peer pressure, that single swallow has haunted him. In *Keep the River*, he writes: "I am a cannibal. . . . No matter into what far corner of my mind I push those words, they flash along the surface of my brain like news along the track that runs around the building at Times Square."

There is one question that everybody asks him. "I can't remember the taste," he says. "All I'll say is that I like my meat well done, and this wasn't." Although he has gotten used to prurient inquiries over the years, they still make him nervous. He prefers to be seen as a bold adventurer, not as Hannibal Lecter.

The unhappy ending of Schneebaum's Peru journey in no way dampened his enthusiasm for seeking out primitive people. "It all turned out so well except for the raid," he says. Upon returning to New York in September 1956, he quit painting for good and got a job folding Christmas cards to amass fresh travel funds. He traversed Borneo, befriending Dyaks along the way. In 1973, he went on the first of many sojourns in New Guinea. Schneebaum spent several years living (and sometimes sleeping) with men of the Asmat tribe. He transferred his artistic energies to drawing, making detailed pen-and-ink records of the Asmat's elaborately carved wooden shields. While becoming one of the world's leading experts on Asmat art, he supported his travels by working as a tour guide in New Guinea.

In 1994, David Shapiro came across an old copy of *Keep the River*, by then long forgotten, lying in a box on Avenue B in Manhattan. He excitedly shared the book with his sister. When the Shapiros discovered that the man they envisioned as a latter-day Cortés was a witty, effete Jewish artist, they asked to chronicle his life story on film. "But to do it right, we knew we had to take him back to Peru," says David Shapiro. "It was his defining moment."

Schneebaum's story is the only personal account of ritual cannibalism on record. There are some dubious "eyewitness" reports from the Age of Exploration, but they serve to demonize more than document. Indeed, though most anthropologists believe that murder followed by cannibalism occurred in some preliterate societies, it has not been easy to prove that the practice ever existed. (Those thousands of cartoons depicting people roasting on spits don't count as evidence.) Despite occupying a recurrent role in the Western collective imagination as a symbol of uncivilized man, flesh-eating has never actually been witnessed by scholars or captured by a camera's lens.

Only in recent years have archaeologists been able to show, for example, that certain fossilized human remains display clear signs of having been cooked. (Bones floating around in a boiling pot, for example, get scratched in a unique way.) And last September, the journal *Nature* published a striking report. Fossilized human excrement located at an Anasazi site in Colorado was found to contain digested human-muscle protein. But what motivated this meal? Starvation? Revenge? Were the bodies already dead, or had they been slaughtered? The closer one gets to proving cannibalism, the harder it can be to say what it really means.

The Shapiros' movie emphasizes that Schneebaum's life should not be reduced to a single grisly meal. At the same time, the second half of the film puts Schneebaum's Peru story to the test, following the same route he followed from Cuzco in 1956. Arriving at the remote outpost of Shintuya, the crew learns that the settlement where Schneebaum lived was abandoned soon after his departure, when missionaries colonized the Arakmbut. But they are told that a village tied to indigenous traditions exists six hours upriver.

At this point Schneebaum protests that he's too frail, physically and emotionally, to continue. The filmmakers, he says plaintively, "are forcing me into doing things I do not want to do." The Shapiros calm him down, however, and the group travels by boat up the Madre de Dios.

San José del Karene is, in some ways, exactly what Schneebaum predicted. The village looks impoverished. A small store is surrounded by a moat of empty soda bottles. There's a communal structure, but it's now a community center; a TV showing *Rambo* flickers in the corner. When Schneebaum warily greets a group of around 30 Arakmbut, he is treated as a stranger. Then, slowly, some elders recognize him. He is embraced once more. (This time, everyone stays clothed.) Through a translator, Arakmbut men merrily recall Schneebaum's pathetic bow-and-arrow skills.

His dreaded trip back suddenly melts into a joyful family reunion. It's a moving sequence, and it confirms that Schneebaum really did go native. Yet amid all the reminiscing, one subject is pointedly not addressed. What happened on the raid?

"We don't want to remember those days," says one Arakmbut man firmly.

It becomes clear that, having been "civilized" by missionaries, the Arakmbut now feel a similar anxiety about their past. Sensing this, Schneebaum tenderly tells the men that he would love to hear their old hunting song. A graying Arakmbut complies. As the beautiful melody fills the air, Schneebaum's eyes flood with tears.

The journey offers a personal catharsis for Schneebaum, but a question lingers: is his tale of cannibalism true? If it is, it means that cannibalism took place in the Amazon well into the 20th century. If it's not, it would be hard to dismiss as a harmless fiction. Last fall, Patrick Tierney condemned anthropologists in his book *Darkness in El Dorado* for turning the Amazon into a playground for their personal fantasies. The writings of Napoleon A. Chagnon, Tierney argued, had projected his own prejudices about "savage" Indians onto the gentle Yanomami of Venezuela.

Has Schneebaum slandered the Arakmbut by calling them cannibals? His response is matter-of-fact: "Some people think I sat in Cuzco and made the whole thing up. But it all happened." Indeed, his endless effusions about the purity of naked man suggest a lack of interest in exposing humanity's dark side. "The raid was a bad thing," he tells me, "and the cannibalism was not for me, but I loved the Arakmbut. And if you think about it, it wasn't so unusual. We have wars all the time."

The only study of the Arakmbut in English was written by the British anthropologist Andrew Gray. (He died two years ago.) His 1996 study notes that "intense warfare" took place between the Arakmbut and rival groups "prior to contact with the missions." Reasons for these raids, he writes, included "raiding for women." Though Gray documents no cannibalism, he observes that some Arakmbut myths feature man-eaters.

It may well be that by going native, Schneebaum witnessed things that no scrupulous anthropologist could ever see. Gray's ethnography, for example, ignores same-sex relations. (Schneebaum says his lovers also slept with women.) But to apprehend the private practices of a foreign culture, one might need to go beyond interviews. To sleep in a pile with natives affords an intimacy that, however unconventionally obtained, may yield genuine knowledge. The ethnographer who remains a "distanced observer" may leave some secret places unexplored. Schneebaum didn't merely ask the Arakmbut about their hunting traditions. He hunted—and ate—with them. Although his actions broke every rule of field research, Schneebaum may have inadvertently beaten ethnographers at their own game.

That said, Schneebaum's memoirs, which in addition to *Keep the River* include accounts of life in New Guinea, could hardly be considered scholarly. His writings are too self-obsessed; one gets little sense of the natives beyond descriptions of their physical glories. (You could learn almost as much by staring at a Gauguin.) But his memoirs are matchless in the way they give voice to a potent desire: namely, the Westerner's yearning for salvation in the primitive. The idea that seeing man in his "natural" state would offer spiritual emancipation can be traced back to Jean-Jacques Rousseau, who coined the term "noble savage." Schneebaum's life has been an attempt to make Rousseau's myth a reality. For him, that impulse doesn't seem strange in the slightest. "In going to live in the jungle," he says, "I did something that almost everybody, at some point or other, has thought of doing or wanted to do."

Growing up in Brooklyn in the 20's, Schneebaum frequently visited Coney Island with his mother. On the boardwalk there was a sideshow attraction called "The Wild Man of Borneo." The tent's poster of a hirsute savage provided one of the first sparks in young Toby's imagination—and libido. As he grew older, he devoured books in the corny *Bomba the Jungle Boy* series. (The prose was classic Ooga-Booga: "From time to time the dreaded headhunters . . . invaded this district in search of the hideous trophies which their name implied wherewith to adorn their wigwams.") Schneebaum was hooked. "The minute I read *Bomba*, he says, "I knew that someday I would go live like him."

Schneebaum is in some ways a historical relic. One suspects that if he were growing up today, he wouldn't feel compelled to escape to the jungle to express his desires. It's too facile, however, to attribute his interest in the exotic to his sexuality. Too many others share his fascination.

"At film festivals," he says, "people keep coming up to me with maps, asking where they can go that's still unexplored by Westerners. I point to a small region of New Guinea and say, 'That's about it.' An Austrian acquaintance, an amateur explorer, sometimes sends him photos he has taken of "uncontacted" people from the central highlands of New Guinea. The photographs are lovely, he says, but they're no substitute for the real thing. "That's what I miss," he says. "When you come upon a native for the first time, if he's all painted and decorated, it's scary. Terrifying, gorgeous and absolutely beautiful."

Schneebaum is glad he went back after all. "I still feel such a connection with the Arakmbut," he says. "To see people you'd been friends and lovers with 45 years ago was astonishing." And though he happily reveals that he now has a boyfriend—a native of exotic Canada—he leans forward and offers a confession. "I still sometimes wonder," he says, "Why am I living here? Why I am not still there, in the forest?"

from Keep the River on Your Right
by Tobias Schneebaum

When Tobias Schneebaum (born 1921) entered the Peruvian Amazon in 1956, he began his stay in the jungle at a mission, where he met a Spaniard named Manolo. An Indian named Wassen stumbled out of the forest, telling of a murderous tribe's raid on his village. Schneebaum set out up the Madre de Dios river to find the killers. He wrote a diary of his journey in the form of letters to "M" and "C."

The excitement of these weeks that have gone by has increased to such a degree that I no longer have the will or strength to allow another day to pass without expelling some of that energy into this diary.

I left the mission with no more than a wave to Father Moiseis, Hermano, and the Indians. Manolo put his hands on my shoulders. "Ciao," is all he said, as if I were to return the next day. Wancho and Alejo were waiting by one of the rafts with my knapsack and food, to take me across the river. I waved again, for the last time. The only thing I said to myself was, Goodbye, when I left the two Puerangas on the other side.

Even so, it was an eloquent, unspoken parting. The clamminess of fear within me at that final break with everything that was part of my recent past, remote past, of all my known life, of everything experienced by my body and mind, was not generated by what lay ahead. Time that is to come and what happens to me within it are speculations that can be invoked only through the whole of myself, within the context of my thought and existence, and limited by all that I have fed into me. So my fears were not so much for the future but for what I left behind. Not for the people or places, but for my knowledge. I was cutting away all that I knew about myself, I was removing my own reflection, and as I walked on, I walked into an incarnation of myself that had always been there, so hidden it had never reached the outer layers of my soul. I lived then, during those few days, in each hour and each day, and they enclosed me like the forest itself. Time separated itself into fragments, each one discarded to make way for my emerging self. Not like those other days when I walked to the mission, when time was fused and exhilarating, but I was allowing my secrets to come forth, shedding the disguise that I had never known was only a screen. I did not look for the Indians now; I simply transferred myself toward them. There were no pictures in my mind of what they would look like, no ideas of what their reactions might be.

It was the fourth day and I was walking along munching on fried bits of yuca that I had soaked in a stream to soften, and I came out from among a huddle of bushes to a long rocky beach, at the far end of which, against a solid wall of green, some spots of red attracted my eye. My first thought was that they must be blossoms of some kind that I had never seen before, but they were too much like solid balls, and they moved slightly, though there wasn't the slightest breeze. A few steps farther on I frowned and shook my head, wondering even more what they could be and then it came over me in a shiver that these spots were faces, and they were all turned in my direction, all unmoving. Still closer, I made out a group of men, their bodies variously painted in black and red, looking tiny against the gigantic backdrop of the jungle that stretched so high above them. No one moved; no one turned his eyes away or looked anywhere but straight at me. They were frozen in place. They were squatting tightly together, chins on knees, arms on one another's shoulders, leaning over resting heads upon another's knee, or thigh or flank. They continued to stare, moving neither a toe nor an eyelash. Smiles were fixed upon their faces, mouths were closed, placid. Some had match-like sticks through their lower lips, others had bone through noses. Their feet and toes curled round stones and twigs in the same way that their hands held vertically bows and long arrows, and axes of stone tied to short pieces of bough. Long, well-combed bangs ran over their foreheads into the scarlet paint of their faces and hair covered the length of their backs and shoulders. Masses of necklaces of seeds and huge animal teeth and small yellow and black birds hung down from thick necks and almost touched the stones between their open thighs.

Still no one moved as I approached. There were thirteen, fifteen of them, I never knew. Off to one side, on the right, without ever taking my eyes from the men, I was able to see two fires burning in front of two small structures of branches and leaves, and I felt rather than saw figures lying within. I came up to the men, stood but a few feet away. Still no one moved, still no one made a gesture of any kind, no gesture of hate or love, no gesture of curiosity or fear. My feet moved, my arm went out automatically and I put a hand easily upon the nearest shoulder, and I smiled. The head leaned over and briefly rested its cheek upon my hand, almost caressing it. The body got up, straightening out, and the frozen smile split open and laughter came out, giggles at first, then great bellows that echoed back against the wall of trees. He threw his arms around me, almost crushing with strength and pleasure, the laughter continuing, doubling, trebling, until I realized that all the men had got up and were laughing and embracing each other, holding their bellies as if in pain, rolling on the ground with feet kicking the air. All weapons had been left lying on stones and we were jumping up and down and my arms went around body after body and I felt myself getting hysterical, wildly ecstatic with love for all humanity, and I returned slaps on backs and bites on hard flesh, and small as they were, I twirled some round like children and wept away the world of my past.

A pair of claw-like hands, black with paint as if they had gloves on them, suddenly were pulling at my shirt, pulling it apart at the neck and buttons popped, while other hands were stretching out the waist of my trousers and I felt a head pushing into my stomach as its eyes tried to look down and a hand went in and scratched my thigh and cupped my testicles and penis. My sneakers were pulled off by someone below me, and he took hold of the legs of my trousers and pushed them up as high as they would go. A handkerchief came out of my pocket and soon covered a head. More hands went into pockets and found a box of matches, which opened by itself and the matchsticks scattered over the ground. We all bent to pick them up and they were removing similar sticks from their lower lips and replacing them with these when a flash of flame appeared between my hands and shrieks of astonishment went up and long whispers of Ooooo-oooooo and two fingers reached out and closed themselves on the fire and a shout of pain gave it reality, and they backed away an instant but returned and I lit another. Ooooo-oooooo, the whispered, and from a lower lip came a match that was examined carefully and the man hit it on the top of the box and broke it in two. Another tried and again it broke in two. I showed them where to strike the match and they looked at me and uttered low clicking sounds.

From behind me someone had finally pulled out my shirttails and was pushing the shirt up and pinching my skin, then rubbing it with the flat of his palm. A cold tongue licked at my back and then came around to my hand and licked again. I unbuttoned the last of the buttons on my shirt and took it off. I removed my trousers. Hands were all over me again, pulling hard at the hair on my chest, pulling at the hair of my groin, lifting my penis and whispering Ooooo-oooooo, spreading the cheeks of my buttocks, and hugging, always hugging me. They each had a turn at touching my whole body, and some came up and held their penises alongside mine, comparing them. My nipples ached from the pinching and it seemed that my body hair would soon be removed, painfully. At last we all squatted down and they spoke to me as if I understood their language fluently.

This was the beginning of my meeting with the Akaramas, and now, living within their lives, I have become what I have always been and it has taken a lifetime, all of my own life, to reach this point where it is as if I know finally that I am alive and that I am here, right now. I have thought back often to that meeting, to when I first knew that those shapes were human, that they were men who had killed other humans and had eaten their flesh, that they were the first men who had ever walked upon the earth, and that my own world, whatever, wherever it was, no longer was anywhere in existence. I walk alone, and have always walked alone. I have walked this time, this last time, where my legs took me, as if the nerves of my body all extended in the one direction that would take me here. In writing, I think. That is, in writing here, it has become necessary to put thoughts together that go down on these pages. But when I walk, I am driven in some inexplicable way, almost as if the way were one I had traveled before, and I put my foot down on crunching leaves, lift the other leg and place the foot forward, stepping where it has always known it would step again. And coming upon my people, now my lovers, my friends, I shed my past as I did my clothes, even knowing inside me that I could never be a Michii or Yoreitone, that a shirt, though now gone in shreds, though it no longer is an object for which I have any desire or need, remains forever something that I know has somewhere a use, and I can never strip myself of the knowledge of how to open a button, how to put my arms in sleeves, how to put the tails inside a pair of pants. To become Michii, I must not only rid myself of the need to write, but also of the very knowledge that writing exists. Whatever self I have opened within me is one which forever must retain a sense of another world. In my hand at this moment is a pen and it is making marks on paper. On my hand is the black paint that comes from the fruit of the huito tree. There are designs painted over my body and I have scraped away with a bone knife all hair below my shoulders. So I sit here writing, naked. Was I in the same way naked before them, before I had removed my shirt and trousers? Had I bared my soul before my body? How is it that they did not kill me? How is it that I was not frightened of them? Again it is questions, and questions without answers. They were there, squatting in front of mahogany trees and the picture of them registered itself upon my brain, clicking like a camera, and there were no thoughts, nothing to tell me to be afraid, that they are cannibals, but it's as if I absorbed them through my flesh, an osmosis whereby they came into me, into me, inside me, ran along with my bloodstream, became white and red corpuscles, the air that entered me, the food of my gullet and stomach, crept along my dermis like a second skin. They entered into my pores. What smell did I exude that allowed them to accept me? It was in Borneo that Mathurin Daim had said, "You are the only Westerner whose smell I have ever been able to bear." There, I knew well that having lived for so long among his people, eating their foods, my body smells were like his own. But here, it is something else, something to do with the fact that I came as I did, that I came alone and in need. I knew that they recognized me, that we recognized each other. We played games and hugged each other. My skin was white and they licked it to see if the paint would come off and were pleased when it remained its strange color. Time after time they ran their hands over my chest and belly and penis. They touched with gentle fingers my nose, my eyes, my ears, my hair, and they prodded into my navel with their noses. They repeated one word over and over, Habe, habe, and it has taken me all this time to understand its meaning: "ignorant one."

It might be that an hour passed and they were still talking to me, and all I could do was shake my head and nod as thoughts of what they might be saying went through my mind. Some of the men stood before me on one leg, resting the other foot on its calf. Perhaps from the very first I knew that they were naked, but it was only later that I looked at them, realized that they wore only paint, and began to some extent to study the designs on their bodies. Some men had a band of black around the waist, buttocks, and sexual parts, as if wearing shorts or bathing suits, and their hair was clipped in crew-cut fashion with a pigtail running down the nape of the neck. Slightly older men, though they too were young, had clean thin paint lines going down from below the neck to the knees, with a design from chest to groin of double inverted vees. The youngest boys were completely black, though their faces too were scarlet. One man seemed out of place; his body was splashed and splattered with red and black as if he were the beginning of a Jackson Pollock. Everyone's hands and feet were black with gloves and shoes. No one looked more than twenty-two.

We were all squatting there, knitted together, and I was talking and laughing, telling them, only because of a need to talk back, whether they understood or not, all about the mission and about my life in New York, when a woman appeared from one of the lean-tos. She could have been fourteen or eighteen. She had small breasts that stood out straight from her chest. She covered her face with one hand and with the other held out a piece of meat. Her hair was cut very short and she was black from neck to toe, except for the upper chest, which was carefully painted in spots of red to form a vee that ended just above her navel. Her face remained hidden until a man took the meat and she turned back to the shelter.

Beside one of the shelters, a large monkey was being cooked over a smoking fire. From the coals, long tubes of yuca stuck out. The sun had gone down and I became silent and listening. Whispers filled the cool night air. A wind brushed against the forest and leaves swayed and rustled. Figures around the fire moved in slow motion as if nudged along by this tranquil breeze. Three other women tended the fire and meat. The oldest carried a baby on her back, wrapped in leaves and vines. They did not look in my direction. The man who I came later to know as Michii (for it was weeks before I knew anyone's name) and who was sitting behind me with his thighs against the sides of my body, so close up that I could rest my elbows on his knees, poked me on the back and I turned around. He was chewing on a piece of the monkey meat, masticating it without seeming to swallow. He opened his mouth and let the meat fall into his hand and held it out to me. A little unsure, I took it, put it into my own mouth, chewed and swallowed. He laughed and tilted his head and then gave me the charred arm from which he had been eating. The singed hairs of the animal stood up like thorns all over it. I bit into the flesh and blood and juice ran out. It was tough, stringy, unsalted, delicious. Michii took a banana from a stalk that had just been dropped there beside him and sank his teeth into the skin, bit along it quickly to split the peel, and with a quick movement, tore it apart and pushed the whole fruit into his mouth. He peeled another and gave it to me, pushing it into my mouth with his own hands. After we had eaten several bananas he reached behind him for a long section of sugar cane, broke it over the top of his head into short lengths, and handed one to me. His front teeth were short and arched, filed down from biting into the hard outer layer of the cane. Each time he handed me something to eat, he said "Baapendée."

I slept intermittently that night, on leaves and bodies and branches. At dawn we breakfasted on more yuca and monkey meat, and when all stomachs were full, all food and weapons were gathered together and we set off into the jungle. I had no idea where we were going. My clothes had disappeared, but I found my knapsack untouched and managed to remove, from the feet of two different men, my sneakers.

Well, Manolo, where are you and what do you say now? "They are fattening you up for the kill," you will think. But I did not feel that, and here I lie on my stomach on the ground, with three young men leaning on me watching each movement of the pen.

Last night, after we came back from a hunting trip, Michii presented me with a bow and six arrows of two types, four wide-bladed bamboo arrows for animals like monkeys and ocelots, and two made of ebony with notched shafts and sharpened ends, for birds. This morning he and Darinimbiak led me out to a field and began to teach me how to use them. I had thought that the day they both sat me by the river and painted me with the same designs they wore themselves, the day also that Michii scraped off the hair on my body, for the first time, with a nutria's tooth, that somehow I had then, with no other ceremony, become a member of the tribe, had become within that short time as close as possible to being an Akarama, to accepting myself as the being I had always dreamt myself to be. Until the bow and arrows were offered, they gave me everything: laughter, food, themselves, time; but with that presentation came also the need to learn their use, a sympathy for the weapons themselves, as if without them it was only my mind that lived here and my body, even with all its pleasures, had remained in other worlds. But oh! what a fiasco I made of that first lesson! I tried pulling the bow, and I pulled and I pulled and I stretched it out a foot and a half. I fitted an arrow and it jumped away. Michii and Darinimbiak rolled with laughter. Darinimbiak's arms came around me and together we shot an arrow into the air, straight up, and it hung there a moment, resting before turning its head and dropping at our feet. Again my arrow flipped away, again the bow made only a slight arch. There was no impatience as time passed, only a lessening of the laughter, and I improved and finally was able to send an arrow straight and somewhat close to its hoped-for distance. For me it was as if I had conquered an earthly element, and there was a glow on their faces that held me staring from one to the other until they placed the bow and arrows in my hand and back we went to the hut and lay down to sleep, one upon the other.

We went off the other morning, yesterday it was, as if we were going for a swim in the river or into the edge of the jungle to find an edible bird or two. The three of us, Michii and Darinimbiak and I, suddenly were inside the forest racing along as if we were already on the track of some great animal. I looked down at my bare feet with shock and pleasure as they moved along, those feet of mine, and trod upon the ground, upon the twigs and debris, with no uncertainty, without the pains of cuts that had been so habitual, and had seemed then to be a part of my feet themselves. We stopped and they examined leaves and earth and sniffed the air, and on we went, slower.

There was another time five or six years ago, when the sky was the rose of that painting I sold to C, and I was following a Murut in Borneo, over a hunting trail. He carried a blowgun in his hand, there was a bone through the bun of his hair, and we were racing along the way we are now, with leeches on my legs and no time then to brush them off as he stopped an instant to bend and test the tiny footprints for their moistness and off again we went, slower then, slowing down

to an absolute silence on a still evening with the air as clear as it can
ever be, and the long tube moved up to his mouth and flutt! the dart
flew out through leaves and branches, moving them along its path, and
suddenly his voice screeching as he rushed back towards me, a mouse
deer slung across his shoulder. I ran a hand over its fur and the Murut
touched a finger on my breast and pointed into the trees above us and
there, staring down, were three orangutans. And still another time,
when C was touching me and pointing up into the jungle of Chiapas
and three Lacandon Indians stood there in the trees in their dirty shifts,
three arrows in their three drawn bows aimed in our direction.

Suddenly again a hand was on my arm pointing. Michii's hand,
pointing to a large grey animal rushing wildly through the brush. We
ran on and came to deep water, into which the animal jumped and
almost hid itself, only a snout and ears above the surface. An arrow,
two arrows, three, splashed the water behind the snout. Michii and
Darinimbiak were swimming before I knew they had moved. They
reached the already dead animal and floated it back to shore.

Out of the water, the huge tapir took on a brownish color. Michii
took hold of its snout and wiggled it back and forth and laughed. With
the long, sharp edge of one of his bamboo arrows, Darinimbiak sliced
through the underside and removed the innards, carrying them into
the river to clean. Michii cut away at the head and soon had it separated from the body. He searched out two thick branches, sharpened an
end of each, staked the head on one and ran the second through the
animal's body. After that first laughter, we made no other sounds but
looked at one another often with smiles as they worked and I watched
and helped when it was possible. The innards were wrapped in leaves
and tied with vines to the stake that held the head and this was given
to me to carry, while they lifted the immense creature onto their shoulders and began to trot their way back to the hut. It was dark when we
reached our village. We crawled through the entrance hole, dragging
the tapir behind us. Michii took the head to Yoreitone, who immediately set it onto the coals of a fire. Darinimbiak opened the package of
innards, held up the liver and ran to the fire in front of the area in

which we slept and began to roast it, holding it over the heat with a long stick. The rest of the animal was cut up into small pieces and distributed among all the others. My shoulder ached where I had held the head and I lay down between Baaldore and Ihuene, who pressed themselves up close and asked about our trip. I whispered out my story, moving my hands and body in description, varying my tone for color, and they were hearing me, listening to me, imitating my gestures to gather into themselves what I was saying, in this way making it more clear to themselves, and though my words in their language were few, my movements were long and changing and as my arms stretched out a bow and an arrow flew, their eyes widened with interest and fascination as they knew it would reach its target. It was not a long story I told, and Michii might have taken two hours to tell it, but it pleased me so to tell this tale and I was feeling more than ever part of this family. Darinimbiak came over as I was finishing my last descriptive movement. He already had in his mouth the pierced liver, biting off a piece to give me. It melted in my mouth.

I was feeling confident in my new language when an evening came that Yoreitone sat outside the hut upon a jaguar skin, surrounded by boys of twelve or fourteen. His parrot-feathered mace lay in his lap. His face was clear of paint, but black lines circled his neck, beginning at the chin and continuing into the strands of jaguar teeth that hung down to his navel, and also covered his upper arms. Wide bands of black reached from his clavicle to his knees, while thinner lines followed the contours of his thighs and calves. His testicles but not his penis were also black and a line ran from there, passing over the anus up to the coccyx, where it ended in a long filled-in inverted vee. He had the match-like stick in his lower lip. All of the boys were painted exactly alike, black from chin to toe, scarlet on their faces.

Yoreitone stretched an arm up to the moon, paused in his whispering until I had settled among them, and continued, "And then you will have the woman and you will see what you must do with her. You have heard our speaking and you know what you must do, and you have seen. The fruit is ready." The boys nodded slowly, expressions of understanding on their faces. I waited for Yoreitone to go on and explain further. He shifted his body off to one side by rolling his thighs and buttocks, sat up in a squat, and defecated loudly, then moved back onto the skin. He did not speak again, but no one left the circle.

I opened my mouth and uttered a sound, hesitated, and then at an opening gesture from Yoritone, his palms up, spreading out his fingers and his arms, I asked in my own whisper, "Tell me, Old One. Tell me from where do men come?"

He patted my forearm and laughed. "You are very ignorant." The boys giggled into their hands as if a great tension had been released, but they stopped as Yoreitone lifted his head, lifted and rattled his mace, replaced it in his lap, and nodded his head up and down several times.

"So you do not know that all men come from the heights? Yes, it was many times ago, many, many times of death ago, that we were all living up there." He pointed the mace toward the sky and moved it as if to encompass the whole of the heavens.

"One day an opening split through the heights and men in wonder came from everywhere to look at it. They looked down from the hole that had split and they liked what they saw. There was light, and there were rivers with fishes in them and under the trees were many animals to hunt, and they wanted to go down. But they had not enough rope to reach to the bottom, and much time, a great deal of time, each day they all worked, and time went by while they made the rope long enough, because the heights were so high that even the strongest arm could not send an arrow to reach them. And when they finished making the rope, they climbed down and began to eat of the hunt and of the fishes of the rivers. But the spirits from above became angry because we had left them and they were all alone and man was not with them. It began to rain and the waters of the rivers boiled, and the men, in order not to be drowned or burned, went out to look for the

tall, tall tree, the huamée, it was called, so they could take refuge there
and they could live and eat, and also the animals lived in the tree with
them. Also the jaguar and his woman, and mama the crocodile too. It
was a long time that they lived there, and when there was no longer so
much water, some of the men wanted to go down from the tree, but the
waters were still hot and it killed them. And later others went down
and then there was no water and there were no fires. Then the mukas,
the wild pigs, came down, and these were the first that man ate, and
last of all came down the jaguar and his woman. But this was many
times ago, many times of death ago, and no one knows where this
huamée tree is. We look for it when we go into the forest, but always it
hides from us, but a time will come to find it."

Here he was, Yoreitone, my chief, sitting and telling me a story and
looking at me with his one eye as he looked upon his family, his body
full of gentleness, a finger now and then resting on my knee, and when
he had finished the tale and sat there simply within the aura of its
meaning, with no movement of any kind, it was as if he had opened
his arms to welcome a child to his breast, and I cannot help but
wonder who this man is, with his wrinkled face and eye that speaks to
all of past and future, and I cannot help but wonder where within him
lay the murder of that family that sent Wassen to the mission. Once, in
childhood, an old man with a skull cap covering a bald patch, and a
long grey beard with curls at its ends, used to sit at a kitchen table in
the back of my father's grocery store, teaching in Hebrew the Five
Books of Moses. With each of my mistakes he cracked a thumb and
finger on my head, and I left those books forever with no feeling for
God, but only full of stories that talked of vengeance, hate, and war.
Yoreitone, within my hearing, had not yet talked of death or war, but
always he told of hunting trips for monkeys and birds, and other creatures that lived and stalked within the forest, tales of spirits that inhabited deer to feed the jaguar and therefore could not be tracked to kill,
and tales that wandered in time and space and seemed to me no legend
or symbol but did no more than tell of walks to new rivers and trees.
Later, I asked Yoreitone what he thought of the white upon the

mountains far in the distance, the mountains that could only be seen on the clearest of days, the mountains that reached up to twenty thousand feet and more. "Flowers," he said. "They are white flowers."

Tell me again, Manolo, the words of Wassen. Tell me how he found them dead. Tell me now the hands that killed were those of Yoreitone and of Michii. I walk within my world a man, I think, and every day confirms my need to live it out with all my senses, not like you, Manolo, living only the moments of the days for which you said you waited. My friends are real and solid, to be slapped and bitten, friends to race with along the jungle floor to shoot an arrow into food. What did you say to me the night before I left? We will both of us die here, deep in a jungle we grow around ourselves. No day of death has yet entered me and I see my friends as proof of my own aliveness, no reflection of them, but a response all my own that wakes me up with no alarm ringing in my ears and takes me through the day with no dream thoughts to tell me what I hope will come. Michii's face is round, his eyes are always narrowed with a squint or a smile, his head of hair is blown by wind and filled with bits of dried leaf, his lips are thin, his body straight from shoulder to hip, and his thighs widen with muscle. Darinimbiak's smile is sad and thoughtful, there's a hint of a mustache above his heavy lips, his bangs are cut often, to keep them well above his eyebrows, and each night he brushes his hair before we lie down to sleep. Baaldore is thick and square, with eyes and mouth wide open, a belly button protruding from a protruding belly, hair tied back with fiber, a small nose and an almost flat face. Reindude is always splashed with red and black, his body and his cheeks, and his face is the squarest of all the men; his nose is widest, sometimes it has a bone inside it; and his bangs are longest. Ihuene is the most elegant. He arranges his hair in a mirror of water. His cheekbones are high and his nostrils are small in the perfectly straight, short nose. All eyes are the same color of brown, all hair the same black, and all the men stand about five feet five, small for ease and speed inside the jungle. The others too have their individuality, but these I know best, having sketched them most, having spent each night sleeping against the textures of their skin. It would not be right to say their personalities are as various as their faces, nor is it possible to say they are all the same. Michii is a maker of quick decisions, Darinimbiak is always eating and searches out palm shoots each time we go into the forest, Baaldore loves birds and has taken over the feeding of my parrots, Reindude is a follower and never goes anywhere alone, and Ihuene frowns and ponders an hour after daylight before he thinks of a plan for the day, as if the day had need of plans.

The women, then, had been by the river for two days, making large clay pots and drying them in the sun. They brought small, ripe pineapples from a field where they grew with yuca and peanuts and wild bushes. They cut the fruit apart, chewed it, and spit the juice into the clay pots and threw away the pulp. The juice leaked out through cracks that were then stopped up with more clay. The pots were covered with leaves and left in the shade another day. Morning came. Michii got up and brought me a bowl of the fermenting juice, very sour and tasting of the clay. We ate no other food. There were fires outside and Yoreitone sat at the central one, whittling the small matchsticks. Small slivers of ebony lay at his side. A piece of tree trunk stood up in front of him like a chopping block. The women brought out gourds of liquor and left them at the fires and the men all came out to drink. They brought with them the huito fruit, which they pounded and put into the embers. The boys crawled out of the hut and lined up in front of Yoreitone. These were the boys who had sat and listened to him the other day, the day I heard the end of his talk of women. They were as silent now as then. Yoreitone held up his mace and, in a loud voice, began to chant.

"Fill the emptiness!"

A man of thirty or thirty-five came up and took hold of the shoulders of the first boy and pushed his head down to the edge of the tree trunk. Yoreitone, still chanting, put a sliver of ebony into the coals of the fire, twirling it there with both hands for some seconds, then pulled out the lower lip of the boy so that it rested firmly on the flat of the trunk and pushed the sliver through the flesh, removed it immediately and shoved a small match-like stick into the hole. "Fill the emptiness!"

No cry was heard as the ebony pierced the lip and the boy got up, blinking his eyes and smiling happily. The man, his father, led him to one of the fires and scrubbed his body clean with a bundle of fibers and thistles. He had looked before as if he had come out from a black bath of ink and now his flesh was a shining light brown, all ready for the new designs, like those on myself, Michii, and Darinimbiak, that were being patiently painted upon him, beginning with the inverted vees on his breast.

The whole of the day went by before the last line of paint had been drawn on the body of the last boy. No one had gone inside the hut, except for the women who brought out the liquor, which we each drank down, bowlful after bowlful. Laughter began with nightfall and from the blackness we crawled into the smoky light of the hut. Some women were in all of our small partitions, others remained around the fires and the newly made men, as well as the others, went up to them without a word, embraced and began to couple. Michii lay down on top of the woman with whom he had fathered a child. We others found arms stretched up in welcome. Strange, inevitable, holy, to feel that soft flesh beneath my hands and body. Sleepless hours passed and I got up and went outside and in my mind took a piece of orange paper and with a pair of scissors cut a small circle, pasted it on a sheet of ultramarine light, cut from black the shape of treetops and stuck them inches below the moon, held out the collage and saw the sky.

Is it to you, M, or to you C, that I wish to address this? Are you now all become one, my friends and diary, so that I can barely distinguish you one from the other? Or is it only the terror or horror that came over me that day of murder that binds together your world into one, having faded into the mist of my memory and you float there at this moment of writing with but a single mind, and I lie here ready to cry out and scream my innocence to you, to myself, to Michii, Manolo, Darinimbiak, to every leaf and animal, to every sky and every moon, to every cloud and drop of rain, to every day and night, to every painting that I've ever painted? What had I released from inside me that day I first set foot inside a jungle and I could not see the violence of those strangling vines, of plant life fighting for a bit of sun, nor insects sending forth venom? Instead perhaps a dybbuk entered me, the spirit waiting for the day I crossed a threshhold of unknown self, lying dormant all these years in patience until a time it knew would come, the time perhaps when I prepared myself with practice every morning with my friends, to shoot my bow and arrows till I felled a flying toucan, two wild turkeys, and another bird they called a mee-ekana, with orange breast and wide black wings. For years I had practiced on a violin, making music heard by none but me; for weeks I practiced with a different bow and those birds that I impaled were sources for a hundred joys that covered me with gooseflesh and sent sensations through my groin.

There came another hunting trip with many men, and me among them freshly painted, going farther and farther into the forest, carrying in my hand my bow and arrows, while they carried theirs, too, and axes of stone as well. The rains of the season had already begun and sheets of water drenched the jungle and flooded the rivers. Streams turned into raging torrents, and we would cross them slowly, leaning against the current, the water rushing violently over our legs; quickly it reached our waists and we strained to make headway, holding our weapons above our heads. Michii grabbed my hand and ran at an angle with the current until there was no bottom and we were suddenly being swept downstream and finally jolted into a far bank. Thick mud was everywhere and we sank deep into marshes and struggled in slime, pulling ourselves out by grasping vines. It was any day and any time of my life, the rain a little heavier. The scarlet of our faces was streaked with water and dropped in stains that paled upon our bodies. A silence came over the whole of us and we stood in a small open area on wet leaves and formed a circle around our propped-up arrows and axes, our arms on each other's shoulders, so close our hips were touching, and we swayed back and forth, heads leaning to one side. "Ooooo-ooooo," we whispered in a low growl. "Ooooo-ooooo," the sound cane out from deep inside, sending a shiver along the line of arms. Michii broke from the circle and stepped inside, the gap closing in a smack of flesh. He held up his penis and began to rub it hard. He walked to the man beside me who was himself then half erect, and touched the ends of their penises together, then moved in a counter-clockwise fashion from one to another, pressing slightly on each penis with his own, ending up with mine, and re-entering the circle at my side. We growled once again in whispers and I wondered at this ceremony, performed so far from home, thinking not where it might end or why no one had shot the nutria we had startled in its sleep, but only thinking in the present and allowing all to enter in.

The rain had stopped, the sun had long gone down, no moon had risen. Small animals rustled on leaves, a monkey howled, a bird shrieked. We walked noiselessly. The smell of smoke drifted toward us and I heard the muffled sounds of a village, not our own. My companions, twenty-three of them, went on in single file, and then broke into groups as the forest opened into a clearing, each group moving toward one of the several huts. Michii took me by the elbow and pulled me along with Darinimbiak and Ihuene, Baaldore and Reindude, all those among whom I spent each night. Great cries of EEEEE-eeeee!! hit the air and ears as we ran into a fire-lit hut and animal arrows in front of my eyes were used as spears, and axes split into skulls. I stood and watched, no word or sound from me, but shaking, trembling with cold, my breathing coming in gasps. No time was passing, but seven men lay there dead, bellies and chests open, still pouring out hot blood, heads crushed and dripping brain, while women huddled far in a corner, chanting in deep moans and holding the fright-filled faces of their children into the red paint of their breasts. The bowels of the men had opened and their feces oozed out and mixed with their blood. They stared at me, the dead, their eyes wide or half opened, one with a line of white running from his mouth crossing over the black triangles painted on his face, another with a hand resting in the fire and his back curving over a log, a pair of them wound together as if about to begin an act of love and held one upon the other with a single spear. The others were strewn around and lay like dummies carelessly dropped, except that skin was torn and cut and dark red bubbled up from holes. The living laughed and threw their arms around me, and Michii took an arrow from my hand and plunged it through an inert breast. With another arrow he sliced through the string that held a penis stiff against an abdomen, and the penis curled and slipped between its thighs. Outside, my stomach turned upside down, but I went on with them to look in other huts, where other dead lay in other positions, and against the background of the unending moaning of the women, the crying of the children, was the laughter of my people. Not one had a scratch on him, it was over so quickly, and once, even, I laughed with them.

One body from each hut was brought out and dismembered. The heads were cut off and tossed by the hair to the edge of the compound. All viscera was removed, cleaned, and wrapped in leaves and placed with its body. The torso and limbs were tied to poles. A few of what seemed to be the healthiest women and children, those that weighed the most, were rounded up, none protesting and no longer moaning, and we all set out for home, in a long, chattering, lively procession.

We did not sleep that night, but walked on until the early morning, when we reached our river, where we washed, and then we rested. In the light of day, in the thoughts that ran through me, I could not sleep, but rested my head on Michii's chest, with Darinimbiak's legs woven with mine. It was evening, and I had dozed at times before I felt Michii move out from under me and we three got up and crossed with all the others to where fires were burning in the open and human flesh was already roasting, not tended by women now, but by the younger boys who had not come with us. Yoreitone held out his feathered mace. He circled each fire and grunted out words that soon became a chant. The men went into the hut and brought out their own maces and decorations, the first I had seen of them, and joined him to form a huge oval that encompassed all the fires, and all began to sing.

Mayaarii-há, mayaarii-há

Eyorii-kihuat

Ihuenuayken

Hinkaá-hinkaá

Ihuenuayken, ihuenuayken

Mayaarii-há, mayaarii-há . . .

It was chanted in low hoarse voices, with long drawn-out syllables in only three notes. The refrain was repeated over and over and the last line had no ending so that the song could go on with no break before the first word began again. They bounced in dance up and down, twice on one foot, twice on the other.

Roaring jaguar, roaring jaguar

Who wanders over the bank of the river Eyori

There you are saying

This is how I growl, this is how I growl

Here I am, here I am

Roaring jaguar, roaring jaguar . . .

They wore headdresses of red and yellow macaw feathers, and rings of long feathers were looped over their shoulders and in movement they spread and waved like wings. They carried the long maces, topped with bunches of short parrot feathers glued together with wild black beeswax and tied on loosely with fibers, ten or twelve bunches to a mace that hit one against the other, as the mace bounced up and down, hard wax cracking against hard wax to the same movement and rhythm that their necklaces of bone rattled round their necks, all of it together making a spectral sound, rustling, clattering. The figures hovered about the fires, black silhouettes, or blazing copper and gold when the flames' reflection struck their bodies. They danced without tiring, sometimes undulating and swaying, the long plumes blurring from their backs in flight, and when I entered the circle, I was hypnotized by movement always up and down, kaleidoscopic lights that flickered through my iris, a chant that soon became a roar that drained out thoughts that came my way, and hours later when I sat with Michii and with Darinimbiak, the three of us alone at the fire with others dancing, singing around us, I took a piece of meat that Michii held out and ate and swallowed and ate some more, and entered the circle again to dance. Mayaarii-há, mayaarii-há!!

A curve of moon came up and lined a black cloud with grey. Its light covered us all with blue as we sat or lay around the fires, eating, moaning the tones of the chant, swaying forward and back, moving from the hip, forward and back. Calm and silence settled over us, all men. Four got up, one picked a heart from the embers, and they walked into the forest. Small groups of others rose, selected a piece of meat, and disappeared in other directions. We three were alone until Ihuene, Baaldore and Reindude were in front of us, Reindude cupping in his hand the heart from the being we had carried from so far away, the heart of he who had lived in the hut we had entered to kill. We stretched out flat upon the ground, lined up, our shoulders touching. Michii looked up at the moon and showed it to the heart. He bit into it as if it were an apple, taking a large bite, almost half the heart, and chewed down several times, spit it into a hand, separated the meat into six sections and placed some into the mouths of each of us. We chewed and swallowed. He did the same with the other half of the heart. He turned Darinimbiak onto his stomach, lifted his hips so that he crouched on all fours. Darinimbiak growled, Mayaarii-há! Michii growled, Mayaarii-há!, bent down to lay himself upon Darinimbiak's back and entered him.

It is written down on paper now and there's no turning back, no erasing, no washing out the brain with turpentine, no telling myself it was all a dream. I can read it here myself. In Singapore, I met a man, a doctor married to a heathen Chinee, a beautiful, brilliant woman who bore him equally beautiful, brilliant children. He himself was British, with a Russian name, and he had been sent the year before by the British authorities to make a study of the Murut people, who lived in the center of what was then called North Borneo. He was a medical doctor and went there as such, to find out why the tribe was dying out. He lived some months with them and came away with no certain knowledge, but only a theory that met with derisive laughter. The Muruts had been headhunters, and when I myself went on to stay with them, there were still heads hanging from beams and set on shelves under eaves. They had been a fertile tribe, babies plopping out of wombs each year to grow up healthy and strong, with nothing more than outbreaks of malaria to keep them from overrunning the island. The war came and the Japanese offered other types of heads, their own, for them to slice and hang. When the British returned and took control, the cutting off of heads was stopped and then, according to my doctor, then, the tribe began to waste away. He had no evidence but the year of sterility's beginnings, the talks with elders of the kampongs, and examinations that might have showed a weakening of muscles but no lack of strength in other areas of the body. No evidence, but somehow, coincidental with the British law, a lack of children being born.

"It could not have been clearer," he said to me, "but they laughed as if I'd told a joke."

Darinimbiak has been ill for the past two days with diarrhea. I had brought along inside my knapsack, as I always do wherever I go and luckily have never had to use for myself, a tube of enterovioform tablets, and the six I've already given to him have had no effect. It doesn't seem serious, but it has been disturbing him to get up at night, and once he got no further than a few feet from us before he had to squat and empty himself, groaning with pain. It hurts to hear his groans, but others laugh and he laughs too.

Here I'd been so closed inside my own contentment that it occurs to me only now that in all my time living my time, there have been no deaths within our hut. I have never counted heads, which I might have done during my first days, and was never aware of any disappearances that could have taken place before I came to know each face so well. There were two pregnant women whom I noticed one day with flatter bellies and no babies on their backs, but there was no sign of grief, no service of which I was a part. No older man has fallen in his tracks, grasping at a convulsing heart, no hunter has returned all shredded from the claws and teeth of a jaguar, no fever has yet kept anyone bedded down. Awaipe has sores creeping along his back and side as if he'd somehow contracted syphilis, and young Pendiari has a lump on the back of his head that seems a little larger every day, but neither one complains, and they are sources more for curiosity than embarrassment or disgust. Even if I had the medicines of Manolo's pharmacy with me, I wouldn't know what to do with them. It is strange now to be thinking of illnesses and death again. No, not so strange.

I am a cannibal.

That four-word sentence doesn't leave my head. No matter into what far corner of my mind I push those words, they flash along the surface of my brain like news along the track that runs around the building at Times Square. So thoughts of death are natural now as love, I tell myself, and I repeat it on and on, hoping some impression will be made. It is a simple truth of this life, and Michii and Darinimbiak can live in no other way that would keep them as they are, the way in which I continue and will forever love them. What monster do I become that I can write and think so cruel a combination of words! Better let me lie sleepless again another night like last, when I chanted to myself Shema, Hear, Ysroel, O Israel, Adonoi, The Lord, Elohenu, our God, Adonoi, The Lord, Echod, is One. There was a certain element of comfort thinking out excuses for those killings, but none would hold in any way, and I cannot help but judge myself even in the role of onlooker, helpless for a moment, yes, helpless to react, but later surely taking part. In that past life of mine in which I could not live the norm and take an ordinary job, marry and have children, I set myself apart, seeing no pleasure in the marriage covenant, or in a TV set or bridge or in owning any kind of car. And then I came out here and for the first time joined a real community, immersing myself within their lives as best I could, not deeply enough I see now to go deeper into their whole way, to become an honest one of them, not thinking back to that other day on which I wrote I'd always necessarily have knowledge they could never know or feel, but going even where I never thought to travel into inner consciousness and asking my flesh and blood to turn my centuries back to their beginnings. This is a limitation of my own, not theirs, and if I sit in judgment on myself, it must remain only me whom I judge, for I have come here into a new world, from a world as strange in other ways, a world which always troubled me.

Cannibalism in the Cars

by Mark Twain

This story by Mark Twain (1835–1910) appeared in Sketches, New and Old *(1875). William Dean Howells reviewed the book for the* Atlantic Monthly. *Howells remarked upon a "growing seriousness of meaning in the apparently unmoralized drolling, which must result from the humorist's second thought of political and social absurdities."*

I visited St. Louis lately, and on my way west, after changing cars at Terre Haute, Indiana, a mild, benevolent-looking gentleman of about forty-five, or maybe fifty, came in at one of the way-stations and sat down beside me. We talked together pleasantly on various subjects for an hour, perhaps, and I found him exceedingly intelligent and entertaining. When he learned that I was from Washington, he immediately began to ask questions about various public men, and about Congressional affairs; and I saw very shortly that I was conversing with a man who was perfectly familiar with the ins and outs of political life at the Capital, even to the ways and manners, and customs of procedure of Senators and Representatives in the Chambers of the National Legislature. Presently two men halted near us for a single moment, and one said to the other:

"Harris, if you'll do that for me, I'll never forget you, my boy."

My new comrade's eyes lighted pleasantly. The words had touched upon a happy memory, I thought. Then his face settled into thoughtfulness—almost into gloom. He turned to me and said, "Let me tell you a story; let me give you a secret chapter of my life—a chapter that has never been referred to by me since its events transpired. Listen patiently, and promise that you will not interrupt me."

I said I would not, and he related the following strange adventure, speaking sometimes with animation, sometimes with melancholy, but always with feeling and earnestness.

On the 19th December, 1853, I started from St. Louis in the evening train, bound for Chicago. There were only twenty-four passengers, all told. There were no ladies and no children. We were in excellent spirits, and pleasant acquaintanceships were soon formed. The journey bade fair to be a happy one, and no individual in the party, I think, had even the vaguest presentiment of the horrors we were soon to undergo.

At 11 p.m. it began to snow hard. Shortly after leaving the small village of Weldon, we entered upon that tremendous prairie solitude that stretches its leagues on leagues of houseless dreariness far away towards the Jubilee Settlements. The winds unobstructed by trees or hills, or even vagrant rocks, whistled fiercely across the level desert, driving the falling snow before it like spray from the crested waves of a stormy sea. The snow was deepening fast, and we knew, by the diminished speed of the train, that the engine was ploughing through it with steadily increasing difficulty. Indeed it almost came to a dead halt sometimes, in the midst of great drifts that piled themselves like colossal graves across the track. Conversation began to flag. Cheerfulness gave place to grave concern. The possibility of being imprisoned in the snow, on the bleak prairie, fifty miles from any house, presented itself to every mind, and extended its depressing influence over every spirit.

At two o'clock in the morning I was aroused out of an uneasy slumber by the ceasing of all motion about me. The appalling truth flashed upon me instantly—we were captives in a snow-drift! "All hands to the rescue!" Every man sprang to obey. Out into the wild night, the pitchy darkness, the billowing snow, the driving storm, every soul leaped, with the consciousness that a moment lost now might bring destruction to us all. Shovels, hands, boards—anything, everything that could displace snow, was brought into instant requisition. It was a weird picture, that small company of frantic men fighting the banking snows, half in the blackest shadow and half in the angry light of the locomotive's reflector.

One short hour sufficed to prove the utter uselessness of our efforts. The storm barricaded the track with a dozen drifts while we dug one away. And worse than this, it was discovered that the last grand charge the engine had made upon the enemy had broken the fore-and-aft shaft of the driving-wheel! With a free track before us we should still have been helpless. We entered the car wearied with labor, and very sorrowful. We gathered about the stoves, and gravely canvassed our situation. We had no provisions whatever—in this lay our chief distress. We could not freeze, for there was a good supply of wood in the tender. This was our only comfort. The discussion ended at last in accepting the disheartening decision of the conductor,—viz.: That it would be death for any man to attempt to travel fifty miles on foot through snow like that. We could not send for help, and even if we could, it could not come. We must submit and await, as patiently as we might, succor or starvation! I think the stoutest heart there felt a momentary chill when those words were uttered.

Within the hour conversation subsided to a low murmur here and there about the car, caught fitfully between the rising and falling of the blast; the lamps grew dim; and the majority of the castaways settled themselves among the flickering shadows to think—to forget the present if they could—to sleep, if they might.

The eternal night—it surely seemed eternal to us—wore its lagging hours away at last, and the cold grey dawn broke in the east. As the light grew stronger the passengers began to stir and give signs of life, one after another, and each in turn pushed his slouched hat up from his forehead, stretched his stiffened limbs, and glanced out at the windows upon the cheerless prospect. It was cheerless indeed!—not a living thing visible anywhere, not a human habitation; nothing but a vast white desert; uplifted sheets of snow drifting hither and thither before the wind—a world of eddying flakes shutting out the firmament above.

All day we moped about the cars, saying little, thinking much. Another lingering, dreary night—and hunger.

Another dawning—another day of silence, sadness, wasting hunger, hopeless watching for succor that could not come. A night of restless slumber, filled with dreams of feasting—wakings distressed with the gnawings of hunger.

The fourth day came and went—and the fifth! Five days of dreadful imprisonment! A savage hunger looked out at every eye. There was in it a sign of awful import—the foreshadowing of a something that was vaguely shaping itself in every heart—a something which no tongue dared yet to frame into words.

The sixth day passed—the seventh dawned upon as gaunt and haggard and hopeless a company of men as ever stood in the shadow of death. It must out now! That thing which had been growing up in every heart was ready to leap from every lip at last! Nature had been taxed to the utmost—she must yield. RICHARD H. GASTON, of Minnesota, tall, cadaverous, and pale, rose up. All knew what was coming. All prepared—every emotion, every semblance of excitement was smothered—only a calm, thoughtful seriousness appeared in the eyes that were lately so wild.

"Gentlemen,—It cannot be delayed longer! The time is at hand! We must determine which of us shall die to furnish food for the rest!"

Mr. JOHN J. WILLIAMS, of Illinois, rose and said: "Gentlemen,—I nominate the Rev. James Sawyer, of Tennessee."

Mr. WM. R. ADAMS, of Indiana, said: "I nominate Mr. Daniel Slote, of New York."

Mr. CHARLES J. LANGDON: "I nominate Mr. Samuel A. Bowen, of St. Louis."

Mr. SLOTE: "Gentlemen,—I desire to decline in favor of Mr. John A. Van Nostrand, jun., of New Jersey."

Mr. GASTON: "If there be no objection; the gentleman's desire will be acceded to."

Mr. VAN NOSTRAND objecting, the resignation of Mr. Slote was rejected. The resignations of Messrs. Sawyer and Bowen were also offered, and refused upon the same grounds.

Mr. A. L. BASCOM, of Ohio: "I move that the nominations now close, and that the House proceed to an election by ballot."

Mr. SAWYER: "Gentlemen,—I protest earnestly against these proceedings. They are, in every way, irregular and unbecoming. I must beg to move that they be dropped at once, and that we elect a chairman of the meeting and proper officers to assist him, and then we can go on with the business before us understandingly."

Mr. BELKNAP, of Iowa: "Gentlemen,—I object. This is no time to stand upon forms and ceremonious observances. For more than seven days we have been without food. Every moment we lose in idle discussion increases our distress. I am satisfied with the nominations that have been made—every gentleman present is, I believe—and I, for one, do not see why we should not proceed at once to elect one or more of them. I wish to offer a resolution—"

Mr. GASTON: "It would be objected to, and have to lie over one day under the rules, thus bringing about the very delay you wish to avoid. The gentleman from New Jersey—"

Mr. VAN NOSTRAND: "Gentlemen, I am a stranger among you; I have not sought the distinction that has been conferred upon me, and I feel a delicacy."

Mr. MORGAN, of Alabama: "I move the previous question."

The motion was carried, and further debate shut off, of course. The motion to elect officers was passed, and under it Mr. Gaston was chosen Chairman, Mr. Blake, Secretary, Messrs. Holcomb, Dyer, and Baldwin, a Committee on nominations, and Mr. R. M. Howland, purveyor, to assist the committee in making selections.

A recess of half an hour was then taken, and some little caucusing followed. At the sound of the gavel the meeting reassembled, and the committee reported in favor of Messrs. George Ferguson, of Kentucky,

Lucien Hermann, of Louisiana, and W. Messick, of Colorado, as candidates. The report was accepted.

Mr. ROGERS, of Missouri: "Mr. President,—The report being properly before the House now, I move to amend it by substituting for the name of Mr. Hermann that of Mr. Lucius Harris, of St. Louis, who is well and honorably known to us all. I do not wish to be understood as casting the least reflection upon the high character and standing of the gentleman from Louisiana—far from it. I respect and esteem him as much as any gentleman here present possibly can; but none of us can be blind to the fact that he has lost more flesh during the week that we have lain here than any among you—none of us can be blind to the fact that the committee has been derelict in its duty, either through negligence or a graver fault, in thus offering for our suffrages a gentleman who, however pure his own motives may be, has really less nutriment in him—"

THE CHAIR: "The gentleman from Missouri will take his seat. The Chair cannot allow the integrity of the Committee to be questioned save by the regular course, under the rules. What action will the house take upon the gentleman's motion?"

Mr. HALLIDAY, of Virginia: "I move to further amend the report by substituting Mr. Harvey Davis, of Oregon, for Mr. Messick. It may be urged by gentlemen that the hardships and privations of a frontier life have rendered Mr. Davis tough; but, gentlemen, is this a time to cavil at toughness? is this a time to be fastidious concerning trifles? is this a time to dispute about matters of paltry significance? No, gentlemen, bulk is what we desire—substance, weight, bulk—these are the supreme requisites now—not talent, not genius, not education. I insist upon my motion."

Mr. MORGAN (excitedly): "Mr. Chairman,—I do most strenuously object to this amendment. The gentleman from Oregon is old, and furthermore is bulky only in bone—not in flesh. I ask the gentleman from Virginia if it is soup we want instead of solid sustenance? if he would delude us with shadows? if he would mock our suffering with an Oregonian spectre? I ask him if he can look upon the anxious faces around him, if he can gaze into our sad eyes, if he can listen to the beating of our expectant hearts, and still thrust this famine-stricken fraud upon us? I ask him if he can think of our desolate state, of our past sorrows, of our dark future, and still unpityingly foist upon us this wreck, this ruin, this tottering swindle, this gnarled and blighted and sapless vagabond from Oregon's inhospitable shores? Never!" (Applause.)

The amendment was put to vote, after a fiery debate, and lost. Mr. Harris was substituted on the first amendment. The balloting then began. Five ballots were held without a choice. On the sixth, Mr. Harris was elected, all voting for him but himself. It was then moved that his election should be ratified by acclamation, which was lost, in consequence of his again voting against himself.

Mr. RADWAY moved that the House now take up the remaining candidates, and go into an election for breakfast. This was carried.

On the first ballot there was a tie, half the members favoring one candidate on account of his youth, and half favoring the other on account of his superior size. The President gave the casting vote for the latter, Mr. Messick. This decision created considerable dissatisfaction among the friends of Mr. Ferguson, the defeated candidate, and there was some talk of demanding a new ballot; but in the midst of it, a motion to adjourn was carried, and the meeting broke up at once.

The preparations for supper diverted the attention of the Ferguson faction from the discussion of their grievance for a long time, and then, when they would have taken it up again, the happy announcement that Mr. Harris was ready, drove all thought of it to the winds.

We improvised tables by propping up the backs of car-seats, and sat down with hearts full of gratitude to the finest supper that had blessed our vision for seven torturing days. How changed we were from what we had been a few short hours before! Hopeless, sad-eyed misery, hunger, feverish anxiety, desperation, then—thankfulness, serenity, joy too deep for utterance now. That I know was the cheeriest hour of my eventful life. The wind howled, and blew the snow wildly about our prison-house, but they were powerless to distress us any more. I liked Harris. He might have been better done, perhaps, but I am free to say that no man ever agreed with me better than Harris, or afforded me so large a degree of satisfaction. Messick was very well, though rather high-flavored, but for general nutritiousness and delicacy of fibre, give me Harris. Messick had his good points—I will not at attempt to deny it, nor do I wish to do it—but he was no more fitted for breakfast than a mummy would be, sir—not a bit. Lean?—why, bless me!—and tough? Ah, he was very tough! You could not imagine it,—you could never imagine anything like it.

"Do you mean to tell me that—"

Do not interrupt me, please. After breakfast we elected a man by the name of Walker, from Detroit, for supper. He was very good. I wrote his wife so afterwards. He was worthy of all praise. I shall always remember Walker. He was a little rare, but very good. And then the next morning we had Morgan, of Alabama, for breakfast. He was one of the finest men I ever sat down to,—handsome, educated, refined, spoke several languages fluently—a perfect gentleman—he was a perfect gentleman, and singularly juicy. For supper we had that Oregon patriarch, and he *was* a fraud, there is no question about it—old, scraggy, tough—nobody can picture the reality. I finally said, gentlemen, you can do as you like, but *I* will wait for another election. And Grimes, of Illinois, said, "Gentlemen, *I* will wait also. When you elect a man that has *something* to recommend him, I shall be glad to join you again." It soon became evident that there was general dissatisfaction with Davis, of Oregon, and so, to preserve the good-will that had prevailed so pleasantly since we had had Harris, an election was called, and the result of it was that Baker, of Georgia, was chosen. He was splendid! Well, well—after that we had Doolittle, and Hawkins, and McElroy (there was some complaint about McElroy, because he was uncommonly short and thin), and Penrod, and two Smiths, and Bailey (Bailey had a wooden leg, which was clear loss, but he was otherwise good), and an Indian boy, and an organ-grinder, and a gentleman by the name of Buckminster—a poor stick of a vagabond that wasn't any good for company and no account for breakfast. We were glad we got him elected before relief came.

"And so the blessed relief *did* come at last?"

Yes, it came one bright sunny morning, just after election. John Murphy was the choice, and there never was a better, I am willing to testify; but John Murphy came home with us, in the train that came to succor us, and lived to marry the widow Harris—"

"Relict of—"

Relict of our first choice. He married her, and is happy and respected and prosperous yet. Ah, it was like a novel, sir—it was like a romance. This is my stopping-place, sir; I must bid you good-bye. Any time that you can make it convenient to tarry a day or two with me, I shall be glad to have you. I like you, sir; I have concieved an affection for you. I could like you as well as I liked Harris himself, sir. Good day, sir, and a pleasant journey.

He was gone. I never felt so stunned, so distressed, so bewildered in my life. But in my soul I was glad he was gone. With all his gentleness of manner and his soft voice, I shuddered whenever he turned his hungry eye upon me; and when I heard that I had achieved his perilous affection, and that I stood almost with the late Harris in his esteem, my heart fairly stood still!

I was bewildered beyond description. I did not doubt his word; I could not question a single item in a statement so stamped with the earnestness of truth as his; but its dreadful details overpowered me, and threw my thoughts into hopeless confusion.

I saw the conductor looking at me. I said, "Who is that man?"

"He was a member of Congress once, and a good one. But he got caught in a snow-drift in the cars, and like to been starved to death. He got so frost-bitten and frozen up generally, and used up for want of something to eat, that he was sick and out of his head two or three months afterwards. He is all right now, only he is a monomaniac, and when he gets on that old subject he never stops till he has eat up that whole car-load of people he talks about. He would have finished the crowd by this time, only he had to get out here. He has got their names as pat as A, B, C. When he gets them all eat up but himself, he always says:—'Then the hour for the usual election for breakfast having arrived, and there being no opposition, I was duly elected, after which, there being no objections offered, I resigned. Thus I am here."

I felt inexpressibly relieved to know that I had only been listening to the harmless vagaries of a madman, instead of the genuine experiences of a bloodthirsty cannibal.

Across the Plains
in the Donner Party
by Virginia Reed Murphy

The Donner Party's travails during the winter of 1846 and 1847 led to one of the 19th century's most sensational scandals. Survivor Virginia Reed Murphy's (1833–1921) account barely mentions the cannibalism that made the Donner Party infamous, but is more convincing than many sensational versions of the story.

I was a child when we started to California, yet I remember the journey well and I have cause to remember it, as our little band of emigrants who drove out of Springfield, Illinois, that spring morning of 1846 have since been known in history as the "Ill-fated Donner party" of "Martyr Pioneers." My father, James F. Reed, was the originator of the party, and the Donner brothers, George and Jacob, who lived just a little way out of Springfield, decided to join him.

All the previous winter we were preparing for the journey—and right here let me say that we suffered vastly more from fear of the Indians before starting than we did on the plains; at least this was my case. In the long winter evenings Grandma [Sarah] Keyes used to tell me Indian stories. She had an aunt who had been taken prisoner by the savages in the early settlement of Virginia and Kentucky and had remained a captive in their hands five years before she made her escape. I was fond of these stories and evening after evening would go into grandma's room, sitting with my back close against the wall so that no warrior could slip behind me with a tomahawk. I would coax her to tell me more about her aunt, and would sit listening to the recital of the fearful deeds of the savages, until it seemed to me that everything in the room, from the high old-fashioned bedposts down even to the shovel and tongs in the chimney corner, was transformed into the dusky tribe in paint and feathers, all ready for the war dance. So when I was told that we were going to California and would have to pass through a region peopled by Indians, you can imagine how I felt.

Our wagons, or the "Reed wagons," as they were called, were all made to order and I can say without fear of contradiction that nothing like our family wagon ever started across the plains. It was what might be called a two-story wagon or "Pioneer palace car," attached to a regular immigrant train. My mother, though a young woman, was not strong and had been in delicate health for many years, yet when sorrows and danger came upon her she was the bravest of the brave. Grandma Keyes, who was seventy-five years of age, was an invalid, confined to her bed. Her sons in Springfield, Gersham and James W. Keyes, tried to dissuade her from the long and fatiguing journey, but in vain; she would not be parted from my mother, who was her only daughter. So the car in which she was to ride was planned to give comfort. The entrance was on the side, like that of an old-fashioned stage coach, and one stepped into a small room, as it were, in the centre of the wagon. At the right and left were spring seats with comfortable high backs, where one could sit and ride with as much ease as on the seats of a Concord coach. In this little room was placed a tiny sheet-iron stove, whose pipe, running through the top of the wagon, was prevented by a circle of tin from setting fire to the canvas cover. A board about a foot wide extended over the wheels on either side the full length of the wagon, thus forming the foundation for a large and roomy second story in which were placed our beds. Under the spring seats were compartments in which were stored many articles useful for the journey, such as a well filled work basket and a full assortment of medicines, with lint and bandages for dressing wounds. Our clothing was packed—not in Saratoga trunks—but in strong canvas bags plainly marked. Some of mama's young friends added a looking-glass, hung directly opposite the door, in order, as they said, that my mother might not forget to keep her good looks, and strange to say, when we had to leave this wagon, standing like a monument on the Salt Lake desert, the glass was still unbroken. I have often thought how pleased the Indians must have been when they found this mirror which gave them back the picture of their own dusky faces.

We had two wagons loaded with provisions. Everything in that line was bought that could be thought of. My father started with supplies enough to last us through the first winter in California, had we made the journey in the usual time of six months. Knowing that books were always scarce in a new country, we also took a good library of standard works. We even took a cooking stove which never had had a fire in it, and was destined never to have, as we cachéd it in the desert. Certainly no family ever started across the plains with more provisions or a better outfit for the journey; and yet we reached California almost destitute and nearly out of clothing.

The family wagon was drawn by four yoke of oxen, large Durham steers at the wheels. The other wagons were drawn by three yoke each. We had saddle horses and cows, and last but not least my pony. He was a beauty and his name was Billy. I can scarcely remember when I was taught to sit on a horse. I only know that when a child of seven I was the proud owner of a pony and used to go riding with papa. That was the chief pleasure to which I looked forward in crossing the plains, to ride my pony every day. But a day came when I had no pony to ride, the poor little fellow gave out. He could not endure the hardships of ceaseless travel. When I was forced to part with him I cried until I was ill, and sat in the back of the wagon watching him become smaller and smaller as we drove on, until I could see him no more.

Never can I forget the morning when we bade farewell to kindred and friends. The Donners were there, having driven in the evening before with their families, so that we might get an early start. Grandma Keyes was carried out of the house and placed in the wagon on a large feather bed, propped up with pillows. Her sons implored her to remain and end her days with them, but she could not be separated from her only daughter. We were surrounded by loved ones, and there stood all my little schoolmates who had come to kiss me good-by. My father with tears in his eyes tried to smile as one friend after another grasped his hand in a last farewell. Mama was overcome with grief. At last we were all in the wagons, the drivers cracked their whips, the oxen moved slowly forward and the long journey had begun.

Could we have looked into the future and have seen the misery before us, these lines would never have been written. But we were full of hope and did not dream of sorrow. I can now see our little caravan of ten or twelve wagons as we drove out of old Springfield, my little black-eyed sister Patty sitting upon the bed, holding up the wagon cover so that Grandma might have a last look at her old home.

That was the 14th day of April, 1846. Our party numbered thirty-one, and consisted chiefly of three families, the other members being young men, some of whom came as drivers. The Donner family were George and Tamsen Donner and their five children, and Jacob and Elizabeth Donner and their seven children. Our family numbered nine, not counting three drivers—my father and mother, James Frazier and Margaret W. Reed, Grandma Keyes, my little sister Patty (now Mrs. Frank Lewis, of Capitola), and two little brothers, James F. Reed, Jr., and Thomas K. Reed, Eliza Williams and her brother Baylis, and lastly myself. Eliza had been a domestic in our family for many years, and was anxious to see California.

Many friends camped with us the first night out and my uncles traveled on for several days before bidding us a final farewell. It seemed strange to be riding in ox-teams, and we children were afraid of the oxen, thinking they could go wherever they pleased as they had no bridles. Milt Elliott, a knight of the whip, drove our family wagon. He had worked for years in my father's large saw-mill on the Sangamon River. The first bridge we came to, Milt had to stop the wagon and let us out. I remember that I called to him to be sure to make the oxen hit the bridge, and not to forget that grandma was in the wagon. How he laughed at the idea of the oxen missing the bridge! I soon found that

Milt, with his "whoa," "haw," and "gee," could make the oxen do just as he pleased.

Nothing of much interest happened until we reached what is now Kansas. The first Indians we met were the Caws, who kept the ferry, and had to take us over the Caw river. I watched them closely, hardly daring to draw my breath, and feeling sure they would sink the boat in the middle of the stream, and was very thankful when I found they were not like grandma's Indians. Every morning, when the wagons were ready to start, papa and I would jump on our horses, and go ahead to pick out a camping-ground. In our party were many who rode on horseback, but mama seldom did; she preferred the wagon, and did not like to leave grandma, although Patty took upon herself this charge, and could hardly be persuaded to leave grandma's side. Our little home was so comfortable, that mama could sit reading and chatting with the little ones, and almost forget that she was really crossing the plains.

Grandma Keyes improved in health and spirits every day until we came to the Big Blue River, which was so swollen that we could not cross, but had to lie by and make rafts on which to take the wagons over. As soon as we stopped traveling grandma began to fail, and on the 29th day of May she died. It seemed hard to bury her in the wilderness, and travel on, and we were afraid that the Indians would destroy her grave, but her death here, before our troubles began, was providential, and nowhere on the whole road could we have found so beautiful a resting place. By this time many emigrants had joined our company, and all turned out to assist at the funeral. A coffin was hewn out of a cottonwood tree, and John Denton, a young man from Springfield, found a large gray stone on which he carved with deep letters the name of "Sarah Keyes; born in Virginia," giving age and date of birth. She was buried under the shade of an oak, the slab being placed at the foot of the grave, on which were planted wild flowers growing in the sod. A minister in our party, the Rev. J. A. Cornwall, tried to give words of comfort as we stood about this lonely grave. Strange to say, that grave has never been disturbed; the wilderness blossomed into the city of Manhattan, Kansas, and we have been told that the city cemetery surrounds the grave of Sarah Keyes.

As the river remained high and there was no prospect of fording it, the men went to work cutting down trees, hollowing out logs and making rafts on which to take the wagons over. These logs, about twenty-five feet in length, were united by cross timbers, forming rafts, which were firmly lashed to stakes driven into the bank. Ropes were attached to both ends, by which the rafts were pulled back and forth across the river. The banks of this stream being steep, our heavily laden wagons had to be let down carefully with ropes, so that the wheels might run into the hollowed logs. This was no easy task when you take into consideration that in these wagons were women and children, who could cross the rapid river in no other way. Finally the dangerous work was accomplished and we resumed our journey.

The road at first was rough and led through a timbered country, but after striking the great valley of the Platte the road was good and the country beautiful. Stretching out before us as far as the eye could reach was a valley as green as emerald, dotted here and there with flowers of every imaginable color, and through this valley flowed the grand old Platte, a wide, rapid, shallow stream. Our company now numbered about forty wagons, and, for a time, we were commanded by Col. William H. Russell, then by George Donner. Exercise in the open air under bright skies, and freedom from peril combined to make this part of our journey an ideal pleasure trip. How I enjoyed riding my pony, galloping over the plain, gathering wild flowers! At night the young folks would gather about the camp fire chatting merrily, and often a song would be heard, or some clever dancer would give us a barn-door jig on the hind gate of a wagon.

Traveling up the smooth valley of the Platte, we passed Court House Rock, Chimney Rock and Scott's Bluffs, and made from fifteen to twenty miles a day, shortening or lengthening the distance in order to secure a good camping ground. At night when we drove into camp, our wagons were placed so as to form a circle or corral, into which our cattle were driven, after grazing, to prevent the Indians from stealing them, the campfires and tents being on the outside. There were many expert riflemen in the party and we never lacked for game. The plains were alive with buffalo, and herds could be seen every day coming to

the Platte to drink. The meat of the young buffalo is excellent and so is
that of the antelope, but the antelope are so fleet of foot it is difficult
to get a shot at one. I witnessed many a buffalo hunt and more than
once was in the chase close beside my father. A buffalo will not attack
one unless wounded. When he sees the hunter he raises his shaggy
head, gazes at him for a moment, then turns and runs; but when he is
wounded he will face his pursuer. The only danger lay in a stampede,
for nothing could withstand the onward rush of these massive creatures, whose tread seemed to shake the prairie.

Antelope and buffalo steaks were the main article on our bill-of-fare
for weeks, and no tonic was needed to give zest for the food; our
appetites were a marvel. Eliza soon discovered that cooking over a camp
fire was far different from cooking on a stove or range, but all hands
assisted her. I remember that she had the cream all ready for the churn
as we drove into the south fork of the Platte, and while we were fording
the grand old stream she went on with her work, and made several
pounds of butter. We found no trouble in crossing the Platte, the only
danger being in quicksand. The stream being wide, we had to stop the
wagon now and then to give the oxen a few moments' rest. At Fort
Laramie, two hundred miles farther on, we celebrated the fourth of July
in fine style. Camp was pitched earlier than usual and we prepared a
grand dinner. Some of my father's friends in Springfield had given him
a bottle of good old brandy, which he agreed to drink at a certain hour
of this day looking to the east, while his friends in Illinois were to drink
a toast to his success from a companion bottle with their faces turned
west, the difference in time being carefully estimated; and at the hour
agreed upon, the health of our friends in Springfield was drunk with
great enthusiasm. At Fort Laramie was a party of Sioux, who were on the
war path going to fight the Crows or Blackfeet. The Sioux are fine
looking Indians and I was not in the least afraid of them. They fell in
love with my pony and set about bargaining to buy him. They brought
buffalo robes and beautifully tanned buckskin, pretty beaded moccasins, and ropes made of grass, and placing these articles in a heap
alongside several of their ponies, they made my father understand by

signs that they would give them all for Billy and his rider. Papa smiled and shook his head; then the number of ponies was increased and, as a last tempting inducement, they brought an old coat, that had been worn by some poor soldier, thinking my father could not withstand the brass buttons!

On the sixth of July we were again on the march. The Sioux were several days in passing our caravan, not on account of the length of our train, but because there were so many Sioux. Owing to the fact that our wagons were strung so far apart, they could have massacred our whole party without much loss to themselves. Some of our company became alarmed, and the rifles were cleaned out and loaded, to let the warriors see that we were prepared to fight; but the Sioux never showed any inclination to disturb us. Their curiosity was annoying, however, and our wagon with its conspicuous stove-pipe and looking-glass attracted their attention. They were continually swarming about trying to get a look at themselves in the mirror, and their desire to possess my pony was so strong that at last I had to ride in the wagon and let one of the drivers take charge of Billy. This I did not like, and in order to see how far back the line of warriors extended, I picked up a large field-glass which hung on a rack, and as I pulled it out with a click, the warriors jumped back, wheeled their ponies and scattered. This pleased me greatly, and I told my mother I could fight the whole Sioux tribe with a spy-glass, and as revenge for forcing me to ride in the wagon, whenever they came near trying to get a peep at their war-paint and feathers, I would raise the glass and laugh to see them dart away in terror.

A new route had just been opened by Lansford W. Hastings, called the "Hastings Cut-off," which passed along the southern shore of the Great Salt Lake rejoining the old "Fort Hall Emigrant" road on the Humboldt. It was said to shorten the distance three hundred miles. Much time was lost in debating which course to pursue; Bridger and Vasques, who were in charge of the fort, sounded the praises of the new road. My father was so eager to reach California that he was quick to take advantage of any means to shorten the distance, and we were assured by Hastings and his party that the only bad part was the forty-mile drive through the desert by the shore of the lake. None of our party knew then, as we learned afterwards, that these men had an interest in the road, being employed by Hastings. But for the advice of these parties we should have continued on the old Fort Hall road. Our company had increased in numbers all along the line, and was now composed of some of the very best people and some of the worst. The greater portion of our company went by the old road and reached California in safety. Eighty-seven persons took the "Hastings Cut-off," including the Donners, Breens, Reeds, Murphys (not the Murphys of Santa Clara County), C. T. Stanton, John Denton, Wm. McClutchen, Wm. Eddy, Louis Keseburg, and many others too numerous to mention in a short article like this. And these are the unfortunates who have since been known as the "Donner Party."

On the morning of July 31 we parted with our traveling companions, some of whom had become very dear friends, and, without suspicion of impending disaster, set off in high spirits on the "Hastings Cut-off"; but a few days showed us that the road was not as it had been represented. We were seven days in reaching Weber Cañon, and Hastings, who was guiding a party in advance of our train, left a note by the wayside warning us that the road through Weber Cañon was impassable and advising us to select a road over the mountains, the outline of which he attempted to give on paper. These directions were so vague that C. T. Stanton, William Pike, and my father rode on in advance and overtook Hastings and tried to induce him to return and guide our party. He refused, but came back over a portion of the road, and from a high mountain endeavored to point out the general course. Over this road my father traveled alone, taking notes, and blazing trees, to assist him in retracing his course, and reaching camp after an absence of four days. Learning of the hardships of the advance train, the party decided to cross towards the lake. Only those who have passed through this country on horseback can appreciate the situation. There was absolutely no road, not even a trail. The cañon wound around among the hills. Heavy underbrush had to be cut away and used for making a road bed. While cutting our way step by step through the "Hastings

Cut-off," we were overtaken and joined by the Graves family, consisting of W. F. Graves, his wife and eight children, his son-in-law Jay Fosdick, and a young man by the name of John Snyder. Finally we reached the end of the cañon where it looked as though our wagons would have to be abandoned. It seemed impossible for the oxen to pull them up the steep hill [Donner Hill] and the bluffs beyond, but we doubled teams and the work was, at last, accomplished, almost every yoke in the train being required to pull up each wagon. While in this cañon Stanton and Pike came into camp; they had suffered greatly on account of the exhaustion of their horses and had come near perishing. Worn with travel and greatly discouraged we reached the shore of the Great Salt Lake. It had taken an entire month, instead of a week, and our cattle were not fit to cross the desert.

We were now encamped in a valley [Tooele Valley] called "Twenty Wells." The water in these wells was pure and cold, welcome enough after the alkaline pools from which we had been forced to drink. We prepared for the long drive across the desert and laid in, as we supposed, an ample supply of water and grass. This desert had been represented to us as only forty miles wide but we found it nearer eighty. It was a dreary, desolate, alkali waste; not a living thing could be seen; it seemed as though the hand of death had been laid upon the country. We started in the evening, traveled all that night, and the following day and night—two nights and one day of suffering from thirst and heat by day and piercing cold by night. When the third night fell and we saw the barren waste stretching away apparently as boundless as when we started, my father determined to go ahead in search of water. Before starting he instructed the drivers, if the cattle showed signs of giving out to take them from the wagons and follow him. He had not been gone long before the oxen began to fall to the ground from thirst and exhaustion. They were unhitched at once and driven ahead. My father coming back met the drivers with the cattle within ten miles of water and instructed them to return as soon as the animals had satisfied their thirst. He reached us about daylight. We waited all that day in the desert looking for the return of our drivers, the other wagons going on out of sight. Towards night the situation became desperate and we had only a few drops of water left; another night there meant death. We must set out on foot and try to reach some of the wagons. Can I ever forget that night in the desert, when we walked mile after mile in the darkness, every step seeming to be the very last we could take! Suddenly all fatigue was banished by fear; through the night came a swift rushing sound of one of the young steers crazed by thirst and apparently bent upon our destruction. My father, holding his youngest child in his arms and keeping us all close behind him, drew his pistol, but finally the maddened beast turned and dashed off into the darkness. Dragging ourselves along about ten miles, we reached the wagon of Jacob Donner. The family were all asleep, so we children lay down on the ground. A bitter wind swept over the desert, chilling us through and through. We crept closer together, and, when we complained of the cold, papa placed all five of our dogs around us, and only for the warmth of these faithful creatures we should doubtless have perished.

At daylight papa was off to learn the fate of his cattle, and was told that all were lost, except one cow and an ox. The stock, scenting the water, had rushed on ahead of the men, and had probably been stolen by the Indians, and driven into the mountains, where traces of them were lost. A week was spent here on the edge of the desert in a fruitless search. Almost every man in the company turned out, hunting in all directions, but our eighteen head of cattle were never found. We had lost our best yoke of oxen before reaching Bridger's Fort from drinking poisoned water found standing in pools, and had bought at the fort two yoke of young steers, but now all were gone, and my father and his family were left in the desert, eight hundred miles from California, seemingly helpless. We realized that our wagons must be abandoned. The company kindly let us have two yoke of oxen, so with our ox and cow yoked together we could bring one wagon, but, alas! not the one which seemed so much like a home to us, and in which grandma had died. Some of the company went back with papa and assisted him in cacheing everything that could not be packed in one wagon. A cache was made by digging a hole in the ground, in which a box or the bed of a wagon was placed. Articles to be buried were packed into this box, covered with boards, and the earth thrown in upon them, and thus they were hidden from sight. Our provisions were divided among the company. Before leaving the desert camp, an inventory of provisions on hand was taken, and it was found that the supply was not sufficient to last us through to California, and as if to render the situation more terrible, a storm came on during the night and the hill-tops became white with snow. Some one must go on to Sutter's Fort after provisions. A call was made for volunteers. C. T. Stanton and Wm. McClutchen bravely offered their services and started on bearing letters from the company to Captain Sutter asking for relief. We resumed our journey and soon reached Gravelly Ford on the Humboldt.

I now come to that part of my narrative which delicacy of feeling for both the dead and the living would induce me to pass over in silence, but which a correct and lucid chronicle of subsequent events of historical importance will not suffer to be omitted. On the 5th day of October, 1846, at Gravelly Ford, a tragedy was enacted which affected the subsequent lives and fortunes of more than one member of our company. At this point in our journey we were compelled to double our teams in order to ascend a steep, sandy hill. Milton Elliott, who was driving our wagon, and John Snyder, who was driving one of Mr. Graves's became involved in a quarrel over the management of their oxen. Snyder was beating his cattle over the head with the butt end of his whip, when my father, returning on horse-back from a hunting trip, arrived, and, appreciating the great importance of saving the remainder of the oxen, remonstrated with Snyder, telling him that they were our main dependance and at the same time offering the assistance of our team. Snyder having taken offense at something Elliott had said declared that his team could pull up alone, and kept on using abusive language. Father tried to quiet the enraged man. Hard words followed. Then my father said: "We can settle this, John, when we get up the hill." "No," replied Snyder with an oath, "we will settle it now," and springing upon the tongue of a wagon, he struck my father a violent blow over the head with his heavy whip-stock. One blow followed another. Father was stunned for a moment and blinded by the blood streaming from the gashes in his head. Another blow was descending when my mother ran in between the men. Father saw the uplifted whip, but had only time to cry: "John, John," when down came the stroke upon mother. Quick as a thought my father's hunting knife was out and Snyder fell, fatally wounded. He was caught in the arms of W. C. Graves, carried up the hill-side, and laid on the ground. My father regretted the act, and dashing the blood from his eyes went quickly to the assistance of the dying man. I can see him now, as he knelt over Snyder, trying to stanch the wound, while the blood from the gashes in his own head, trickling down his face, mingled with that of the dying man. In a few moments Snyder expired. Camp was pitched immediately, our wagon being some distance from the others. My father, anxious to do what he could for the dead, offered the boards of our wagon, from which to make a coffin. Then, coming to me, he said: "Daughter, do you think you can dress these wounds in my head? Your mother is not able, and they must be attended to." I answered by saying: "Yes, if you will tell me what to do." I brought a basin of water and sponge, and we went into the wagon, so that we might not be disturbed. When my work was at last finished, I burst out crying. Papa clasped me in his arms, saying: "I should not have asked so much of you," and talked to me until I controlled my feelings, so that we could go to the tent where mama was lying.

We then learned that trouble was brewing in the camp where Snyder's body lay. At the funeral my father stood sorrowfully by until the last clod was placed upon the grave. He and John Snyder had been good friends, and no one could have regretted the taking of that young life more than my father.

The members of the Donner party then held a council to decide upon the fate of my father while we anxiously awaited the verdict. They refused to accept the plea of self-defense and decided that my father should be banished from the company and sent into the wilderness alone. It was a cruel sentence. And all this animosity towards my father was caused by Louis Keseburg, a German who had joined our company away back on the plains. Keseburg was married to a young and pretty German girl, and used to abuse her, and was in the habit of beating her till she was black and blue. This aroused all the manhood in my father and he took Keseburg to task—telling him it must stop or measures would be taken to that effect. Keseburg did not dare to strike his wife again, but he hated my father and nursed his wrath until papa was so unfortunate as to have to take the life of a fellow-creature in self-defense. Then Keseburg's hour for revenge had come. But how a man like Keseburg, brutal and overbearing by nature, although highly educated, could have such influence over the company is more than I can tell. I have thought the subject over for hours but failed to arrive at a conclusion. The feeling against my father at one time was so strong that lynching was proposed. He was no coward and he bared his neck, saying, "Come on, gentlemen," but no one moved. It was thought more humane, perhaps, to send him into the wilderness to die of slow starvation or be murdered by the Indians; but my father did not die. God took care of him and his family, and at Donner Lake we seemed especially favored by the Almighty as not one of our family perished, and we were the only family no one member of which was forced to eat of human flesh to keep body and soul together. When the sentence of banishment was communicated to my father, he refused to go, feeling that he was justified before God and man, as he had only acted in self-defense.

Then came a sacrifice on the part of my mother. Knowing only too well what her life would be without him, yet fearful that if he remained he would meet with violence at the hands of his enemies, she implored him to go, but all to no avail until she urged him to remember the destitution of the company, saying that if he remained and escaped violence at their hands, he might nevertheless see his children starving and be helpless to aid them, while if he went on he could return and meet them with food. It was a fearful struggle; at last he consented, but not before he had secured a promise from the company to care for his wife and little ones.

My father was sent out into the unknown country without provisions or arms—even his horse was at first denied him. When we learned of this decision, I followed him through the darkness, taking Elliott with me, and carried him his rifle, pistols, ammunition and some food. I had determined to stay with him, and begged him to let me stay, but he would listen to no argument, saying that it was impossible. Finally, unclasping my arms from around him, he placed me in charge of Elliott, who started back to camp with me—and papa was left alone. I had cried until I had hardly strength to walk, but when we reached camp and I saw the distress of my mother, with the little ones clinging around her and no arm to lean upon, it seemed suddenly to make a woman of me. I realized that I must be strong and help mama bear her sorrows.

We traveled on, but all life seemed to have left the party, and the hours dragged slowly along. Every day we would search for some sign of papa, who would leave a letter by the way-side in the top of a bush or in a split stick, and when he succeeded in killing geese or birds would scatter the feathers about so that we might know that he was not suffering for food. When possible, our fire would always be kindled on the spot where his had been, but a time came when we found no letter, and no trace of him. Had he starved by the way-side, or been murdered by the Indians?

My mother's despair was pitiful. Patty and I thought we would be bereft of her also. But life and energy were again aroused by the danger that her children would starve. It was apparent that the whole company would soon be put on a short allowance of food, and the snow-capped mountains gave an ominous hint of the fate that really befell us in the Sierra. Our wagon was found to be too heavy, and was abandoned with everything we could spare, and the remaining things were packed in part of another wagon. We had two horses left from the wreck, which could hardly drag themselves along, but they managed to carry my two little brothers. The rest of us had to walk, one going beside the horse to hold on my youngest brother who was only two and a half years of age. The Donners were not with us when my father was banished, but were several days in advance of our train. Walter Herron, one of our drivers, who was traveling with the Donners, left the wagons and joined my father.

On the 19th of October, while traveling along the Truckee, our hearts were gladdened by the return of Stanton, with seven mules loaded with provisions. Mr. McClutchen was ill and could not travel, but Captain Sutter had sent two of his Indian vaqueros, Luis and Salvador with Stanton. Hungry as we were, Stanton brought us something better than food—news that my father was alive. Stanton had met him not far from Sutter's Fort; he had been three days without food, and his horse was not able to carry him. Stanton had given him a horse and some provisions and he had gone on. We now packed what little we had left on one mule and started with Stanton. My mother rode on a mule, carrying Tommy in her lap; Patty and Jim rode behind the two Indians, and I behind Mr. Stanton, and in this way we journeyed on through the rain, looking up with fear towards the mountains, where snow was already falling although it was only the last week in October. Winter had set in a month earlier than usual. All trails and roads were covered; and our only guide was the summit which it seemed we would never reach. Despair drove many nearly frantic. Each family tried to cross the mountains but found it impossible. When it was seen that the wagons could not be dragged through the snow, their goods and provisions were packed on oxen and another start was made, men and women walking in the snow up to their waists, carrying their children in their arms and trying to drive their cattle. The Indians said they could find no road, so a halt was called, and Stanton went ahead with the guides, and came back and reported that we could get across if we kept right on, but that it would be impossible if snow fell. He was in favor of a forced march until the other side of the summit should be reached, but some of our party were so tired and exhausted with the day's labor that they declared they could not take another step; so the few who knew the danger that the night might bring yielded to the man, and we camped within three miles of the summit.

That night came the dreaded snow. Around the camp-fires under the trees great feathery flakes came whirling down. The air was so full of them that one could see objects only a few feet away. The Indians knew we were doomed, and one of them wrapped his blanket about him and stood all night under a tree. We children slept soundly on our cold bed of snow with a soft white mantle falling over us so thickly that every few moments my mother would have to shake the shawl—our only covering—to keep us from being buried alive. In the morning the snow lay deep on mountain and valley. With heavy hearts we turned back to a cabin that had been built by the Murphy-Schallenberger party two years before. We built more cabins and prepared as best we could for the winter. That camp, which proved the camp of death to many in our company, was made on the shore of a lake, since known as "Donner Lake." The Donners were camped in Alder Creek Valley below the lake, and were, if possible, in a worse condition than ourselves. The snow came on so suddenly that they had no time to build cabins, but hastily put up brush sheds, covering them with pine boughs.

Three double cabins were built at Donner Lake, which were known as the "Breen Cabin," the "Murphy Cabin," and the "Reed-Graves Cabin." The cattle were all killed, and the meat was placed in snow for preservation. My mother had no cattle to kill, but she made arrangements for some, promising to give two for one in California. Stanton and the Indians made their home in my mother's cabin.

Many attempts were made to cross the mountains, but all who tried were driven back by the pitiless storms. Finally a party was organized, since known as the "Forlorn Hope." They made snow-shoes, and fifteen started, ten men and five women, but only seven lived to reach California; eight men perished. They were over a month on the way, and the horrors endured by that Forlorn Hope no pen can describe nor imagination conceive. The noble Stanton was one of the party, and perished the sixth day out, thus sacrificing his life for strangers. I can find no words in which to express a fitting tribute to the memory of Stanton.

The misery endured during those four months at Donner Lake in our little dark cabins under the snow would fill pages and make the coldest heart ache. Christmas was near, but to the starving its memory gave no comfort. It came and passed without observance, but my mother had determined weeks before that her children should have a treat on this one day. She had laid away a few dried apples, some beans, a bit of tripe, and a small piece of bacon. When this hoarded store was brought out, the delight of the little ones knew no bounds. The cooking was watched carefully, and when we sat down to our Christmas dinner mother said, "Children, eat slowly, for this one day you can have all you wish." So bitter was the misery relieved by that one bright day, that I have never since sat down to a Christmas dinner without my thoughts going back to Donner Lake.

The storms would often last ten days at a time, and we would have to cut chips from the logs inside which formed our cabins, in order to start a fire. We could scarcely walk, and the men had hardly strength to procure wood. We would drag ourselves through the snow from one cabin to another, and some mornings snow would have to be shoveled out of the fireplace before a fire could be made. Poor little children were crying with hunger, and mothers were crying because they had so little to give their children. We seldom thought of bread, we had been without it so long. Four months of such suffering would fill the bravest hearts with despair.

During the closing days of December, 1846, gold was found in my mother's cabin at Donner Lake by John Denton. I remember the night well. The storm fiends were shrieking in their wild mirth, we were sitting about the fire in our little dark home, busy with our thoughts. Denton with his cane kept knocking pieces off the large rocks used as fire-irons on which to place the wood. Something bright attracted his attention, and picking up pieces of the rock he examined them closely; then turning to my mother he said, "Mrs. Reed, this is gold." My mother replied that she wished it were bread. Denton knocked more chips from the rocks, and he hunted in the ashes for the shining particles until he had gathered about a teaspoonful. This he tied in a small piece of buckskin and placed in his pocket, saying, "If we ever get away from here I am coming back for more." Denton started out with the first relief party but perished on the way, and no one thought of the gold in his pocket. Denton was about thirty years of age; he was born in Sheffield, England, and was a gunsmith and gold-beater by trade. Gold has never been found on the shore of the lake, but a few miles from there in the mountain cañons, from which this rock possibly came, rich mines have been discovered.

Time dragged slowly along till we were no longer on short allowance but were simply starving. My mother determined to make an effort to cross the mountains. She could not see her children die without trying to get them food. It was hard to leave them but she felt that it must be done. She told them she would bring them bread, so they were willing to stay, and with no guide but a compass we started—my mother, Eliza, Milt Elliott and myself. Milt wore snow shoes and we followed in his tracks. We were five days in the mountains; Eliza gave out the first day and had to return, but we kept on and climbed one high mountain after another only to see others higher still ahead. Often I would have to crawl up the mountains, being too tired to walk. The nights were made hideous by the screams of wild beasts heard in the distance. Again, we would be lulled to sleep by the moan of the pine trees, which seemed to sympathize with our loneliness. One morning we awoke to find ourselves in a well of snow. During the night, while in the deep sleep of exhaustion, the heat of the fire had melted the snow and our little camp had gradually sunk many feet below the surface until we were literally buried in a well of snow. The danger was that any attempt to get out might bring an avalanche upon us, but finally steps were carefully made and we reached the surface. My foot was badly frozen, so we were compelled to return, and just in time, for that night a storm came on, the most fearful of the winter, and we should have perished had we not been in the cabins.

We now had nothing to eat but raw hides and they were on the roof of the cabin to keep out the snow; when prepared for cooking and boiled they were simply a pot of glue. When the hides were taken off our cabin and we were left without shelter Mr. Breen gave us a home with his family, and Mrs. Breen prolonged my life by slipping me little bits of meat now and then when she discovered that I could not eat the hide. Death had already claimed many in our party and it seemed as though relief never would reach us. Baylis Williams, who had been in delicate health before we left Springfield, was the first to die; he passed away before starvation had really set in.

I am a Catholic although my parents were not. I often went to the Catholic church before leaving home, but it was at Donner Lake that I made the vow to be a Catholic. The Breens were the only Catholic family in the Donner party and prayers were said aloud regularly in that cabin night and morning. Our only light was from little pine sticks split up like kindling wood and kept constantly on the hearth. I was very fond of kneeling by the side of Mr. Breen and holding these little torches so that he might see to read. One night we had all gone to bed—I was with my mother and the little ones, all huddled together to keep from freezing—but I could not sleep. It was a fearful night and I felt that the hour was not far distant when we would go to sleep—never to wake again in this world. All at once I found myself on my knees with my hands clasped, looking up through the darkness, making a vow that if God would send us relief and let me see my father again I would be a Catholic. That prayer was answered.

On his arrival at Sutter's Fort, my father made known the situation of the emigrants, and Captain Sutter offered at once to do everything possible for their relief. He furnished horses and provisions and my father and Mr. McClutchen started for the mountains, coming as far as possible with horses and then with packs on their backs proceeding on foot; but they were finally compelled to return. Captain Sutter was not surprised at their defeat. He stated that there were no ablebodied men in that vicinity, all having gone down the country with Frémont to fight the Mexicans. He advised my father to go to Yerba Buena, now San Francisco, and make his case known to the naval officer in command. My father was in fact conducting parties there—when the seven members of the Forlorn Hope arrived from across the mountains. Their famished faces told the story. Cattle were killed and men were up all night drying beef and making flour by hand mills, nearly 200 pounds being made in one night, and a party of seven, commanded by Captain Reasen P. Tucker, were sent to our relief by Captain Sutter and the alcalde, Mr. Sinclair. On the evening of February 19th, 1847, they reached our cabins, where all were starving.

They shouted to attract attention. Mr. Breen clambered up the icy steps from our cabin, and soon we heard the blessed words, "Relief, thank God, relief!" There was joy at Donner Lake that night, for we did not know the fate of the Forlorn Hope and we were told that relief parties would come and go until all were across the mountains. But with the joy sorrow was strangely blended. There were tears in other eyes than those of children; strong men sat down and wept. For the dead were lying about on the snow, some even unburied, since the living had not had strength to bury their dead. When Milt Elliott died,—our faithful friend, who seemed so like a brother,—my mother and I dragged him up out of the cabin and covered him with snow. Commencing at his feet, I patted the pure white snow down softly until I reached his face. Poor Milt! it was hard to cover that face from sight forever, for with his death our best friend was gone.

On the 22d of February the first relief started with a party of twenty-three—men, women and children. My mother and her family were among the number. It was a bright, sunny morning and we felt happy, but we had not gone far when Patty and Tommy gave out. They were not able to stand the fatigue and it was not thought safe to allow them to proceed, so Mr. Glover informed mama that they would have to be sent back to the cabins to await the next expedition. What language can express our feelings? My mother said that she would go back with her children—that we would all go back together. This the relief party would not permit, and Mr. Glover promised mama that as soon as they reached Bear Valley he himself would return for her children. Finally my mother, turning to Mr. Glover said, "Are you a Mason?" He replied that he was. "Will you promise me on the word of a Mason that if we do not meet their father you will return and save my children?" He pledged himself that he would. My father was a member of the Mystic Tie and mama had great faith in the word of a Mason. It was a sad parting—a fearful struggle. The men turned aside, not being able to hide their tears. Patty said, "I want to see papa, but I will take good care of Tommy and I do not want you to come back." Mr. Glover returned with the children and, providing them with food, left them in the care of Mr. Breen.

With sorrowful hearts we traveled on, walking through the snow in single file. The men wearing snow-shoes broke the way and we followed in their tracks. At night we lay down on the snow to sleep, to awake to find our clothing all frozen, even to our shoe-strings. At break of day we were again on the road, owing to the fact that we could make better time over the frozen snow. The sunshine, which it would seem would have been welcome, only added to our misery. The dazzling reflection of the snow was very trying to the eyes, while its heat melted our frozen clothing, making them cling to our bodies. My brother was too small to step in the tracks made by the men, and in order to travel he had to place his knee on the little hill of snow after each step and climb over. Mother coaxed him along, telling him that every step he took he was getting nearer papa and nearer something to eat. He was the youngest child that walked over the Sierra Nevada. On our second day's journey John Denton gave out and declared it would be impossible for him to travel, but he begged his companions to continue their journey. A fire was built and he was left lying on a bed of freshly cut pine boughs, peacefully smoking. He looked so comfortable that my little brother wanted to stay with him; but when the second relief party reached him poor Denton was past waking. His last thoughts seemed to have gone back to his childhood's home, as a little poem was found by his side, the pencil apparently just dropped from his hand.

Captain Tucker's party on their way to the cabins had lightened their packs of a sufficient quantity of provisions to supply the sufferers on their way out. But when we reached the place where the cache had been made by hanging the food on a tree, we were horrified to find that wild animals had destroyed it, and again starvation stared us in the face. But my father was hurrying over the mountains, and met us in our hour of need with his hands full of bread. He had expected to meet us on this day, and had stayed up all night baking bread to give us. He brought with him fourteen men. Some of his party were ahead, and when they saw us coming they called out, "Is Mrs. Reed with you? If she is, tell her Mr. Reed is here." We heard the call; mother knelt on the snow, while I tried to run to meet papa.

When my father learned that two of his children were still at the cabins, he hurried on, so fearful was he that they might perish before he reached them. He seemed to fly over the snow, and made in two days the distance we had been five in traveling, and was overjoyed to find Patty and Tommy alive. He reached Donner Lake on the first of March, and what a sight met his gaze! The famished little children and the death-like look of all made his heart ache. He filled Patty's apron with biscuits, which she carried around, giving one to each person. He had soup made for the infirm, and rendered every assistance possible to the sufferers. Leaving them with about seven days' provisions, he started out with a party of seventeen, all that were able to travel. Three of his men were left at the cabins to procure wood and assist the helpless. My father's party (the second relief) had not traveled many miles when a storm broke upon them. With the snow came a perfect hurricane. The crying of half-frozen children, the lamenting of the mothers, and the suffering of the whole party was heart-rending; and above all could be heard the shrieking of the Storm King. One who has never witnessed a blizzard in the Sierra can form no idea of the situation. All night my father and his men worked unceasingly through the raging storm, trying to erect shelter for the dying women and children. At times the hurricane would burst forth with such violence that he felt alarmed on account of the tall timber surrounding the camp. The party were destitute of food, all supplies that could be spared having been left with those at the cabins. The relief party had cached provisions on their way over to the cabins, and my father had sent three of the men forward for food before the storm set in; but they could not return. Thus, again, death stared all in the face. At one time the fire was nearly gone; had it been lost, all would have perished. Three days and nights they were exposed to the fury of the elements. Finally my father became snow-blind and could do no more, and he would have died but for the exertions of William McClutchen and Hiram Miller, who worked over him all night. From this time forward, the toil and responsibility rested upon McClutchen and Miller.

The storm at last ceased, and these two determined to set out over the snow and send back relief to those not able to travel. Hiram Miller picked up Tommy and started. Patty thought she could walk, but gradually everything faded from her sight, and she too seemed to be dying. All other sufferings were now forgotten, and everything was done to revive the child. My father found some crumbs in the thumb of his woolen mitten; warming and moistening them between his own lips, he gave them to her and thus saved her life, and afterward she was carried along by different ones in the company. Patty was not alone in her travels. Hidden away in her bosom was a tiny doll, which she had carried day and night through all of our trials. Sitting before a nice, bright fire at Woodworth's Camp, she took dolly out to have a talk, and told her of all her new happiness.

There was untold suffering at that "Starved Camp," as the place has since been called. When my father reached Woodworth's Camp, a third relief started in at once and rescued the living. A fourth relief went on to Donner Lake, as many were still there—and many remain there still, including George Donner and wife, Jacob Donner and wife and four of their children. George Donner had met with an accident which rendered him unable to travel; and his wife would not leave him to die alone. It would take pages to tell of the heroic acts and noble deeds of those who lie sleeping about Donner Lake.

Most of the survivors, when brought in from the mountains, were taken by the different relief parties to Sutter's Fort, and the generous hearted captain did everything possible for the sufferers. Out of the eighty-three persons who were snowed in at Donner Lake, forty-two perished, and of the thirty-one emigrants who left Springfield, Illinois, that spring morning, only eighteen lived to reach California. Alcalde Sinclair took my mother and her family to his own home, and we were surrounded with every comfort. Mrs. Sinclair was the dearest of women. Never can I forget their kindness. But our anxiety was not over, for we knew that my father's party had been caught in the storm. I can see my mother now, as she stood leaning against the door for hours at a time, looking towards the mountains. At last my father arrived at Mr. Sinclair's with the little ones, and our family were again united. That day's happiness repaid us for much that we had suffered; and it was spring in California.

Words cannot tell how beautiful the spring appeared to us coming out of the mountains from that long winter at Donner Lake in our little dark cabins under the snow. Before us now lay, in all its beauty, the broad valley of the Sacramento. I remember one day, when traveling down Napa Valley, we stopped at noon to have lunch under the shade of an oak; but I was not hungry; I was too full of the beautiful around me to think of eating. So I wandered off by myself to a lovely little knoll and stood there in a bed of wild flowers, looking up and down the green valley, all dotted with trees. The birds were singing with very joy in the branches over my head, and the blessed sun was smiling down upon all as though in benediction. I drank it in for a moment, and then began kissing my hand and wafting kisses to Heaven in thanksgiving to the Almighty for creating a world so beautiful. I felt so near God at that moment that it seemed to me that I could feel His breath warm on my cheek. By and by I heard papa calling, "Daughter, where are you? Come, child, we are ready to start, and you have had no lunch," I ran and caught him by the hand, saying, "Buy this place, please, and let us make our home here." He stood looking around for a moment, and said, "It *is* a lovely spot," and then we passed on.

from A Dangerous Journey
by J. Ross Browne

J. Ross Browne (1821–1875) was a prolific travel writer. His work included an account of his visit to the island where Alexander Selkirk (the inspiration for Robinson Crusoe) was marooned and a report on a gold rush in the Sierra Nevada mountains. His article for the May 1862 Harper's New Monthly *told of his 1849 horseback journey from San Francisco to San Luis Obispo, which included this encounter with Donner Party survivors Patrick and Margaret Breen.*

I stopped a night at San Jose, where I was most hospitably received by the Alcalde, an American gentleman of intelligence, to whom I had a letter of introduction. Next day, after a pleasant ride of forty-five miles, I reached the Mission of San Juan [Bautista]—one of the most eligibly located of all the old missionary establishments. It was now in a state of decay. The vineyards were but partially cultivated, and the secos, or ditches for the irrigation of the land, were entirely dry. I got some very good pears from the old Spaniard in charge of the Mission— a rare luxury after a long sea-voyage. The only tavern in the place was the "United States," kept by an American and his wife in an old adobe house, originally a part of the missionary establishment. Having secured accommodations for my mule, I took up my quarters for the night at the "United States." The woman seemed to be the principal manager. Perhaps I might have noticed her a little closely, since she was the only white woman I had enjoyed the opportunity of conversing with for some time. It was very certain, however, that she struck me as an uncommon person—tall, raw-boned, sharp, and masculine—with a wild and piercing expression of eye, and a smile singularly startling and unfeminine. I even fancied that her teeth were long and pointed, and that she resembled a picture of an Ogress I had seen when a child. The man was a subdued and melancholy-looking person, presenting no particular trait of character in his appearance save that of general abandonment to the influence of misfortune. His dress and expression impressed me with the idea that he had experienced much trouble, without possessing that strong power of recuperation so common among American adventurers in California.

It would scarcely be worth while noticing these casual acquaintances of a night, since they have nothing to do with my narrative, but for the remarkable illustration they afford of the hardships that were encountered at that time on the emigrant routes to California. In the course of conversation with the man, I found that he and his wife were among the few survivors of a party whose terrible sufferings in the mountains during the past winter had been the theme of much comment in the newspapers. He did not state—what I already knew from the published narrative of their adventures—that the woman had subsisted for some time of the dead body of a child belonging to one of the party. It was said that the man had held out to the last, and refused to participate in the horrible feast of human flesh.

So strangely impressive was it to be brought in direct contact with a fellow-being, especially of the gentler sex, who had absolutely eaten of human flesh, that I could not but look upon this woman with a shudder. Her sufferings had been intense; that was evident from her marked and weather-beaten features. Doubtless she had struggled against the cravings of hunger as long as reason lasted. But still the one terrible act, whether the result of necessity or insanity, invested her with a repellant atmosphere of horror. Her very smile struck me as the gloating expression of a cannibal over human blood. In vain I struggled against this unchristian feeling. Was it right to judge a poor creature whose great misfortune was perhaps no offense against the laws of nature? She might be the tenderest and best of women—I knew nothing of her history. It was a pitiable case. But, after all, she had eaten of human flesh; there was not getting over that.

When I sat down to supper this woman was obliging enough to hand me a plate of meat. I was hungry, and tried to eat it. Every morsel seemed to stick in my throat. I could not feel quite sure that it was what it seemed to be. The odor even disgusted me. Nor could I partake of the bread she passed to me with any more relish. It was probably made by her hands—the same hands that had torn the flesh from a corpse and passed the reeking shreds to her mouth. The taint of an imaginary corruption was upon it.

The room allotted to me for the night was roughly furnished, as might reasonably be expected; but, apart from this, the bedding was filthy; and in common with every thing about the house, the slatternly appearance of the furniture did not tend to remove the unpleasant impression I had formed of my hostess. Whether owing to the vermin, or an unfounded suspicion that she might become hungry during the night, I slept but little. The picture of the terrible Ogress that I had seen when a child, and the story of the little children which she had devoured, assumed a fearful reality, and became strangely mingled in my dreams with this woman's face. I was glad when daylight afforded me an excuse to get up and take a stroll in the fresh air.

from The Rage to Survive
by Jacques Vignes

*Catherine Plessz and Lucien Schiltz survived
12 days at sea in a lifeboat without food. This
interview with the pair suggests the strain starvation can put on a relationship. Jacques Vignes
(born 1921) asks the questions.*

C*atherine:* Having come this far, it would be impossible to
go further without mentioning something we have
avoided until now. It's just too bad for the softhearted. If
we are to speak the real truth about this matter, certain
forms of prudery, or rather certain social hypocrisies, are irrelevant. We
must go all the way.

But first of all we should make clear again what our situation was
on Friday the 22nd, the eighth day, difficult though it may be to set
precise boundaries on our thoughts. When I say Friday the 22nd, I'm
no doubt simplifying. What each of us in our little corner imagined
that day, we had no doubt already thought about, more or less confusedly, the day before or even the day before that, if not earlier.

In any case, one thing is certain. That kind of thinking did not
arise in our minds all at once. We reached that point after many
meanderings. We must have thought about similar things earlier, but
without attaching any importance to them since they were specula-

tions of no immediate concern. Then, little by little, those so-called speculations asserted themselves as actual plans. We began to consider them with complacency, until the thing itself was so deeply embedded within us that it became one of the central themes of our thoughts and dreams.

And when I speak of us, I mean each of us taken separately. Anyone will readily understand that in our situation an intellectual or sentimental community was no longer possible. If I spoke, a few moments ago, of the reality of the situation I was referring to this fact. Aside from rare instances of rudimentary exchanges, each of us was enclosed inside his own world. There was no question of allowing the other access to it. Our solidarity, or what was left of it, was only revived for a moment when our survival depended on carrying out some essential act together, like pumping up the raft, bailing, sharing the water, or signaling an eventual rescuer.

I say "we." That's perhaps unfair. After all, Lucien may not have lived through that period in the same way. Yet I think he did. Several indications led me to think that we had reached the same point. The moment when we thought that if the other were to die, it would of course be in many ways dreadfully lonely, but it would also mean the possibility of nourishment again, of regaining strength, of saving one's skin.

Jacques Vignes: In other words, by Friday each of you seriously thought of nourishing yourself with the remains of whoever should die first?

Lucien: As far as I'm concerned, that's right. I had decided that I must survive. I'd always had the impression that Catherine was much weaker than I. Therefore, it was logical that she should die first.

Catherine: I held the opposite point of view. I thought, "Lucien is very low. He won't last long or he'll give in to one of those suicidal urges that overtake him now and then." I saw his body, his face changing. I read death in his look.

Jacques Vignes: "Had you, in any way, referred openly to such plans?"

Catherine: Yes, but in a very hypocritical way, each of us saying that he wouldn't eat the other if he died. That was a way of admitting that we wanted to do it. Yet I admit I was quite surprised when I learned that Lucien held the same ideas on the subject. I didn't think he was capable of it.

Lucien: I was also surprised. I reproached myself. I thought, "How can I think of eating her when she would never dream of doing that to me." And then at other times I was ashamed. I thought of the days we had spent together. I realized that even after she died I would be unable to grapple with her. And yet, little by little, the obsession with food regained the upper hand.

Catherine: I, too, felt ashamed, told myself I couldn't do it and at the same time I thought, "There's no reason why it should be wrong."

Jacques Vignes: "So there came a time when you began to watch each other, to say to yourselves that the death of one of you could mean a kind of salvation for the other?"

Catherine: Yes. And I began to see what had to be done very quickly. We had an absurd little knife, no doubt thought up by some survival expert sitting in his comfy armchair, a knife designed to do everything. There was a bottle opener at one end, as if we'd have brought bottles of soda or mineral water. In short, a knife that's good for nothing.

I saw myself trying to carve with that knife. What piece should I choose? I felt like a cutlet, but that was probably very difficult to remove. What then? The buttock seemed unappetizing. I wondered where steaks were in a human being. Wouldn't it be simplest to cut a piece from the thigh? I was also tempted to suck out all the blood. Could it be done? How should I go about it? I thought about that sort of problem for hours.

From time to time, however, I would come up against a stone wall. First of all, education, accepted notions, the revulsion of a civilized person, although on the eighth day not much was left of the great social taboos. At other times they were more down-to-earth obstacles. For example, I saw myself being saved by a boat with a half-carved body next to me. I was being questioned, I was thrown into prison for the rest of my life. Then I thought of rigor mortis. I pictured this great body, stiff as a board, stretched across the raft, pushing it out of shape.

I wouldn't be able to do anything with it, to drink its blood, to carve that monolith. I'd have to live with it, to let it have the lion's share of room, to step over it continually. Little by little that cadaver consumed everything—an enormous statue too heavy for me to throw into the sea.

But that nightmare lasted only a short while. I soon convinced myself of its ridiculousness. If it came to that, I wouldn't be the first to be in such a predicament. Others had eaten their dead companions in order to survive. We had even heard of people killing one another to provide food. After all, I hadn't reached that point. In all frankness, although it had occurred to me to wish for Lucien's death, I never for a second dreamt of helping to bring it about. The thought never crossed my mind, not even an eventuality that one rejects. It was always, "If he dies," or "He's sure to die." And, starting at that point, the dream unfolded itself more and more precisely as time went by. I took pleasure in the evocation, in the meticulous inventory of the gestures destined to ransom my life.

Jacques Vignes: "What had become of that noble decision not to let yourselves dwell on the thought of food?"

Catherine: It was still there. Please understand. I had always forbidden myself to dream of nonexistent food, to allow myself to succumb to the impossible. But obviously, if by some miracle food had appeared in the raft, I would not have complained about it.

Now, the moment I thought that Lucien was about to die, and that it was not only possible but certain that I would eat his flesh after his death, the food appeared, so to speak, or was about to appear. The living Lucien had ceased, in a way, to be a companion, a human presence—although in another way, of course, he still was—and became, instead, the possibility of food that could be transformed into reality at any moment. So it became natural to picture the new situation and to hope it would happen.

Lucien: I thought along pretty much the same lines, except that I also dreamt about other kinds of food.

When I was dozing, I went to a little restaurant in Beaulieu where we used to go. In the middle of the restaurant there was a table piled with hors d'oeuvres. I helped myself and ate and ate. And then, when I was back in the raft, I saw Catherine opposite me. I had the impression she was growing weaker by the hour. She scarcely moved. She had told me that she felt stiffer all the time, that it was harder and harder for her to make the slightest move. It was obviously the end for her. So why turn down that chance to survive?

I also wondered how to go about carving her up, what piece I should remove first. I thought of her liver. I'm very fond of liver. I had asked her, "Catherine, is your liver healthy?" She had replied yes while looking at me in surprise. She even said, "Why do you ask that question?" I told her, "Because I think one needs a healthy liver in order to survive."

Catherine: I remember. I immediately gathered that he was planning to eat my liver if I died. I think I was sure then that he too was considering feeding on my corpse. Yet I was not unduly impressed by the discovery. I felt like telling him: naive Lucien, you are sadly mistaken if you think I will be the first to die.

Jacques Vignes: "And yet you continued to reassure each other that if one of you died the other would not eat him."

Lucien: Yes, it was one of the basic themes of our rare conversations. From time to time we would talk about death, or rather about our ever more slim chance of survival. We were asking each other how we felt, if we thought we could last much longer, without realizing too clearly that each of us understood perfectly why the other asked those questions. And then that led immediately to our chief preoccupation: "Do you think you would be capable of eating me if I died?" There followed vehement denials which neither one believed, yet which didn't prevent our raising the subject again at the first opportunity. It was as though we wanted to reassure and unmask each other at the same time. We had to know where we stood.

I remember trying to trap Catherine. I said to her, "After all, if I died first and it was your only chance to survive, I don't see why you shouldn't eat me. It wouldn't make much difference to me, once I was dead."

I don't remember anymore exactly what she replied. She must have reassured me that she would not be capable of it, which somewhat set my mind at rest. In effect, I was always trying to convince myself, against all the evidence, that even if I had decided to eat Catherine's flesh when the occasion arose, she certainly wouldn't behave in the same way toward me. She was thinking of it, perhaps, yet when the time came, she wouldn't dare do it. And at the same time I said to myself that the problem wouldn't arise for her in any case, since it was quite obvious that if anyone were to die it could only be she.

Catherine: I had no illusions. I knew very well that if I died first as the result of some unforeseen accident, Lucien would eat me.

Lucien: And yet, perhaps I'd have hesitated. I had a rather dreadful dream several times. I was landing on some shore with the half cut-up body of Catherine in the raft. Luckily the beach was deserted, yet I was afraid someone might come at any moment. I wanted to run, to run as fast as my legs could go to avoid being discovered next to that mutilated corpse. Yet if I abandoned it there, there would be an inquiry about it. It would lead to me in the end. I'd have to live the life of a hunted man. So I decided to get rid of it. I cut up the rest of the corpse and threw the pieces into the sea. Then I began destroying the raft, strip by strip, because of bloodstains. Once having done that, I headed for the interior. I dared not let myself be seen. I hid in the forest. I was going to feed myself by stealing food from the farms at night. I dug up potatoes from the fields. I went inside henroosts, making off with eggs, wringing the necks of chickens.

Jacques Vignes: "And what happened when you woke up and saw Catherine facing you, still alive?"

Lucien: First of all, I was relieved. Compared to that nightmare, the situation in the raft seemed, if not desirable, at least tolerable. Nothing irreversible had yet taken place and there was still hope of getting out alive. And then I began to wonder whether that dream were really a nightmare. It had several ghastly aspects, of course. Yet the potatoes, the eggs, the chickens, renewed strength, one's fill of water—these things were far from unpleasant.

The more I thought about it, the more I was obsessed with the idea of food. Only a few moments before I'd been telling myself: you know quite well it's impossible, that no matter what happens you could never cut up Catherine's body, eat her flesh. And yet, there it was. The temptation was coming back so strongly that there was no question of resisting it.

I saw the problem in very simple terms. As soon as she were dead there would be only two alternatives—to eat her or to die.

Yet wasn't I a bit hasty to reduce it to those two alternatives? More and more often, especially during Saturday evening and night, I wondered whether things would ever happen that way. When the moment came, would I still have any strength left to make the slightest effort? Suppose I died first? I was beginning to consider that possibility. In that case, why not hasten the outcome? Wasn't suicide the only real solution?

I pictured myself dead. I had become something else. Perhaps a seagull. Yes, why not a seagull? Or perhaps another animal. A cow, for example, belly-deep in rich grass, endlessly contemplating an unchanging landscape through vacant eyes. That prospect made me freeze with terror. No, I couldn't run that risk. There was only one solution. To live, whatever the cost.

Catherine: It wasn't death I was afraid of, I mean death as the beginning of something else. For me, death was the end of everything—in other words, the final, absolute end of Catherine. That was what I rebelled against, losing my life, now, so young, while there were still so many things to experience. And losing it that way, almost alone in that raft. No one would ever know what had happened. There was no way to leave my story behind. If only I could have sent a message, at least to say what my life had been like to the last day.

I had the impression of being walled-in. Yet, at the same time, I felt my situation was worse. In the case of someone walled-in, there would be others to know about it. The victim could always hope that at the last moment someone would take pity, would come to rescue him or that he might manage in a final outburst to topple the stones that separated him from the world.

from Shackleton's Forgotten Men
by Lennard Bickel

When the support team for Ernest Shackleton's aborted 1914 attempt to cross Antarctica also lost their ship, they scavenged the remains of earlier expeditions, and six men trudged 2,000 miles across the Ross Ice Shelf to lay supply depots for Shackleton—who never arrived. Lennard Bickel in 1976 interviewed survivor Dick Richards. Here is Bickel's account of how the men—including Captain Aeneas Mackintosh and chaplain Arnold Patrick Spencer-Smith—struggled back toward the coast.

They formed a pathetic procession. In a closed sphere of wildly whirling snow the famished dogs were white moles floundering through the drift, while the men were shadowy figures, their heads bowed in weariness as they leaned in their harness. Ernest Joyce on the lead rope was merely a blur in the distance. On the sledge the figure of the Padre was a bundle lashed in a snow cloth against the flying flakes. At the rear, the Captain tottered piteously on crooked legs. Every man and every dog gulped great lungfuls of chill air, either in exhaustion or in pain. All movement, all effort was a striving of will against weakness of body and the buffeting blizzard wind.

It had been like that from the moment they decided not to lie and wait for death in the tents. When Joyce told Mackintosh they had decided to march rather than submit, Richards had noted Mackintosh seemed to have lost "all initiative and was quite content to remain. However, he agreed to make the effort and we set about digging out our equipment." So great were the layers of snow, 10 to 12 feet deep in places, that they found this work to be a "prodigious effort." It was then, Richards recorded, that they realized the extent to which hunger and inactivity had weakened them, how their strength had been sapped by the blizzard's assault. It took them all morning before they could drag the sledge to the Captain's tent, knock that down, wrap the recumbent Spencer-Smith in the snow sheet and lift him to the sledge. The sick man lost consciousness during the pain of movement.

They were not able to "set sail" until midafternoon, rigging the snow cloth against the bamboo spar to gain some impetus from the wind hammering at their backs. The wind force was as violent as ever, and the air was full of flying drift. Joyce felt apprehensive; they were marching in conditions they never would have faced if they had had adequate supplies of food, knowing that a slight error in direction could turn them from their course, to be lost for ever in the white wasteland. Richards checked the prismatic compass and watched the angle of the lead rope carefully, and he and Joyce tried to shout directions to each other against the howl of the wind.

They had little chance of going far in the afternoon. After a mere half-hour of trudging, Mackintosh collapsed, his head lolling back and the snow falling on his face and clogging his goggles. Richards caught him as he fell. His final shreds of resolution had been eroded by the increasing effect of scurvy and the lack of food, and his voice was so pitiable that Richards thought him delirious. With the agony of helplessness their commander was crying to them, "I'm done, I'm done for!" over and over. And then, "Oh, my hands! My hands are gone."

Richards felt deeply moved. He was to write in his diary, "I have never been so profoundly impressed with the change in a man's condition." Now he tried rough comfort, knowing every hour lost on the trail increased their peril. "Don't be a bloody fool, Mack. We'll get you a hot drink and then we'll go on again."

Mackintosh did not respond. He repeated that he was finished, that he had lost his hands to frostbite and could not go on any longer. Then he told them, "I don't care what happens. I don't care. Wrap me in a snow cloth and leave me here! I'm done for."

Richards comforted him again, still holding his body from falling into the snow. "We'll take care of you, Mack," he said. "We'll see you through."

The anguish of that time was still vivid in the mind of Dick Richards more than 60 years later, and recalling the harrowing situation still brought tears to his eyes. He remembered lifting the wasted body of the Captain and comforting him while the others threw up the tent against the force of the snow-filled wind: "No argument, Mack. We'll put you in the tent and make you comfortable, and then we'll go on to the depot and bring back food and fuel. You'll be right."

Joyce had his own memories of the crisis. He noted how he tried to jolly the Captain into a brighter frame of mind. "I felt I should cheer him at any cost. Some added strength came to my assistance and I remembered the wager we had made on our race to the Bluff a year before. I exclaimed, 'You Scotsman! What about my magnum of champagne?' This remark changed his thought waves. Even the Padre had to smile."

There were two invalids to be left in the tent, incapable of fending for themselves. Joyce and Richards, now in total command, quickly decided what should be done. It was essential, they agreed, to leave a fit man to care for the two scurvy victims. Hayward was now so far along that trail that he, too, might soon be helpless. The strongest men, Joyce and Richards, should make the attempt to reach the depot. That meant Ernie Wild would have to stay and care for the sick men. When they told the Yorkshireman of their plan he accepted reluctantly, acknowledging the wisdom of the decision. He had, after all, been tent mate to the Captain and had also cared for the Padre since his collapse at 83° South.

Richards recorded that the decision to leave Wild with Mackintosh and Spencer-Smith appeared to be the right one at the time. "He had been caring for the Padre all along with the utmost unselfishness, so it seemed the right course to follow. As things turned out it would perhaps have been better to have taken him with us."

The march to the depot and back would take four days at the very least, Joyce calculated. He, Richards and Hayward placed almost all their remaining food in the Captain's tent. This amounted to 16 biscuits, some four ounces of meat cubes, and a little chocolate. Optimistically, he told Ernie Wild to expect them back with rations and fuel by the following Sunday, February 27. "We shall bring you supplies by then if we find the depot," Joyce said. "If not? What then?" asked Wild. Joyce cheerfully replied, "We live in hopes of a fine day. We'll try to be back in four days." That would entail covering seven miles a day for three days, allowing for one day at the depot to stock up on food, feed themselves and the famished animals, and rest. "The situation looks far from promising," he wrote.

The parting was made as cheerful as their doubts would permit. Joyce took the lead rope, and with Richards and Hayward on each side of the dogs—big Oscar straining in the front—they tramped to the north. Within moments the small dome of the tent with the three men inside was lost to their vision, vanished in the swirl of blown drift and snowflakes. "So we left them there," Dick Richards told this writer. "When we left I had no idea whether we would ever see them again. In the blizzard we were not sure we could find that depot; and if we did, whether we would ever find the tent again in that wilderness."

Joyce wrote his version of that parting and of their brief march for the rest of the day, Wednesday, February 23: "We wished them goodbye and gave them a cheery parting. As we left, the blizzard came on us again with unabating fury. Even with an empty sledge, four dogs, sail set, we found we could not do more than half-a-mile an hour. The surface was so bad that sometimes we sank in up to the waist. After the tent was pitched I found my left foot badly frostbitten and blistered. We sat down to our banquet: one cup of tea, half a biscuit. The dogs did not give their cheerful bark that they always do when we camp for the night. Poor fellows—no food for them."

The blizzard was unceasing. All night it blew and blustered around them, the patched tent quaking under its impact. They could not rest too long; hungry and shivering in their thinning skin bags they were up and about soon after 4 in the morning. Richards melted some snow, cursing the nature of the last of the methylated spirits. "In normal times," he would recall, "you could put a match to the spirit and it would burst into flame. Down there it was so cold it had to be coaxed with match after match to start burning." When the water was warm enough, they made a weak infusion of tea and drank it thankfully while munching another half biscuit. They wasted no time in forcing on their frigid finneskoes and breaking camp.

The snow and wind were worse than on the previous day. They had great difficulty laying their course and were so weak now that every 15 minutes or so they would drop gasping for breath, their backs resting against the sledge for brief shelter. They came on banks of soft snow that stopped them in their tracks as though hidden brakes had been applied to their load. Then, with men and dogs heaving and straining, the sledge would be inched forward in a heartbreaking slow advance, each stint measured by only tens of yards. At best, with utmost exertion, they could not cover more than three miles in a good day. All dreams of trudging seven miles per diem were blown away by blasts of wind with a force they reckoned to be between 60 and 80 miles an hour, and were buried in the layers of fresh soft snow laid in their path.

Ernest Joyce remembered how a month previously this same team— three men and four dogs—had hauled a sledge with a lading of 1,380 pounds, covering at least 10 miles in a day. "As a comparison," he noted, "the weight of this sledge is about 200 pounds all told and, with the same team, making only two or three miles in a whole day."

They camped at noon that second day, exhausted from their efforts, and spent more than an hour in the torment of igniting the dribble of methylated spirits in the converted mug-stove in order to melt snow to hot water. They drank their weak tea and were compelled to halve their biscuit ration. Richards and Hayward went out to the sledge to prepare the dogs for another haul, but the battering gale almost blew them off their feet. They dragged the skin sleeping bags back into the tent, admitting it was impossible to march, and they lay there in the shaking tent with the cold and the hunger growing in them as the hours went by.

It was little more than 24 hours since they had left the other tent, and they had covered a miserable distance. Now they were so cold they felt they had to use more spirits to make a warm drink, but they would not make more inroads into their few biscuits. Joyce brought in the canvas tank they had used to haul the dog food, and in utter desperation they scraped the inside and the corners with their metal spoons for any shreds of seal meat and pemmican left adhering to the fabric. Joyce's diary relates that "it is a very scanty meal. I don't think I ever tasted anything worse, but it had to go down. This is the third day the dogs have been without food." Now it dawned on their minds that reaching the depot was critical not so much for themselves as for the starving animals. "Our idea is to push on to the depot to save the lives of the dogs," wrote Dick Richards, sitting in the tent that day. "The reason for this is a selfish one, since we know we cannot get back to safety if they give up."

The starving animals were already losing their spirit, all except the doughty Oscar. When they were bogged down in the deep drift, it had been beyond their strength to budge the stranded sledge. At those times of crisis some new surge of power was dredged from the lead dog, and Richards noted how "massive Oscar would lower his great head and pull as he never did when things were going well." His superb pulling power sometimes managed to add a little run to the sledge movement, and then the big dog would snap at the heels of the others to make them try harder.

"Perhaps that sounds rather fantastic, but it was true," Richards attested. "These dogs were as individual as humans and we had become very close to them indeed. We could recognize their moods. Like us, they had been on very short commons for many days, and it seemed that Oscar was aware that we were looking for something that would give him a full meal once more."

They were bound to slave in order to try and save the dogs, because that meant saving the three men they had left behind in the tent. All their energy, all their strength of being were now bent towards reaching the citadel, the depot near Minna Bluff. So consuming was this fight for distance that they gave little thought to the problem of finding the tent again—it was somewhere back along the trail, but exactly where they did not know.

When the blizzard had first blotted out the world for them, somewhere near Captain Scott's grave, they had lost their guiding cairns. When Mackintosh collapsed they had not known whether they were to the east or the west of that line of snow blocks they had laid on the outward journey. And there was a further uncertainty: In the frenetic drive to cover the distance to 80° South they had discarded any equipment they considered not vital. Among the items dumped was their sledge meter, an apparatus with a wheel attached to the rear of the sledge, which measured the distance they covered. Thus they had no sure knowledge of how far they had gone, or whether they were on one side or the other of the cairns that would guide them to the depot. "We were weak and the gusting wind would make us stagger; we marched into a white void and could see nothing," Richards recalled.

They sat fearful in their fragile tent that night of Thursday, February 24. Joyce, "The wind came on worse than ever at 8:30. I am afraid the tent will be the next thing to go, and then it will be all up with us. . . . Trusting in Providence for a fine day tomorrow." Their very breaths and the faint steam from melting the snow to drink were a menace, for the vapor caked into stiff ice on the tent fabric, making it brittle and ready to split from the severe buffeting. Richards was concerned with the problem of direction and navigation. His diary read, "It is hard to know what course to pursue when a wrong decision means wasting the working efficiency of our meagre food. A false start means a meal wasted. . . . It is very cold." And there was more to it than the danger of wasting a meal. Unsure of how much ground they were covering, they could easily overshoot the depot—and "never find the succour that awaits us in that featureless wilderness."

The blizzard fell away for a few hours that night, but Joyce's fine day did not come. Instead it snowed heavily, blocking all hope of seeing anything beyond a yard or two. Without wind on their backs to give them a sense of direction, they could not march. They could even have gone back on their tracks without being aware of it. When the wind came again, at 4 in the morning, they started to prepare for the trail. It took three hours to make the weak tea, knock down the tent, carefully furl it against the brittle ice splitting the fabric, and set off north again.

They made a faltering cavalcade, forced to stop every five or 10 minutes to catch their breath and check their direction, always with nagging uncertainty in their minds. Setting the scene and their predicament, Richards wrote, "Sun shining somewhere through the murk—we cannot see where it is—heavy wind and snowfall. We do not know how we stand in relation to the depot or whether in thick weather we have strayed from our course. We are very weak. The huskies work pluckily but they are obviously weak—no food for two nights; Con very groggy. The method of heating takes a great deal of time; a meal of a mug of tea doesn't stay with us very long."

The wind and the flight of the blown snow was their guide. Richards recorded, "It was my job, being nearest the sledge, to lay the course. This could only be done when we halted. . . . In the cold, with bare fingers, it was possible only to struggle with the metal of the prismatic compass for a few seconds before it had to be put away and the hands returned to the mittens." He laid the course along the angle of the rope that stretched ahead of the sledge, moving Joyce in the lead trace to right or left each time they halted. "There was nothing to guide him to keep a straight course, and the best we could do was to note how the rope lay in relation to the direction of the wind on our backs, or over our shoulders—to go on for 15 minutes in this way then stop, and check again."

At midday on Friday, February 25, the heaviest snowfall of the long-lasting blizzard fell and the wind rose again to its former savagery. They were now completely out of food of any kind—other than the crumbs from the biscuits they and the dogs had eaten. The young man's diary told a dismal tale: "Impossible to travel. Have to wait until storm abates. We do not know how we stand in regards to the depot or whether we have strayed off course."

Crouched down under the brittle covering of the tent they had scavenged from the dump at Cape Evans, their minds turned to the famous tragedy that had happened hereabouts on this terrible ice plain. Joyce wrote, "We speak often of my late chief, of Captain Scott and his party. . . . If we had prolonged our stay in the tent another day I feel sure we would have remained powerless to get under way again. We would have shared a similar fate. . . . If the worst comes we have made up our minds to carry on and die in harness on the track."

Their danger increased that night. Joyce feared they had already passed the depot. There was no food and no spirits left to heat their drink. Then the tent split again down the front, near the tunnel entrance. Vic Hayward was nearing a breakdown. Formerly a beefy man with a taciturn manner, he was changed. Toil, hunger, and scurvy had eaten away the substance of his resistance. Joyce noted, "I am doubtful if Hayward can stand the strain another day. He is down in the dumps and strange." Chosen by Shackleton for his experience in the cold north of Canada, Hayward was now near to babbling in distraction and distress, and played no part in the torment of repairing the tent. Richards and Joyce took turns squatting in the 60-mile wind, with the temperature down to 20 degrees below freezing, passing the needle back and forth while the calico food bags were stitched over the rent in the fabric.

There was no comfort of a hot drink to be had when the task was finished, and so they curled up in their skin bags to try and restore some warmth in their frozen limbs, and were then shocked to hear Hayward ranting about the food outside the tent, in the snow. "We can have meat," he was saying. "We can kill one of the dogs and eat its flesh. That would keep us alive."

Richards was horrified. Joyce sat upright in his bag and stared at the man. "Don't you know," he asked, "that it will put us all in jeopardy to lose a single one of those dogs? Not just us, Vic, but our comrades back there in the other tent! We depend on them to trek us in. If we lose one then it will mean goodbye for all of us."

Richards tried to cheer the depressed man by saying the blizzard had to let up soon, and that tomorrow could be a clear day in which they would find the cairns and reach the depot. Suddenly Joyce remembered lines from his favorite poet, whom he introduced, much to the delight of Richards, as the Kipling of Canada—Robert Service. He quoted,

> It's the plugging away that will win you the day
> So don't be a piker, old pard!
> Just draw on your grit; it's so easy to quit:
> It's the keeping-your-chin-up that's hard.

The words gave all three of them encouragement. Joyce scribbled in his diary that "after this poor Hayward took in another couple of holes in his belt to stay the gnawings of hunger and was more his old self."

Through the last hours of Friday, February 25, the vicious winds tore at the tattered tent. The three men lay in the skin bags, which were now little more than frosted shrouds; their bodies were ice-cold without food or fuel, and hope was dwindling along with the diminishing warmth of life. Feeble and famished, they no longer had even the luxury of shivering. The fight of internal vital organs to maintain a flow of blood tortured their bodies into violent heaving, a convulsive jerking to force a flow from the slowing blood circulation. Sleep was totally impossible; they were allowed only short periods of exhaustion between the onsets of spasmodic jumping. Their plight was at its most desperate; they were at their lowest ebb, moving inevitably towards surrender into cold death. They fell into apathetic silence; and then, an hour after midnight, the silence extended about them. For the first time in endless days of howling wind and chaotic snowstorms, there was quiet. The tent fabric was limp above their heads, and there was no swish of the frozen flakes on the fabric. There was a stillness that Ernest Joyce found "uncanny."

Suspicious that this was only a momentary lull, they crawled from the tent to stare southward. Without the gale flinging drift into their faces, they could see a break in the southeast, among the lowering snow clouds. It was a hope of the finer weather that Richards had wished for a few hours earlier. Yet he cautioned against being too ready to press onward to the north. They might already have overshot the depot, and so would never find the cairns leading to its location. On reflection, however, they saw they had no alternative to marching, other than to turn into the sleeping bags and stay in this camp until death overtook them or the gales ripped their shelter to shreds.

Breaking camp was a simple operation. There was no fuel to melt snow, no food to be eaten, only the tent to be knocked down and stowed on the sledge with their bags, and the dogs to be readied and harnessed. So great was their weakness, though, that every movement was an effort of will. The start to the north was faltering, with both men and dogs reeling and tottering. Richards recorded, "We could move no more than a few yards at a time, so short was our wind."

This painful process of feeling their way forward was made in a difficult light and no wind, with only the angle of the rope against the sledge to guide them. Then, after nearly an hour, the younger man lifted his eyes to look despairingly at the wasteland ahead and saw a blur, a smudge of dark color against the pervading whiteness. The flag above their depot appeared in the distorting diffraction of light to be only a few yards in front of them. In reality, it was three-quarters of a mile distant. The sighting brought joy and sudden release. The effect on the dogs, said Joyce, "was electric. They gave a joyful howl, the first we had had from them in six days." For the shambling Vic Hayward, however, the sighting relaxed the coil of tension in his mind and he fell against the sledge, yielding to the pain of his swollen legs, his resolution dissolved, his will to go on banished.

This collapse put a new strain on Richards and Joyce. The dogs wanted to race with their last energies to the depot, but Hayward, lolling helplessly, had to be helped onto the sledge and covered with a sleeping bag. Then they had to cross that great gulf of snow and ice that lay between them and the food and fuel that was life for them all.

It was the longest three-quarters of a mile they had ever known. The trek took them two hours to accomplish, and then another hour was spent erecting the tent. "My God," Richards entered in his diary, "but we were terribly weak." Ernest Joyce, describing their simple tasks, remarked how feeble they had become from starvation and toil, for in ordinary circumstances a tent could be spread in five minutes. Joyce reflected: "If this depot had not been sighted today we could never have pitched that tent again. I do not think there has ever been a weaker party to arrive at a depot—Arctic or Antarctic."

There was further cause for depression of their spirits. They had been so many long weeks fighting their way across the ice to the foot of the polar plateau and back that they longed for some contact, some link with other men, with the outside world. There had been an arrangement that if the ship came back to Cape Evans, a party would push down to the Bluff to leave word. Now they found a tin with a note tied to a bamboo pole, but it was from Cope saying how he, Gaze, and Jack had won through to here with their faulty primus. But there was no word other than that reassuring news. No soul had been here with tidings of *Aurora*, and that blank cut deep into their emotions. The ship was their symbol of a link with the world, a symbol that had not materialized. They could only take the most pessimistic view. Dick Richards was gloomy and apprehensive: "I think she must have gone down with all hands." Thus their relief at reaching food and shelter was overshadowed by fears for the future.

The first demand on their strength was now to be the rescue of the three men waiting in the tent back along the southern trail, but before they set out the faithful dogs had to be given food and rest. Hayward was ensconced in the tent, and the other two men began the laborious job of digging through the snow layers for the cases of stores that had been somewhat scattered by the blizzard. First they found dog pemmican and biscuits and fed the animals. The men expected that the dogs would fall on the food with wolfish appetite. Yet some caution inherent in their nature prevailed, and the animals ate slowly and carefully, setting an example to the starving men. The need for restraint became apparent after Richards uncovered the supply of oil and methylated spirits, which had been stored separately to prevent it permeating the food supplies. For the comfort it would bring, they lit the primus and reveled in its roar and blue glow. They melted snow and mixed a dried milk preparation, but when they drank this mixture they could not keep it down. They tried again, this time mixing the drink with oatmeal for substance, and this proved successful. They spent the next few hours repairing their footwear and the new tears in the tent fabric, then they had a weak dish of hoosh and biscuit. "We can feel strength returning to our bodies," Joyce noted, "then we must get our legs in trim for the walk back to our comrades." The food restored Hayward to effective duty. He and Richards worked on arranging the stores in the depot, and selecting and packing those they would haul back to the Captain's tent. The depot was "untidy," Richards found, and it took some effort to put it in order. This done, they determined that they would start back along the trail at 5 the next morning. They retired to their bags fed and warm.

At 8 in the morning the weather defeated their plans. The wind came in at hurricane force and they sat fearful in the shaking tent, waiting for a chance to march south again. "Impossible to see anything," Richards wrote. "We are sitting on our bags, waiting. Dogs and men could not face this, even if a course could be steered. This is awful—held up here knowing that three men are starving—and worse, deathly cold, 10 or 12 miles back."

The blizzard had now raged for more than 10 days, and still great gouts of snow blew over their shelter, smothering their equipment and dogs under toilsome layers, which would demand more strenuous work to remove before their journey of relief could begin. The comforting roar of the primus was little competition against the howl of the angry polar wind. Joyce made an entry in his diary: "Weather continues with fury. Expecting any minute to have the tent blown from over us. This is the longest blizzard I have ever experienced in this country. We have not had one real travelling day in eleven days. The amount of snow that has fallen is incredible, and it is essential that we track south.

The Skipper and his party have been without food now for at least five days. We must reach our companions soon." And this was Sunday— February 27, the day he had assured Ernie Wild they would be back with supplies—and here they sat in the shaking tent waiting for conditions to abate just enough so that they could sight the angle of the rope against the alignment of the sledge.

The delay was not without its benefit, however. They had time to eat another mug of hoosh and drink tea, enabling them to recuperate further after their ordeal of traveling while starved. They had time to inspect one another's condition as well, all three aware that their hope of life depended to different degrees on the others. Each man bore the unmistakable stamp of advancing scurvy. All three had swollen gums falling down over their teeth and turning jet black. Vic Hayward claimed to be feeling much better, but he found it painful to move and obviously could not walk properly. Richards examined the man's legs and saw he had great areas of blue-black bruising from ankle to hip, the same signs they had seen on Padre and Mackintosh. The young Australian spent an hour using his strong hands to massage doses of methylated spirits into the affected legs, and afterward Hayward claimed the treatment had improved his condition.

By noon they had finished the hours of slow preparation. Joyce decided to hitch on an empty sledge that had been left at the bluff depot, fully expecting that they would have two invalids to drag across the 100-odd miles to Safety Camp. The main sledge was no longer the featherweight it had been when they arrived; they now had more than 200 pounds weight of food and fuel aboard, and with their equipment and extra sledge were dragging a total weight of 500 pounds. Not suprisingly, they found they could not shift their load. "We were unaware till then of the full extent the march to Beardmore had weakened us and robbed us of condition," Dick Richards recorded. "The lay-up and the march to the Bluff searched out our weakness." And he recalled, "We had joked at times about how we had taken the Captain's party with us to the Beardmore to see the southernmost depot. We had been confident then in our strength. We wished we had more of it now."

They fought for 20 minutes and covered only 10 yards; then they upended the sledges and scraped and cleaned the runners to start again. The dogs were angry, ready to fight each other, snarling at the men, and unwilling to pull. They would not start south again. Richards declared, "The beggars know the way to Hut Point. Turn them to the north, Joyce! Then we can make a circle and track back." The tactic worked, and Joyce wrote later, "They are cute. They had seen enough of the glories of the southern trail and knew the northward was homeward bound. I turned them northward and at once I was on my back with my legs in the air!"

Although the dogs were fooled into breaking a homeward trail, the blizzard had laid a barrier of snow that restricted their progress to less than half a mile for each hour of slaving toil. The scurvied legs of the men sank into the soft surface, and each yard made the sledge load seem heavier. Joyce grew increasingly irritable and uncomfortable. "His finneskoes are more hole than foot," Richards noted, "and all day he had frozen snow coming in on his feet. It was impossible to mend them at night because the light has gone from the evening. This has been one of the hardest days I have put in."

All the long afternoon they butted southwards with the relentless blizzard flinging the sheets of snow at them. Then the sky began to darken, and they had no means of lighting. They were forced to camp at last in the late evening, while they could still see well enough to pitch the tent, tether and feed the four dogs, and cook their own meal. Hayward was "painfully stiff," and Richards spent the last of the daylight rubbing methylated spirits into his legs. They crawled into the iced sleeping bags to gain some rest during the dark hours, the gale slapping the tent against the bamboo poles.

They were up again at six on the morning of February 28, but their chores took them three hours to accomplish: Joyce sewing food bags over his footwear, Richards rubbing more spirits into Hayward's legs, then feeding dogs and men and digging out their equipment. Joyce ached to make a forced march to reach the stranded men, and so they struggled against the bad surface for the remaining hours until noon, then a torrent of snow clogged their faces, the wind rose again and they could not see to steer. Laboriously they put up the tent, weary and dispirited that they had not reached their goal, though they believed they were in the vicinity. Hoping against hope, they stood outside the tent and yelled into the south wind, but heard nothing in answer except the howl of the blizzard.

The enmity of the hostile ice shelf turned more menacing that night. Hour after hour they had been watching the snowstorm in the wind from the south, waiting and hoping for a break in which they could search for the other tent. Richards kept watch while Hayward and Joyce tried to sleep. To occupy his mind, Richards made one of the lengthier entries in his diary: "Heavy snow . . . Have shouted with no response. A last hope. We knew we could not go farther as we might overshoot their tent. . . . I know I cannot sleep with the thought of those men starving and cold, perhaps within a short distance of help. One keeps wondering how it will all end." And then he recaptured all the travail and disasters that had struck them since they went on from 83° South to lay the Mount Hope depot with food and fuel they now so badly needed. "And now here we are, waiting for this [word undecipherable] to cease. And this seems the end of Mackintosh's folly in going South when done himself and in the company of another done man . . . And now it is too cold on the fingers and I'll stop."

Concern deepened again when he massaged Hayward's legs and then examined his own. The youngest and strongest man left in the party, he had to write, "I'm sorry—I have the dreaded black appearance on the back of my legs, although up to the present it has given me no trouble." In his mind's eye he could see Spencer-Smith starting to falter and the way the condition had slowly defeated the Captain and crushed his will to persist. The young Australian wrote in his diary again, "Hayward is in the same condition, as I fear I will be shortly." And then, "It is distressing to reach here and be prevented by the thick weather from rendering them aid. We can only wait here and look out at 10-minute intervals. I fear what we will find on arriving . . ."

The dark thought was with him as he stared across the space of flying, whirling snow. Death was almost certain to have come to that tent by now. In retrospect Richards would say, "Spencer-Smith was already very weak when we left them there six days previously and they had very little food. I thought he was probably dead. It didn't take much imagination to think that he had slipped his cable."

The days had been without end in the lonely tent. The battering of the blizzard wind had been ceaseless for nearly 11 days, except for one brief let up when Wild was able to peer from the tunnel and discern the hazy shape of Minna Bluff, the point of rescue for which Joyce, Richards and Hayward had set off more than a week before. The stricken Padre had not moved in all that time, and all his needs had been attended by Ernie Wild. Defiantly, with great restraint, they had eked their scrap of food out across the days of the week while they were storm-bound.

It was Monday, February 28, and Mackintosh had recovered enough to get to his feet without help. He now calculated that the other party had been gone a full four days, to cross a distance he reckoned was about nine miles. With that thought, and in his illness, a sense of impending doom settled on his mind. He sat in his sleeping bag and—not too many miles from where Captain Scott, four years earlier, had done this same thing—took from his canvas holder a writing pad, the same lined pad on which he had written the agreement with Richards regarding the southern journey, and on which he had inscribed the formal instructions to Ernest Joyce to proceed south.

In pencil, Mackintosh wrote his letter of farewell to the world. "I leave this record in the event of anything happening to the party. Today we have finished the last of our food. A blizzard has been blowing for 11 days with the exception of one day when the wind fell light, when the horizon could be discerned as well as land round the Bluff. We were left here four days previously in order that Joyce, Hayward, and Richards could travel with dogs and a light sledge to Bluff Depot more easily, returning to us with food of which there is a plentiful supply at the Bluff."

When a week had elapsed on a round-trip journey of less than 20 miles, he still clung to the notion that each hour brought relief nearer, "We now expect succour to reach us any time from today, in which case we shall be saved from starvation and these lines will be unnecessary. Yet, I take precaution to leave this should I become too weak and the cold make it harder to write. Smith and myself are stricken with scurvy, the former being helpless and weak. I am able to stand, yet becoming more feeble daily. Wild has signs of scurvy, but is still able to move his hands and feet, and with a meal could travel, and this I am afraid cannot be the same with Smith and myself."

His hands were cold, his fingers stiffening, and the writing straggled as he continued: "We have not yet given up hope, for we trust our comrades. Time passes, in spite of empty stomachs, and we argue, sing and talk during the day and anyone coming along would imagine us to be a picnic party."

Ernie Wild was the unsung hero of this effort to maintain morale in the tent, leading them into songs, prompting discussion on what had happened in the war, avoiding the worrisome question of what had happened to the ship, and regaling them with tales of his boyhood in Yorkshire. He told them how his eldest brother, Frank, had run away to sea at the age of 16 and had been to Australia in the wooden sailing ship *Sobraon*, before joining the Royal Navy and winning a place on Antarctic expeditions, and how he had marched with Shackleton to within 97 miles of the South Pole. If anyone gave their perilous position the character of a picnic party, it was most certainly Ernie Wild. Mackintosh paid his own tribute to Wild's service as he continued his farewell letter, explaining how they'd reached the edge of disaster.

"Briefly, and I feel glad to say that it has not been due to any lack of organization. We have done the work we came down here to do, the laying of a depot at Mount Hope for Sir Ernest Shackleton. We made splendid progress travelling homeward, as much as 18 miles a day (geographical) and this with Smith on the sledge. We filled up with a fortnight's provisions at 80° South as our previous experience had warned us against this region Moore Bay. Instead of doing the trip in a week we have been 11 days getting to within nine miles of the big depot on 18 February, since which date we have been camped."

Now he had to record the painful fact of his own collapse. He wrote, "With the exception of Smith we were able to travel until the blizzard came upon us, when we were laid up six days. After that period when we made a fresh start, I had to admit defeat owing to my inability to stand the strain, our lay-up making me weaker—legs black and blue, gums black and swollen." And that was it—there was no more about his condition, and nothing on the loss of the ship, nor of the loss of the main dog teams in the previous season and its contribution to the danger they all now faced.

"The above roughly explains how we were left here," he continued. "Wild, who could have gone on, preferred to stay here and help us, good unselfish fellow that he is. It must be explained that with the exception of the first trip from the Bluff we have had no fresh food since 9 October. Hence the disease has taken a stronger hold on us than the other party who had the opportunity of reaching Hut Point.

"Yet I leave it on record that all have done their duty, nobly and well. The rest of our simple adventures can be explained by this note, also by other members of the party. This is all that I can say—and if it is God's will that we should have given up our lives then we do so in the British manner as our tradition holds us in honour bound to do. Goodbye, friends. I feel sure my dear wife and children will not be neglected. Signed Aeneas Mackintosh: Commander, I.T.A.E."

This tragic letter was not the last thing that Shackleton's southern commander would write. It was, however, his last message to survive.

Soon after striking camp on the morning of the last day of February in that leap year of 1916, the keen eyes of Dick Richards saw the blur in the white rolling drift to the south—less than half a mile distant from where they had spent the past anxious night. At once the dogs had an objective and started to yelp with excitement. In the tent, Ernie Wild heard their barking above the sound of the wind and clambered through the tunnel entrance to stand staring at the hazy figures of the men and dogs hauling the sledge towards him.

After living on starvation rations for a week, haggard from the strain of caring for two invalids, he at once reached for his sledge harness and tottered towards the three men to help pull the sledge across the remaining distance. Richards and Joyce were touched by this gesture. Richards noted in his brief diary, "Thank the fates all are alive. Wild is a great chap. What broke us up on meeting was the fact that when he heard the dogs he unemotionally reached for his harness to come and help us in. We had had three days' food by then but he had had little or nothing for six days. Some of us broke down and cried."

The noise brought Captain Mackintosh from the tent and Joyce recorded the reunion. "Poor Mack, he crawled from the tent very weak, could just stagger and started to thank us profusely for our journey. He told me they owed their lives to us. I told Wild to cook them some food . . . but not to eat too much in case of reaction."

Joyce had fully expected to find at least one death in the tent. Instead, he wrote, "The Padre, poor fellow, has had to stay in his wet sleeping-bag and is very weak." The urge was to leave the sick man undisturbed for as long as possible, but they could not risk delay; every hour was now crucial in the fight to reach Hut Point some 100 miles to the north. They had no choice but to start as soon as possible. With three sick men—two almost helpless and one totally incapable—they would have to push on and travel in all weathers. Although these men had been without a hot meal for nine days and had lived on scraps for a week, Joyce decided they would try to move at once. It took them an hour to dig the Captain's dome-shaped tent free from the wall of snow, and then they prepared the two sledges toggled together, each one to be a couch for a sick man.

Mackintosh again decided to try and walk, and with the aid of ski-poles he went hobbling ahead in a half-squatting stance. By the time he had covered about 50 yards and had fallen into the snow, they were lifting the figure of the long-suffering Padre onto the sledge. In pain from all movement, the brave man reminded Joyce that they had made a tryst to meet in London to take some cheer to the homeless men who slept on London's Embankment.

Richards and Joyce carefully strapped him into his sleeping bag on the sledge, so that the jolting would not dump him in the snow; then they lifted the tent floor cloth to put over him as protection against the blown drift. Beneath the cloth they saw a deep recess which the Padre's unmoving body had melted away during the 12 days he had lain there. It had the shape of a human form; and they knew that if they had missed finding the Bluff depot, and failed to return with food, that recess would have formed a coffin in the ice for the uncomplaining clergyman.

from Let Me Survive: A True Story
by Louise Longo with
Marie-Thérèse Cuny

Frenchwoman Louise Longo in 1994 sailed from the French port of Rochefort with her ex-husband Bernard and their five-year-old daughter Gaëlla. Louise and Bernard hoped a three-week cruise would help them reconcile. Six days later a violent storm forced the family into their lifeboat 40 miles off the Spanish coast. Bernard died soon after.

We have reached the depths of horror. Gaëlla is curled up against me and we are trying to keep as far away as possible from the body. I am afraid the raft will tilt and that he will fall upon us. The water is icy, the air is icy. My mind has great difficulty in accepting what has happened to us. Up until now things were relatively easy to explain: the storm, hunger, thirst, drifting, anxiety—but not death. I have never seen a dead person before. I understand nothing.

I inflate the rings, making superhuman efforts not to fall onto him. At times I place my hand on him, to touch him, perhaps to try and realize, as if I were waiting for him to wake up. This deep final sleep, his silence, horrify me.

We almost never stopped talking. We had to talk, to stifle fear, to keep our brains working. All those sentences we said, all the memories, reproaches, comments, have left with him. I would like to remember them, word for word, talk again about life, find what went wrong. I dropped a stitch in the knitting.

I no longer count the days—the 11th, or the 12th—I no longer cross them off on the gauze strip calendar. This must be what is called an emotional shock. If someone were to ask me what I felt, I would be incapable of describing it in any other way than by saying: "I just didn't understand."

It was on the 13th that I got such a fright. His feet were blue, his body soft to the touch. Suddenly I thought he was going to empty himself and that it would be awful. The only thing I knew about death was that a body empties itself afterwards.

I wanted to close his eyes, and I didn't know how. I thought it would be enough to place my fingers on his eyelids for them to close on their own, like in the movies. My symbolic gesture did nothing. I was confused. I had to force them shut. His eyelids closed, then opened again. As if he were looking at me, leering. He couldn't stay there any longer, I could wait no longer. Suddenly, a violent urge to clean the space of our lives took hold of my brain. An obsession. To live without that body.

I had to get him into the water, and explain to my daughter why. I did so, gently.

"Gaëlla, the freighter is not coming, there's no one to help us, and when a sailor dies you have to put him into the water, that's the way it is. It's safer. So I'm going to put Daddy in the water. Do you understand? Three days and two nights. I've kept him as long as possible, but now we must."

"If you have to, then do it, Mommy."

"If you have another solution, another idea, then tell me, Gaëlla."

As if my daughter could help me, encourage me. As if she were an adult. I need her approval to get on with this job. I coax myself in silence. You're going to take him and tip him over the edge.

It took me all afternoon to get it done. You don't just take a body as if it were a bag and tip it over the edge, simple as that, oh no. First of all you recoil, you're terrified to actually touch the body. I was going crazy. Because there were clothes it was still possible, just a rapid gesture. But to grasp him round the torso—that I couldn't do.

To take him by the ankles was beyond my mental capacities. His ankles were bare and his skin frightened me. So I tried to take him by the calves so that the cloth would protect me from the terrifying contact.

"Gaëlla, sweetheart, you must give Mommy some strength, some courage."

"I love you, Mommy, very very much."

"You might have to help me push."

"Oh no, Mommy, I can't . . . I can't help you."

Move my legs, sit down, breathe out, breathe in, look outside, and begin again. He is on one side, I'm on the other. I force myself, unthinking, to grasp his legs, pull a bit, and take a breath. Keep my balance, maintain stability with each movement. I have no more strength. My arms refuse to make the effort. The raft moves around so much: how can I have a hold? I'm struggling against so many things at the same time, inertia, fear, the rolling of the raft.

I stop, realizing that his weight is balancing the raft. The moment I tip him off the edge, if I manage to, there's a risk we'll capsize. And yet I absolutely must do it. Absolutely.

I begin tugging on his legs again, in vain. I talk to my daughter to give myself some courage.

"How can I do it, Gaëlla? What do you think? How?"

"Well. Try another way. If you can't do it with his feet, try some other way."

Poor baby. What sort of perverse destiny has decided to inflict this nightmarish situation on my little girl. It's her father who lies there, cumbersome, terrifying, the father who loved her and whom she loved. She would dance for him, she would laugh, throw herself into his arms, and now here I am asking her what I should do to get rid of him. My brain is made of concrete, I'm going mad. I must act; action is the only thing that will save me from this madness hanging over me.

I try once again to raise his torso, and that doesn't work either. He is now in a sitting position, and it is even more terrifying.

"Gaëlla, shout with me, shout!"

She calls weakly, "Go on, Mommy," and I shout so that she will shout.

"Louder! Help Mommy! Shout louder! We have to do it today."

The light is fading; I refuse to spend another night with him on board. I refuse. Gaëlla shouts, "Go on, Mommy, go on! I love you, you can do it!"

"Think about Daddy, Gaëlla. Think about him, it will be good for him."

What madness, this disjointed dialogue, this intense panic which just won't give me the necessary rage. I have managed to swing him round and pass his feet through the opening of the raft. It's already better but I'm still no further ahead. I have to tip him off the edge. One way or another. I'm back to square one, really.

I take a long time to catch my breath, maybe half an hour. I talk to him, I ask him to help me; he's the dead one, can't he do something, give me an idea. And suddenly, it comes. The positive rage which surges at last, which makes me take a jacket and pass it under Bernard's waist, knot it by the sleeves, so that I manage to lift him at last. A victory.

Gaëlla is still shouting to encourage me. I have found the maneuver; like this I won't have to touch his body, and the jacket will give me a hold. Until the moment when I realize I will still have to use my hands. If I don't, there's a risk I too might fall in the water, and the vision of Gaëlla all alone on the raft acts as a stimulus. I see myself swimming, her screaming, the raft drifting away, the separation, the loss.

"Help me, Bernard, for heaven's sake!"

I am angry with the entire world. With God, with the land, with the sky, I curse the universe, until at last the body falls into the water and I recoil, terrified and breathless, my arms outstretched to keep my balance. I watch as the body turns over onto its back, as if he had decided to be in that position forever with his arms crossed over his stomach.

"Gaëlla, do you want to watch Daddy going away?"

"No."

He is wearing his yellow foulies; someone might see him. A freighter might locate him, go round in circles, and come to get us.

She didn't want to keep anything of his, not even the ring I gave him. Not even a piece of clothing.

We were vagabonds together, the two of us. The sea brought us together, and now it has separated us.

I am trembling with exhaustion. With cold. With relief. Gaëlla is in her corner. I have to make her walk, move around to keep the blood circulating. I have to bail, inflate, wring. I have work on board this fucking orange raft. My bum hurts, I have rashes everywhere, my stomach is a hellhole of cramps. Gaëlla, who was constantly asking for food, has become a bit calmer since Bernard left. The leitmotif seems to occur less often. A weaker refrain.

"I want to eat. I want a freighter."

If only I could fish. A hideous fish showed up and it has been obstinately following us for a while; we would gladly devour it raw. If I could make a hook. There is the hoop which hangs from a lanyard to be used to right the raft if it capsizes; but that's the problem, what if I make a fish hook with it and then we capsize? What about the bucket, then? Careful, Louise, what if you fall. If only . . . Always *if*, I have no other language than if.

That fish is irritating me. It has been there since I put Bernard in the water. It is swallowing the crumbs of tobacco I mopped up with the water. A ridiculous fish; it is ugly, gray, with globular eyes.

"Gaëlla, say hello to the fish."

"What are we going to do now, Mommy?"

"I'm going to teach you things by heart."

"What for?"

"So that you can learn them . . . go on, answer, where does Grandma live?"

"Near the school."

"Where is the school?"

"Well, next to Grandma's house."

I'll have to do better; her childish logic has caught me unawares. I'll start with the town, the street, the number of the house. At times it annoys her but I stick with it.

The rubber bottom of the raft ripples; I feel a presence.

"What is it, Mommy?"

"Ssh . . ."

It's a shark, or sharks. It's rubbing its back, just beneath us. It could flip us over with one wiggle of its back.

"What is it?"

I force her to be quiet. Without using the word "shark," which might frighten her. All my senses on the alert, I observe the threatening movement, silently praying. Don't let us be eaten by sharks, my God, I beg of you . . . Silent, we sit huddled together. God is listening to me: there is a nervous, aggressive rippling beneath my legs, one last thrust, then nothing. Gone. But for a long time I lie listening with my entire body, Gaëlla stretched out on top of me.

Now I must think of the rain, too strong, and the roof of the raft which is getting softer, and the bottom which is getting even more soaked. Great quantities of seawater are coming in through the flap. The improvised sea anchor is no longer there, chewed off by the shark. The awful fish is gone, too. It must have followed us for three, four or five days. It must be . . . October 15.

It was the 15th, but from that day on I lost all notion of time. An hour is as long as a day. I made a doll out of a gauze strip, drew her eyes and mouth. We play tea party to trick our hunger. We have to talk about food to forget it. Talk about it until we're nauseous.

My father had a vegetable garden. He grew peas, carrots, lettuce, tomatoes, leeks. He also raised hens and ducks, and a pig. His motto was, "Eat healthy food." He was a peasant in Sicily before he became a worker in France, and he really only knew the land, the security it gave. What he had grown and raised could be found in a big cupboard filled with supplies; in case of emergency, if you wanted to eat, all you had to do was open that cupboard door. We never wanted for anything. He would buy an entire calf or a sheep and then cut it up to put it in the freezer. He made sausages, blood pudding. My mother made pasta with every imaginable sauce.

I tell Gaëlla about my childhood meals. We make up menus. Sausages, hot chocolate, steak and French fries, oranges, raviolis in tomato sauce.

"Draw a pork chop for me."

We can last a long time drinking rain water, that I know. My resistance is good, too, perhaps better than average. My peasant origins, no doubt. The hard land of my Sicilian ancestors.

"Mommy, where does the moon go? Why are we small? Why do we grow up? Why are there men and women? Mommy, why do we have babies in our tummies and not our backs?"

She will be married in a white dress, to have a baby. I will find a daddy, to make a little sister, that way she'll have someone to play dolls with. The best would be a daddy who is a grocer or a baker, who would give her cakes and chocolate eggs with toys inside.

"You know, you mustn't choose someone just for what you want. The main thing is to love him."

"Why do we love people, Mommy? Why are there some we don't love?"

We talk continuously about the whys. The horizon is still empty. This morning I saw a bird, very high in the sky. Maybe the land is near. The land, full of grocery stores and restaurants and supermarkets and bakeries. Talking about food is like negotiating with one's hunger. Tricking it. You know you're hungry, the cramp is there, but you manage to live with it. Just knowing there are human beings who have lasted fifteen days or three weeks in atrocious conditions: if they lasted, so can we. You drink something to ease the spasms. You can feel your stomach shrinking. We have drunk so much water that my stomach is bloated. Gaëlla had diarrhea, and that frightened me, but it's stopped now.

"Mommy, my wee-wee is really clear."

Another little victory. The rainwater has saved us, for the moment. In the end we drank very little seawater. I did a lot of house cleaning one day when it was pouring. There were still those damned brownish crumbs of tobacco everywhere. I am careful to keep the bottle constantly filled, just in case the bucket tips over.

Bernard is sleeping somewhere, on the water. I talk to the sea. I tell it that it has hurt me so much that I hate it. I think about my mother.

Does she know we have disappeared? If they found the boat afloat, she knows. She could not understand how I could leave with Bernard.

"How can you go off with a man you've divorced?"

She didn't like him. He had drawn me into an adventurous and unstable lifestyle. He had hurt me. She couldn't understand that we remained friends all the same. Bernard was, once and for all, her only daughter's bad genie. When it's time for me to face her, he will stand guilty for having dragged Gaëlla and me into this terrible adventure. I will also stand guilty for having followed him. I am angry with myself. I am angry with him. But he is dead.

What is the point of being angry with someone who is dead? In the end I refuse both my guilt and his. The guilt lies with fate, or God, the sea, the land which abandoned us, the ships which have not passed our way.

"Mommy, do you think God has punished me because I didn't always finish my plate? I'll always finish it from now on."

She is fussy about food. Cleaning her plate—that has often been our little daily battle.

"Why is there no ship?"

She doesn't scream, doesn't cry; just a plaintive little voice, wanting something when she can't understand what's happening to her. Whose fault, my God, how can it be my fault? Impossible. I left with her father, precisely for her sake, so that they could be together and share their love.

"We'll get out of this. We have to be patient, that's all. When you believe in something hard enough, it happens."

The ship that will come will have a beautiful swimming pool. We sing. Gaëlla adores Patrick Bruel. *Casser la voix.* She used to sing it with her father, who would clown around, imitating the singer hanging from his microphone, At times I wondered who was the more childish of the two. He used to take her for piggyback rides and they would laugh themselves silly.

The last picture of tenderness remains carved in my memory. He was in pain and couldn't move, so she crawled over to him to give him a kiss and said, "I love you, my Daddy."

"Mommy, you're the most beautiful mommy."

She is caressing my face; she needs to be on top of me, to touch me all the time, because my protection, my breast, are vital. Sometimes I can't even sleep.

On land she never used to leave me either. Often she wanted to sleep with me; I should have refused but I always gave in. Bernard often said, "You overdo it, she's forever in your skirts, she clings too much. You have to make her more independent."

Overdo it? What is overdoing it? The simple fact of looking at her, letting my gaze settle on her, gives me the feeling I am protecting her and giving her everything. I look at her in the way my mother looked at me, she looks at me as I looked at my mother, the umbilical cord has never been cut among the three of us, it is a silent thing, indestructible, and it needs no words in order to exist. To take a hand, to kiss, touch, caress—we all need physical contact, warmth, gazes. It's an animal thing.

"How many brothers does Mommy have?" I ask.

She lists them: Michel, Paul, Mario and Angelo. Grandma lives in a country called France, in a little village which is called . . . the postal code is . . . the phone number is . . . One day Grandma gave me a little goat.

"Could I have one? When we get back on land we'll live with animals. We'll go to Grandma's; she knows how to do everything, Grandma does, lots of cooking too."

"Get up, Gaëlla, I have to see if there is a ship."

"No, Mommy, I don't want to . . . I want to stay like this, it's nice."

The little hole is still there between the first and the second ring; there is a leak. What if the rain submerges the raft, what if the roof is no longer waterproof . . . Could I make fishing lines with the zippers from our jackets?

My feet are so swollen I can't get them into my boots. I have to use Bernard's. It's all that's left of him.

"Let's cook some rice. We need a saucepan, some water, and salt . . . And if we made some pancakes?"

"Be careful, Gaëlla, your pancake has flipped up to the ceiling!"

Today we're going into a supermarket to steal everything we feel like eating. We can't go during the day, of course, so we'll go at night. We'll hide in the clothing department until everyone's gone, and then, where shall we begin?

"First yogurts and cream cheese, then sausages."

"Wait, don't go so fast, begin at the beginning. You open the yogurt."

She opens it, eats, licks the spoon, then takes a swig of fruit juice.

Food, snacks, anything edible, an obsession.

She is so good at pretending to eat; I admire her. On land she would stamp her foot, she was so fussy; here she puts up with the situation better than an adult would.

"Do you want some cake?"

"Yeah!"

"Don't say yeah, Gaëlla, say yes . . ."

Nothing is happening. Yesterday we saw a rainbow and Gaëlla made a wish. So did I. I said, "I wish this would end."

And she said, "I wish I could have a sausage."

She is sleeping in her foul weather jacket, with the hood; I put a plastic bag on my head. My perspiration and breathing keep up a sort of warmth inside the bag.

And you, up there, Bernard: you're not doing much to help us. What the hell are you doing? You don't answer. I'm going to ask my grandmother. She had the gift of healing, her name was Louise, like me.

"Listen, Grandmother, there are only two possibilities left. Either a freighter goes by and doesn't see us, and it's all over for us, forget it, or it goes by fifteen feet away and it has to see us. So go on, do something."

I have spoken to everyone I know, even people I don't know. Jeannie Longo, for example, who shares my last name; an extraordinary sportswoman. I said to her, "We'll show them that Longos are tough women. Longos are strong . . ."

A slogan for my daughter, Longos are strong . . .

I have stopped marking the passage of days on the rag doll's apron.

Night and day have become drowned in the same fetid water, the same rotting dampness. I have taught Gaëlla how to fill the bottle, how to inflate the three valves, how to bail. She hardly wants to move anymore. I don't actually realize how exhausted she is. I mustn't.

Survive, hang on, keep one's brain working, stay free of delirium. The aim is to hang on. Longos are strong . . .

We have been gliding through these phantom days, all identical, on a flat ocean. But the swell has risen. A long swell. Outside, the sky is beautiful. In the northwest, fine white filaments of cloud announce the coming of wind.

I blow up the rings as tight as they'll go, emptying my lungs. One of the valves is identical to the nozzle of the pump. A curse on whoever thought up anything so stupid. If he were here, the idiot . . .

The raft is sturdy, all the same, even though it is getting worn. Night is coming, I can feel the weather changing. Strong wind somewhere. I pray it doesn't come our way.

"Are you okay, Mommy?"

"Yeah, I'm okay."

"Don't say yeah, Mommy, say yes."

We have to sleep. My head in the plastic bag, Gaëlla bundled up in her foulie, with the hood pulled down. We have to sleep, to hang on. To dream.

I dreamt of a farm with a large orchard and lots of animals. I saw myself in the sun, like some organic farmer, with goats, cheese, bouquets of flowers, baskets of fruit and vegetables. Gaëlla was running in the grass. There were trees, land. It was solid, beneath our feet. I was standing. That's what land is, it doesn't move, and you can stand on it.

I have slept. Gaëlla curled up beside me. The same leaden sleep.

It was the last night. My daughter's last night. I thought I had reached the limits of horror, that I had been subjected to inconceivable punishment, but we were alive, and I had lost neither hope nor strength, nor my trust in "something." I had recited the Lord's Prayer as often as I had insulted the heavens. I had dreamt up all the possible solutions, used my intelligence to the limits of its strength. I had managed not to panic. Bernard was dead. I had forgotten him out of vital necessity. I had tidied things up in my mind and on the raft. But the sea had not finished tidying things up with me.

The freighter came upon us in the morning, brutally, while we were still fast asleep.

A monster.

At first I don't understand what's happening to us; the raft has spun round, three hundred and sixty degrees, and there before me, twelve or fifteen feet away, I see a brick-colored hull. A wall of metal with enormous propellers. I wave my arms, shouting like a madwoman: "We've won! Gaëlla, we've won! Look!"

It turns around, the hull passes us, closer, to get into a position to pick us up. I think immediately of the rope ladder we will have to climb. I pull off my boots, to be more agile.

Gaëlla seems fine. She has even made a joke, which surprises me:

"Is that the ship? I wanted an ocean liner!"

The sea is fairly choppy, but the sky is blue and the visibility is excellent. The ship is called the *Petrovski*.

I wonder what language I'll be able to speak. Spanish, French, or English? The ship is moving on, under its own momentum, and I know it will take some time before it can swing round. I'm not at all worried. It's finished, finished; the nightmare is finished.

Now it is coming back, slowly steaming ahead. I am on its port side and I can hear the muted rumbling of the engines. I had thought it was a huge ship, surprised by the closeness of the hull, but I can see it is actually fairly small.

I help Gaëlla remove her boots, we put on our lifejackets, and I explain to her that we are surely going to have to climb up separately.

"They're going to drop a rope ladder, we'll help you, don't be scared."

It seems so long. The freighter goes by the raft again, a bit further away so that its wake does not cause us to rock over. Leaning out the opening I can see a sailor on the bridge throwing a lifebelt overboard. Just a ring buoy, without a rope to the ship: what's the point? It's idiotic. I grumble, "Stupid idiot."

But I catch the buoy anyway, even if it's useless. The swell is rising, the *Petrovski* has cut its engines and is coming nearer. I cannot make out what flag it's flying. So I shout, confusedly, "Throw a line! A rope! *Corde! Ligna!*"

I can't stop moving. Bernard used to say, "If you see a freighter, show them that you're alive." I wave my arms, I shout, I put my head back in to talk to my daughter, I stick it out again like a jack in the box, I wait hopefully for a rope, for the rope ladder, I'm in a hurry to have Gaëlla grasp onto something, to tear her from this raft; I can already picture her up on the deck, and see myself climbing behind her.

I don't understand what they're doing. A sailor in a wet suit is in the process of sliding down the rope, as fast as he can, to splash in the water before my very nose. I don't notice that he has let go of the rope. As I help him to climb onto the liferaft I pray to heaven that the sea won't throw us against the steel hull. He climbs aboard with some difficulty and begins speaking English with a terrible accent. He places his hand on my head as if to reassure me.

"I've won!"

He doesn't seem to understand.

"I've won, the birthday, on October 29 . . . it's the 22nd today, I've won."

The poor fellow doesn't understand that I've been obsessed by the idea of Gaëlla's birthday. I had promised myself that we would spend it at my mother's house. By October 29 it would be all over. So I've won, that's obvious, but how can he know any of that? He looks at me with big round eyes, patting me on the head.

"It is the 20th of October . . ."

"We'll go to Grandma's, I've won!"

October 20? There are two days missing in my head. I look at our rescuer, impatiently, annoyed. I explain in broken English that I have lost my husband, that we are French; I tell him the name of the sailboat. And he repeats that everything will be fine and that I'll be able to rest.

He is relatively young, thirty or forty, thin, strong and fairly tall. He is so kind to Gaëlla; he was surprised to find her there. They must have thought I was alone. He says he is Russian; we have some difficulty understanding each other.

"Gaëlla, put your boots on, put your boots on, I don't want you to scrape your feet when you climb up."

I have to put them on her myself, and bail, but she pulls them off again.

"Gaëlla, help Mommy."

She refuses. And yet she is happy, at that moment. She is smiling.

The raft, suddenly heavy with the weight of the sailor, is taking on water again; he is bailing, shouting words I don't understand in the direction of the hull. There is indeed a ladder against the hull, but it is fixed and only comes halfway down, impossible to reach. The swell has caused us to spin off to one side and we are paddling to try to come closer. They toss him a line, he manages to catch it, but it's a struggle to try and attach us; he doesn't manage and has to let go. Between the movement of the freighter and the swell, it's impossible. I begin to see it's not going to be as easy as I had thought. When this man dropped so easily from his rope I thought it would be just as simple for us. Not at all the case. He repeats: "We'll manage." But every maneuver the ship makes is incredibly slow, and as soon as it gets closer to us it has to stop its propellers. Finally I grab hold of a line with a big knot at the end. I am so happy to have succeeded that it takes me a few minutes to realize that if I don't let go it's going to pull my arm off. The freighter tries to reposition itself, time is wasting, it takes forever, forever, and the sea is getting rougher, it's dangerous. I'm getting annoyed.

More than once I manage to catch the rope, only to let go again. The sea is too rough, there is no way I can do this maneuver. I expected a rope with a harness, for the fellow to tie Gaëlla and hoist her up.

They should jettison some fuel onto the water to calm the sea. Why hasn't the captain thought of this? I shout at him to do that, but no one up on deck understands me. Then I think of a crane. A freighter has to have a crane, to load its cargo. I tell my rescuer:

"The crane . . . use the crane . . ."

"No, it's okay . . . no problem . . ."

At one point I yell at him in French: "Take the paddle, dammit!"

Yet the poor guy is trying. When he got here, I felt that at last I would be taken care of, there was someone alive, a strong man, he was going to fix everything. But this bitch of a sea just won't let us, it just won't let us.

"Bitch, can't you stop for just a moment? Just a tiny bit, a little tiny bit . . ."

Now I am frightened. These people don't really seem to know what to do. There must be a certain technique to rescue operations. Since they can't drop a whaleboat, they should think of how to hoist us with their crane. I can't stop shouting at the crew with my fist raised.

I no longer understand what they're playing at. Figures, bundled up, stare at us from the deck without being able to do a single thing. It's terrible, we can see life so close and yet we still can't reach it. At one point the raft drifts dangerously close to the hull, I could reach out and touch it; the freighter wavers and almost crushes us, I just have time to put my hands on Gaëlla's head to get her to duck down quickly.

The raft rubbed against the steel hull, covered with barnacles and studded with huge bolts. I hope the raft has not been torn. Not now! It has to hold on a bit longer. The opening gives onto the waves running along the side of the hull. Suddenly I cry, "Watch out!"

It's useless, and too late. The raft flips over. Usually it rights itself fairly easily, but for the first time it remains tipped over. Here we are, sitting on the roof, our feet in the water. I am holding onto Gaëlla, she is clinging to me, her little legs seeking out a place to lodge against mine. It's not easy because my feet are pressing against the hoop which is supposed to support the roof like a tent. The water is up to my chest and I have to keep my balance like a floater.

The sailor manages to get out of the upturned bubble. The water is not all that cold; I thought it would be worse.

We cling onto the straps. There is very little space left to breathe, between the surface of the water and the canvas. You have to put your head to one side to get air. Gaëlla says nothing. I'm the one who's shouting.

I can hear some scraping noises above us. I hope the sailor is going to right the raft, and quickly; no, instead of that he climbs on top of it! We try to talk through the canvas. I want him to get off there, he has a wetsuit on, he can hang on and swim around, but we can't.

I want him to help me right the raft, but he refuses, and just goes on saying that everything will be fine, that I mustn't worry!

I don't know what's going on outside now. I just have to trust him. But Gaëlla is having a hard time keeping her balance and she won't be able to hold on like that for long. I can also see that we lost everything when we capsized; there is nothing left to bail with if the fellow does manage to get us upright again.

Time goes by. The dialogue continues, broken, surrealist. In English or in Spanish; I use all the words that come to mind. The suddenly a silence. He doesn't answer. I ask:

"Are you there? Is someone there?"

The horror of it—he's not there anymore, the bottom of the raft above my head is soft. He let go. He left.

"Gaëlla, listen to Mommy, we're going to do like at Eurodisney, do you remember? Mommy's going to turn the raft over . . . Hold on tight . . ."

She doesn't answer, but I manage the maneuver without any problem. My foul weather jacket is gone, my boots, the bottle, nothing left but the scarf around my neck, my jacket, nothing left to bail with, and we're taking on water.

I am furious, on the verge of hysteria, shouting at the freighter. There is no way I will let this one get away, I'll go to the limits of my strength but I won't let go! It pulls away, returns, pulls away again, I still can't figure out what it is doing. I remember the story of that Greek freighter where they tossed the stowaway immigrants into the sea. Who is on board this one? Rescuers or assassins?

They must have realized they would not be able to pick us up and they would rather slip off and leave us there—could that be it? They must be thinking: "They'll just die, and no one will ever know . . ."

I shout at God, I shout at Bernard. I call him an idiot.

"You've got it easy up there. You don't risk a thing now. Can't you help us a bit?"

Gaëlla is still silent. She has no strength left; the time in the water, clinging to the straps, balancing on my legs, was really too much for her. Her face is quite pale, and her enormous eyes are a dreadful reproach. I talk and talk, reassuring her, trying to paddle, to follow the freighter, getting nowhere. I raise the flap to make it into a sail; I'm going mad, insane. How could it have failed—we were so close! Impossible!

The raft is once again by the hull, I can see the men on deck, I don't know what they're doing, but they have been busy, without paying any attention to me, so it seems. I no longer exist, they don't give a damn! I shout my lungs out:

"*Yo tengo una niña!* I got a baby! *J'ai un enfant! Un enfant!* Baby!"

The enormous shape in front of me, the rising sea, tossing me close to the propeller. Will it ever end? I insult the sea, tell it to calm down, but it doesn't care. I insult the freighter, and it doesn't care either; it is leaving, clearing out, the bastard!

"If you let me down, if you just leave like that, without doing a thing, you'll remember me! I swear it!"

And now comes the most awful moment of my life. I don't know what's going on, on board the freighter; nobody has told me a thing. They've just abandoned me, without a word, or a hope, and, as I turn back to my daughter I notice for the first time since our struggle together on the raft began that there is something wrong.

I've lost my foulies, I'm very cold, I must be trembling, but the only thing which makes me sick with anger is that I have nothing left to shelter her with. She can't lie down on the bottom any more, there's too much water, she is standing up, a tiny, stiff body, hanging to the straps, with her back to me.

Her hands are gripping so tightly to keep from falling that I have difficulty freeing them. I want to hold her close to me.

"Turn around, sweetheart . . . Come to Mommy . . ."

My daughter is stiff as a board. Her eyes are wide open, staring, her long lashes sticking to her cheeks. It's as if she has frozen herself into this position by a superhuman effort of will.

As I turn her face toward me I see drool on her lips. I draw her to me, she doesn't react. I call her, my head in her soaking, salty hair.

"Gaëlla . . . it's Mommy . . . sweetheart . . . I'm going to sit you down, Mommy has to see where the freighter has gone."

The time to look through the flap to see that goddam ship sailing away toward the horizon, disappearing in the swell; the time of nothingness. A few seconds. My little girl has slumped into the water, stretched out on the bottom of the raft, she is floating, her eyes staring ahead; she isn't fighting anymore. It's over. Like Bernard. All at once, before I had time to see death arrive.

Maybe I am screaming, but maybe I'm not. The shock is too sudden, the evidence too violent. It seems I am thinking about her father, that I am angry with him for taking her from me. She is leaving with him. I see myself pick her up, growing desperate, losing it. Why now, just like that, all of a sudden?

I don't know what to do. I try mouth to mouth, but I don't manage to bring her back. I know, anyway, that she is no longer alive. I know it. And I cannot stand this face in the water, these eyes full of water. It's beyond anything I can accept. Later I was told that the freighter found us at 8:30 a.m.; I don't know what time it left us, it felt like the afternoon to me, and in fact it was about one o'clock. We must have tried for five or six hours. But I didn't realize. It tried, I fought so hard, so long, the hours no longer make any sense. All I know is that the sea is empty, we've been abandoned, and Gaëlla is gone. It's the end of this horrid, insane story. The end.

from The Place Where the World Ends
by Richard Cunningham

Forty-five Uruguayan rugby players chartered an airplane in 1972 to take them to a match in Chile. The plane crashed in the Andes. The subsequent events were made famous by Piers Paul Read's 1974 book Alive! *Richard Cunningham (born 1939) invented a diary based on the survivors' accounts, and added his own narrative of events. Twenty days after the crash, 19 people remained alive—and some of them had begun to eat the bodies of the dead.*

November 1

We have started rationing; according to Canessa, a body should last four to five days, depending on its size. Most of us still have difficulty with raw meat. Everyone, however, can eat the dried fat and intestines, which do not have an unpleasant taste.

Both Arturo Nogueira and Rafael Etchevarren have developed gangrene. Arturo's condition is worse because he eats so little. Canessa has begun treating their wounds in a bizarre manner; he hung two amputated and skinned legs in the forward cargo area over a basin to catch the oil that drips as they thaw. He then uses the oil to coat their wounds. He recommended that we rub it on our lips and skin to prevent them from cracking open. Although it is difficult to explain, for some of us that seemed worse than eating the dead.

There is more room to sleep now, and we all have warm coats, heavy shoes, and sufficient blankets. We are still planning an expedition. Roberto Canessa will go, along with Fernando Parrado and Antonio Vizintin.

The majority of us still do not sleep at night, but we are becoming accustomed to the cold. Gustavo Zerbino's vision is almost back to normal. He has been in low spirits since Marcelo Pérez, his best friend, died in the avalanche.

Carlos Miguel led us in telling the rosary tonight.

November 5th
Sunday. Warm. For the first time in four days we could go outside to sleep in the sun. Carlos Miguel conducted religious services this morning.

We have lost so much weight that everyone is called *"flaco"* (skinny). Gustavo Zerbino claims that with our beards, our long hair, our dirty faces, and shabby clothing we look like hippies.

The oil Roberto collects from the limbs hanging in the cargo area does not seem to be helping Nogueira or Etchevarren. But it is good medicine for our chapped skin.

Javier Methol is still depressed about his wife's death. Ramón Sabella, our official "water boy," has grown very attached to Methol, whom he calls "Torito" (little bull) because of his size.

This afternoon Canessa cooked some brains and kidneys. Then he chopped them up and put the pieces into a makeshift aluminum bowl. He set the bowl over the flames and poured in water to make a soup. He burned part of our only book, *The Woman Pilot*, and a number of passports along with the fuel. The soup was warm and tasted faintly of urine, but no one complained.

November 9th

Thursday. Calm this morning, after three days of high winds and snow. We are beginning to wonder if spring will ever come.

On bad days we talk, generally about our families, what they must be going through. Sometimes we play cards. We have an incomplete Argentinian deck, three cards missing, but we can play a game called *Truco*, and poker. We have collected about four thousand dollars from the dead, which is distributed evenly among the players before each game. The stakes are high. Occasionally, we play baccarat. We speculate about what we are going to do when we get out of here. Pedro Algorta made us laugh today by saying the first thing he's going to do is go horseback riding. Someone else said the first animal he intends to ride is a girl. Both of you will have to watch out for saddle burns, Gustavo Zerbino suggested.

We spent the day outside in the sun. Parrado, Canessa, and Vizintin exercised, playing catch with our rugby ball, which will soon be deflated so that they can use the bladder to carry water on their journey.

They will also need food—Canessa figures about fifteen pounds per man. Today Gustavo chopped up a pile of intestines and spread the pieces on top of the plane to dry. He also dressed out several large strips of fat and muscle, and removed the pectoral muscles in long slices. Most of this meat is for the journey.

While Zerbino was working, Alfredo Delgado went to relieve himself in the deep trench we dug off to the right of the nose of the aircraft. On the way back, he almost walked into Zerbino because of the glare. Zerbino was kneeling over a headless, open trunk. He had smashed the sternum bone in order to remove the pectoral muscles. He did not look up at Delgado, who walked quickly away.

Late in the afternoon we heard an avalanche crash over to the east. We spent a bad night, sitting up, listening.

November 14th
Tuesday. The weather has been freakish, fluctuating hourly until today, which was so warm that some of us took off our shirts to sunbathe. We spent the past few bad days indoors, preparing for tomorrow's expedition. To keep from having to climb, Canessa and the others have decided to follow the valley east around the mountain we crashed against, on the theory that it will wind back west toward Chile. Fernando Parrado has convinced us that we are in the foothills of the Andes. All three will have back packs, a traveling bag with two safety belts slung through the grip—Canessa's idea.

Arturo Nogueira was feverish this evening. He did not feel like eating, and Roberto had to force him.

The weather was still clear when we went to bed. Gustavo Zerbino said it looks like Algorta's cabdriver knew what he was talking about.

November 15th
Wednesday. A blizzard began just before dawn. Parrado was in an angry, cursing mood all afternoon. We'll leave the first good day, and to hell with the weather, he told Canessa.

November 18th
Saturday. Cold but clear today. Canessa, Parrado, and Vizintin set out at six o'clock this morning. They prayed with Carlos Miguel before leaving and then said goodbye to everyone. Canessa told Nogueira and Etchevarren that he would bring help soon. They

made good time on the hard crust, and were out of sight in less than two hours.

Arturo Nogueira is running a high fever. He has a deep, racking cough and is very weak. Gustavo believes it is pneumonia. The gangrene in Rafael Etchevarren's legs is spreading into his thighs. Gustavo cleaned a cupful of pus from his wounds today. By evening, Nogueira was delirious and talked incoherently. Carlos Miguel sat with him, praying. He also prayed for the three compañeros who have gone for help.

Within five hours of leaving the plane, Canessa and the others came upon the tail—a fifteen-foot shell still attached to the tall vertical stabilizer which was sitting upright in a snowbank. There were some twenty suitcases scattered around the rear cargo area, where, under the floorboard, they found the two 24-volt, cadmium-plated batteries the mechanic had told them about. The kitchen was cut in half; they ransacked it for an hour, turning up fourteen tiny bottles of whisky, three bottles of wine, one hundred and thirty cartons of cigarettes, and a handful of sugar packets.

They spent most of the afternoon going through the suitcases. By four o'clock they had accumulated a number of heavy windbreakers, six pairs of sunglasses, another rugby ball, and enough needles and thread to make sleeping bags. They loaded their supplies into three suitcases then went outside to see what they could find in the snow. Vizintin uncovered a torn carton of cigarettes, Parrado dug up a bottle of wine, but Canessa searched in vain for Dr. Nicola's medical bag. At dusk they went back inside and spent the night huddled under the blankets.

November 19th
Sunday. Arturo Nogueira is dying. He spent the morning shouting for his mother to bring him something to eat, or remembering scattered incidents from his childhood. Most of the time he does not recognize

us, thinking he is at home. He could not swallow when Gustavo tried to feed him. Finally, at one o'clock, he fell asleep.

Canessa, Vizintin, and Parrado returned unexpectedly this afternoon. They brought good news—they found the tail, and the batteries appear to be in good condition. They were too heavy to carry, so we will have to dismantle the VHF radio and take it down there. Roy Harley is certain that he can hook it up so it will transmit.

They also found some little bottles of whisky and four bottles of wine, but no food. The kitchen was destroyed. Parrado brought back a metal waste container to store our water in, and many plastic cups. Best of all, they discovered some needles and thread in the women's suitcases. Adolfo Strauch went to work on the design for two two-man sleeping bags. Everyone is excited by the news.

Around dusk Arturo Nogueira awoke, still delirious. He began laughing wildly, crying that we couldn't eat him because his meat was bad. Carlos Miguel sat with him, praying. Just before dawn he became clear-headed, and confessed to Carlos Miguel in a weak voice.

November 20th
Monday. Arturo Nogueira died at seven o'clock this morning just as day was breaking. We stored his body alongside the plane.

It was warm today, and we spent several hours packing snow around the bottom of the plane. Adolfo Strauch has cut the pattern for the sleeping bags out of seat covers. A number of us are busy sewing them together. Adolfo and his brother, Eduardo, are helping Roy Harley remove the VHF radio. They claim there are thirty-two separate wires which have to be disconnected before they can pull it out; then, of course, they will have to reconnect them. It will be a slow job, even with the tool kit.

This afternoon Zerbino and Canessa cut off the pilot's head and removed the brains. They made a soup, burning a little fuel and the rest of *The Woman Pilot.*

November 23rd
Thursday. After two days of light snow, the sky was clear this morning.

Today was Roberto Francois' twenty-fifth birthday. We celebrated it with a bottle of wine. Roberto is a strange one. None of us have seen him cry. He has a small infection in his right eye that causes him to squint; but he has never had any problem with the meat, and is the fattest one in the group.

Javier Methol's knee is stronger. Alvaro Mangino still cannot walk, but Roberto says that his leg will heal in a few weeks. Numa Turcatti is very thin. He still has to wash the meat down with snow, and as a consequence eats very little. Alfredo Delgado told him not to feel guilty, because God had sanctified the flesh. Numa said that he was not bothered by the fact that the meat was human, but that it was raw.

Rafael Etchevarren is very despondent. His gangrene is spreading, and he has very little feeling in his legs. Roberto cleans the wounds as best he can, but he cannot stop the infection. The only thing that can save Rafael is an amputation, but under these conditions he would die before the legs were off.

Roy Harley and the two Strauch brothers finally got the radio out this afternoon. Now begins the slow process of reconnecting the wires.

November 25th
Saturday. Light snow this morning, but the sky cleared by afternoon. The sleeping bags are finished. Adolfo lined them with foam rubber.

Rolled up, they fit on the back just like a hiking pack. The radio is ready, too. Our four *compañeros* are leaving for the tail in the morning.

This evening Carlos prayed that the expedition is a success.

November 26th

Sunday. Windy, but clear this morning. We held mass early because our four *compañeros* left before six o'clock. Roberto told Etchevarren not to worry, that they would get help over the radio.

In the afternoon a light plane flew over us several times. We ran around, shouting and throwing snow, but they apparently didn't see us. Everyone wondered who it was. We have heard nothing on the transistor radio about the search being resumed.

Harley, Canessa, Parrado, and Vizintin were to spend seven days—and several nights, after rigging up a light bulb—trying to transmit on the VHF radio without success. No one knows if the radio was broken or if the batteries were too weak. It doesn't matter; in the end, on December 3rd, they returned to the plane.

They brought with them some more supplies—a few pounds of chocolate and some alka-seltzer tablets to curb their craving for salt. Fernando Parrado chanced upon the idea of using the fibrous, asbestos insulation around the refrigeration unit as lining for the sleeping bags; he pulled it out and carried it back to the plane. The main thing they discovered was that they were running out of time. The trip to the tail exhausted Harley's strength; he had to be supported on the return to the plane. Canessa knew that they, like Harley, were all getting weaker. It would not be long before the slightest protracted effort would bring on a complete physical collapse. They would have to leave soon, before they lacked the strength to walk....

December 3rd

Sunday. A bright, clear day. Carlos Miguel conducted mass this morning. Canessa, Parrado, and Vizintin are preparing for another expedition. All three are eating extra rations, generally the organs, the parts richest in vitamins and protein. We have relieved them from any duties. They exercise in the morning and sleep in the sun during the afternoon.

The days are warmer now, and we seldom have any storms. The snow is thawing rapidly. We measure the rate by checking the level around the back of the fuselage. According to our marks, twelve inches have melted so far.

Roberto Canessa estimates that they will need eighty pounds of meat to make the trip. This should be enough for ten days, and Fernando Parrado is certain they will reach a village before then.

Rafael Etchevarren is slowly dying, and there is nothing we can do about it. He is very brave and only complains that he would like to die in Uruguay.

Adolfo Strauch is making a three-man sleeping bag. It will be lined with the insulation Fernando Parrado brought from the tail. Adolfo spent the afternoon carefully removing the thread from the other two bags.

Numa Turcatti is weak and can barely walk. Both Roy Harley and José Luis Inciarte are very thin. Alvaro Mangino is able to stand up, but he cannot walk unassisted. Javier Methol has a slight limp.

December 6th

Wednesday. We have had some snow, but today was nice and warm. Gustavo Zerbino has used up one body so far to prepare the food supply for our expedition. Adolfo Strauch is concerned about the number of bodies we have in reserve, so this afternoon a detail went up the mountain and dragged Carlos Valeta down. We put him alongside the plane.

One thing we have in abundance is cigarettes. There were 130 cartons in the tail. We have various brands: La Paz, Nevada, and Kendall. Only thirteen of us smoke, but Adolfo Strauch (who is one of them) has begun to ration the supply: one pack every two days.

The melting snow forces us to rebury the bodies daily. We must also pack snow around the plane every morning, shoveling it out of the big trench on the right side where Zerbino and Canessa cut the meat. There are three large piles of bones, lungs, and other parts which we have to cover when they are exposed to the sun.

This afternoon Rafael Etchevarren made Roberto Canessa promise that his body would be buried in Uruguay. Canessa said that they would find help in time to save him. Just promise, Rafael said.

Carlos Miguel led us in prayer before we bedded down at seven o'clock. It was a cold night.

December 7th
Thursday. Clear but chilly because of the wind. Adolfo Strauch has the sleeping bag ready. We have gathered our warmest clothing and best sunglasses for the three *compañeros* who are going for help. They will each take two pairs of shoes: rugby cleats for walking in the snow and heavy shoes to sleep in. Fernando Parrado, as always, is ready to go. Vizintin, too.

Roberto Canessa, however, argues that they should exercise and rest and, above all, eat for a few more days. But privately, Roberto admits that he does not want to leave Rafael Etchevarren. Rafael has been running a high fever for twenty-four hours. Canessa and Zerbino have tried to break it with ice packs, but they can't.

Another fight broke out this afternoon. This time between Roberto Canessa and, surprisingly, Carlos Miguel. It didn't last long. They exchanged several punches then stopped suddenly, both of them at once. Then they burst into tears and hugged one another. We have always had fights, little ones, but they are becoming more frequent.

Numa Turcatti fell down today and could not get back up. Gustavo and Roberto had to carry him inside the plane.

December 8th

Friday. Light snow this morning. Rafael Etchevarren was in and out of a coma all day, calling to his father. Turcatti has barely strength enough to eat. He is so thin, one can clearly see the outline of the bones in his arm. José Luis Inciarte and Roy Harley are almost as thin.

Canessa, Parrado, and Vizintin are ready to leave. The meat is dry and can be packed at any time. The snow level has been reduced by twenty inches according to the marks on the plane.

Fernando Parrado has decided that they will have to climb the big mountain to the west. From the top, they will be able to decide on the best route. Adolfo Strauch pointed out that the mountain is at least a thousand feet higher than the one we hit. Then we'll be able to see farther, Fernando said.

This evening Carlos Miguel prayed for the success of our three *compañeros*. He spent the night with Rafael Etchevarren, who was delirious and loud. The last clear thing he said was Nena, the name of his sister.

December 9th

Saturday. A sunny day, no wind. Rafael Etchevarren died around five o'clock in the morning. We buried him in the snow. Roberto said it would not be safe to eat him.

We spent the day preparing for tomorrow's journey. Ramon Sabella filled the two bladders with water, mixing in a little wine. Roberto and Gustavo stored the meat in the leather suitcases Adolfo converted into back-packs. Our three *compañeros* rested in the sun all afternoon.

Numa Turcatti was able to eat some of the dried fat Gustavo Zerbino fed him today. He also drank some water. Later, while two of us were helping him to the tail to urinate, he lost control of his bladder.

December 10th

Sunday. For the journey, a warm day. Carlos Miguel prayed in the dark this morning. Afterwards, we said goodbye to our *compañeros*, who left before it was light. Before leaving, Parrado gave us permission to eat his mother and sister, if it is necessary.

Roy Harley could not stand up this morning. He managed to eat some of the meat Zerbino cut for him. Zerbino tried to feed Turcatti, but he is so weak the food fell out of his mouth.

Canessa, Parrado, and Vizintin climbed for three days. At night they slept wadded together in the big sleeping bag, hugging the two bladders close to their bodies to keep the water from freezing. By noon on December 12th, they were less than a hundred yards from the top. They were exhausted. All day they had been forced to rest ten minutes for every five spent climbing, and both Canessa and Vizintin were ready to turn back. Enraged at the idea, Parrado managed to claw his way alone to the top in thirty minutes. All he could see at first, in every direction, was cordillera. Then, in the distance, he saw the long black line of a river cutting down to where, far off, it branched into a Y.

When he came back down, Parrado told Canessa and Vizintin that one of them would have to go back, explaining that the journey would take longer than he had anticipated. Together, they decided that Vizintin should return and begin organizing another expedition, to the east, if nothing had been heard of Canessa and Parrado in ten days. Vizintin transferred his food supply to their packs and started back down the mountain.

He descended in a highly unorthodox manner. He slid down on the two snowshoe cushions, using them as a sled. It took him only forty-five minutes to reach the bottom, and he arrived back at the plane by dusk.

He never learned that Parrado had duped him—deciding at the last minute that he and Canessa stood a better chance with the extra meat. He never even suspected. Besides, he had other things to worry about. Upon his return to the plane, he discovered that his companions had begun eating rotten meat because they thought it had more salt. On the 14th of December, the condors found the plane.

Before setting out, Canessa and Parrado ate. Then they climbed slowly to the top and rested, dizzy from the effort. While they sat there, a figure appeared below on the valley floor. It had to be Vizintin, of course; but at first they couldn't believe their eyes.

They staggered down the other side of the mountain, falling several times. That night they slept at the base of the mountain. It was cold, and the wind blew hard until morning, bouncing off the high wall behind them and punishing them as they clung together in the sleeping bag. By dawn, Parrado no longer felt guilty about duping Vizintin.

On the afternoon of December 13th, they reached the mouth of the river. It was seven feet wide and the water was paralyzingly cold. They followed the left bank until dark, watching the river grow wider and faster, beginning to roar. They camped well back from it in a snowdrift. The temperature was ten degrees lower near the water.

By nightfall on December 14th, they decided to ford the river. All day they had slogged through deep snow across uneven terrain gouged by narrow crevasses running at right angles to the river.

At ten o'clock the next morning they found a spot where there were boulders large enough to allow them to cross. After changing into flat-soled shoes, Parrado went over first. On his turn, Canessa slipped and fell hard on his right hip, losing one of the water bladders. He was up quickly, but by afternoon he had started to limp.

The river was all rapids now, and twenty feet wide, boiling blue-green and white, and tossing large chunks of ice along like corks. It was hotter, too, and they walked along the bank where the spray frosted the air. At six o'clock on December 15th, they saw, up ahead, a cactus. It was a big mountain *kisco* with yellow and white blossoms. By the time they reached it, they were in the *precordillera*. In the distance there were trees, the dream that all of them had carried for so long in their hearts.

from Shipwreck and Adventures of
Monsieur Pierre Viaud
by Pierre Viaud

Pierre Viaud joined the merchant ship Le Tigre
in 1766, sailing from St. Domingue (present-day
Haiti) to New Orleans. A storm marooned Viaud
and five shipmates on Dog Island, near Florida.
Two men went for help and another, age 15,
died. Viaud with his African slave and the boy's
mother reached the mainland on a raft.

W e stood on a ridge. On all sides we saw a boundless skyline. On our right was the sea and our left a forest stretching as far as the eye could see. In front of us, in the direction in which we had determined to go, was a dry empty plain on which could be seen only the traces of wild beasts and nothing which could sustain us. This sight threw us into bitter despair. Our battered spirits lost all remnants of courage. We abandoned our originally intended route because we could not see how it could end well and because it contained no promise of comfort or nourishment. Instead we walked downhill to the left, directing our steps toward the nearby forest. It was frighteningly dense. The trees were oppressively close to each other; in some places we could not pass between them. The path we had wanted to follow petered out after a few yards. We found alternative tracks which often doubled back to where we had begun. Others would have taken us deep into the woods and left us without a chance of ever getting out, certain of dying from hunger or animal attacks.

None of these trees apparently offered what we needed to survive. Most of them had the same kind of leaves which had made us so sick.

"It's all over," I said to myself, as anguish stabbed me. "It's all over. We must die. We can't go on any more."

Muttering these words, I threw myself on the ground. Madame La Couture lay down next to me. My black placed himself at our feet a little distance from us. Without looking at each other, we all began to weep. Sunk in gloomy thought, we stayed bitterly silent. We understood each other's preoccupations perfectly. They exclusively concerned our frightful situation. We had no need to talk.

The gloomiest ideas occurred to me then. Is there anyone, I asked myself, who has ever seen himself reduced to my extremity? What other man has found himself in a desert, lacking everything, and ready to die of hunger? I then began to recall the adventures of some travelers driven off course by a storm. Adverse winds and dead calms had kept them in unknown waters, and they had used up their stock of provisions without the possibility of replenishing them. I remembered that, having suffered hunger to the point where they were dying of starvation, the only recourse left to those unfortunates was to sacrifice one of their number in order to save the rest of them. Sometimes it was by lot that the choice was made of a victim who, in losing his own life, prolonged his companions' by giving them his corpse to eat.

Dare I confess it to you, my friend? You are going to shudder when reading what remains for me to tell but, believe me, your horror cannot possibly be as great as mine. You will see to what excess despair and starvation can drive us and you will pity me, perhaps, for the suffering which I had endured.

While I was remembering the harrowing experiences of other voyagers, my wandering eyes fell on my black. They lingered there with a kind of greed. "He is dying," I said to myself madly. "A quick death would be a blessing for him. He is dying by inches and all human efforts are powerless to protect him. Why shouldn't his death be made useful to me?"

I will admit that my mind did not reject this possibility. Affected by the weakness of my body, my reason was warped. Starvation under-mined me. I felt searing pangs in my innards. The urgent need to appease them completely dominated me. Alternative ways of doing it were out of the question. There was only one, it seemed. My disturbed mind could not reflect and examine coolly. It formed horrible desires and provided me with countless sophisticated arguments to justify them.

"What crime will I be committing?" I muttered. "He is mine. I brought him to serve me. Of what greater service could he ever be?" Madame La Couture had been entertaining murderous ideas similar to mine. She caught my final words. She did not know what train of thought had led up to them and the reasoning which had preceded them but necessity made everything clear. She attracted my attention in a low voice and when I looked her way she pointed both with her eyes and hand in the direction of my black. Her eyes then turned back to me. They had a literally deadly look and she made an even more expressive gesture with her hand—which I fully understood.

To be unleashed it seems that my madness awaited only the approval of a backer. I did not hesitate for a second. Delighted to see that she thought as I did, I felt justified. I started up and, seizing a knobbly stick which I had used to lean on during our marches, I went up to my black. He was dozing. I brought him out of his stupor by bringing the stick down with stunning force on his head. My hand trembled and I did not dare to hit him again. My heart palpitated. My latent humanity screamed an appeal, depriving me of the strength to go on.

On coming round, the black rose to his knees, clasped his hands together and, looking at me with anguish, said beseechingly and sadly, "What are you doing, master? What have I done to you? Won't you at least spare my life?"

I could not help softening. I wept and for two minutes I could not reply. I could not do anything. At last my hunger pangs overcame the voice of reason. A mournful shout and another signal from the eye of my female friend reequipped me once more with frenzied resolution.

Beside myself, distraught, affected by an unprecedented delirium, I hurled myself at the wretched black and threw him to the ground. I yelled aloud, both to numb myself and so that I would not hear the black's screaming, which might have blunted my cruel determination. I tied his hands behind his back. I called for my companion, who came to my help in this savage procedure. She knelt on the head of my poor black, while I drew my knife and, with all my strength, sank it in his throat and widened the wound. He died at once.

There was a fallen tree near us. I dragged the black to it and hung him on it head down, so that his blood could drain out. Madame La Couture helped me.

This horrible act had exhausted both our strength and our determination. Our fearful eyes lingered on the bleeding body which, a moment before, had been a living being. We shuddered at what we had just done. We quickly ran to a nearby spring to wash our blood-stained hands, which we could not look at except with horror. We fell to our knees to ask God's forgiveness for the inhuman crime we had just committed. We also prayed for the poor wretch whose throat we had just cut.

Nature manages to combine extremes. Completely opposite feelings gripped us at almost the same time. Although devout sentiment followed on the heels of savagery, it was the latter that soon regained the upper hand. Urgent hunger pangs interfered with our prayers. "Lord," we exclaimed, "you know our situation, our overwhelming wretchedness which pushed us into committing murder! Pardon us in our misfortune and at least bless the vile food we are going to eat. Make it nourish us. We have already paid enough for it."

With these words we got up, lit a great fire, and carried out our monstrous determination. I scarcely dare record the details: the very memory of them turns my stomach. No, my friend, except for this period of my life I have never been a barbarian. I was not born for it. You know me well and I have no need to apologize to you, but you must be the only reader of these words. I would suppress this part of my narrative if I imagined that there would ever be other readers. What an idea they would have of my character! Of what other atrocities would they not suspect me capable? Only by reasoning that, thanks to severe hardships, my sense of right had deserted me might they, perhaps, claim that they understood my actions. Few, however, would be fair enough to ponder my misfortunes and to realize that horrors of the kind which I endured actually effect radical changes in a man's character and that the deviations into which they may lead him should not be classed as crimes.

As soon as our fire was ready, I immediately cut off the black's head. I impaled it on the end of a stick and set it up in front of the blaze. Although I took care to turn it frequently so that it would be thoroughly cooked, our raging hunger did not allow us to wait until it was properly roasted. We ate it quickly and, once we were full, made arrangements to pass the night where we were and to protect ourselves from attacks by animals. We rightly expected that the noise of their approach would prevent us from sleeping and therefore spent the night in dismembering the corpse of our black. We cut his flesh into suitable pieces for grilling on the embers or held them in smoke in the hope of preserving them from decay. We had already suffered appallingly from hunger. The only insurance against it was to secure provisions which would not spoil. We stayed in the same place all the next day and the following night, hoarding our food, eating only what would be difficult to preserve and which, consequently, we would be unable to take with us. We parceled the rest, wrapping it in our remaining handkerchiefs and in swatches of cloth from our garments. We hung these packages from our bodies with the makeshift ropes from our raft.

On 24 April or thereabouts we resumed our journey. The break we had taken had rested us and the food we had eaten had restored our strength. Certain of a supply for some time, we did not fear to move onto the plain which had seemed so frightening on the day when we killed the black. We walked slowly and, now just the two of us, did not set out without remorse for the companion who had previously followed us and whose grisly remains we now carried about us. For several days we walked, enduring great strain and meeting many difficulties. Crossing through canebrakes near the sea or in the middle of bramble patches or thorn bushes and other equally hostile plants, we bloodied our feet and legs.

This annoyance, though less serious than hunger, frequently delayed us. The bites of gnats, mosquitoes, and a host of other insects which we met on the coast so disfigured us that we became quite unrecognizable. The bites covered our faces, hands, and legs, causing them to swell monstrously. In an attempt to avoid them, if possible, we made for the seashore, deciding to follow it thereafter, in the hope too of lucky finds in the shape of edibles to supplement the provisions we carried. We were not mistaken in this expectation. When the tide was out and the weather fine, we sometimes found on the beach small mollusks and little flat fish which we speared with a sharpened stick. All the same we happened on them very seldom and there were never enough to fill us. They were, however, not to be despised and we gratefully accepted them as a gift from God with deep emotion.

I cannot give you the details, day by day, of the painful and apparently endless odyssey which we doggedly pursued. The canebrakes, with which the shore was covered in many places, and through which we were forced to travel, were as wicked as the brambles which we had wanted to avoid. Dry canes, splintered by the wind, tore at our legs, cutting them most cruelly. Wild beasts scared us every night, and even more frightening was the frequent need to prepare and eat loathsome meals. Our murderous madness had receded along with our hunger. Reason had resumed control of our minds and reason recoiled at the very idea of cannibalism. We resorted to it only at times of extreme need, when we had managed to find absolutely no other food and when reborn hunger overcame disgust.

One evening, as we made our customary halt, I felt so weak that I could scarcely summon the strength to collect the wood needed for our fire. It proved beyond my power to build it in stacks around our camping place as I always did at night. My monstrously swollen legs could no longer support me. Luckily it then occurred to me that I could do the job better by burning the canes and briars in our vicinity and letting the wind spread the blaze. Not only would it keep wild animals away, but it would have the additional advantage of easing our journey. It would burn all those awkward canes off our intended path and we would be able to walk more conveniently along the shore by following the fire's traces. We found, the following day, that the fire had literally blazed our route for us. I regretted that I had not thought sooner of this expedient to save us from the leg wounds which gave great discomfort and compelled us to cover only short distances daily.

As a bonus we found lying in our path very appetizing food: two rattlesnakes. One had fourteen joints; the other twenty-one. Thus we at once knew their age, if it is true that they grow an extra ring at the end of each year. The snakes were very fat. The fire had surprised them while they slept and its smoke had choked them. They provided us with fresh meat all that day and the one that followed. We also dried part of their flesh for later consumption and added it to our stock of provisions.

During our journey I found yet another means of increasing our store of food. One morning I spotted a sleeping alligator in a nearby pool. I went toward it for a closer look. The beast did not frighten me, although I knew how dangerous it was. The only idea in my mind was how great an addition to our rations the alligator would make, if only I could kill it. For a moment I hesitated to attack it, not because of fear, but simply from uncertainty as to the best way of killing it.

I went forward armed with my stick, which was of a hard and heavy wood. With it I struck the beast sharply on the head three times with such force that I made it capable neither of attacking nor retreating. It merely opened its frightful maw, into which I promptly sank the end of my stick which was fairly well pointed. I probed for and transfixed his throat and pushing downwards at once to the full length of my arm, I pinned the monster to the ground. He leapt and moved in such a frantic fashion that, if my stick had not been firmly and deeply driven into the sand, it would have been impossible to hold the fierce beast, and I would have become the victim of my daring.

Simply keeping the alligator where he was took all my strength. I was fixed in an awkward posture which prevented me from adjusting my stance to improve my chances of killing the monster. I shouted for Madame La Couture, begging her to come and help. She did not dare to assist directly. She did, however, look for and bring me a piece of wood three or four feet in length. I used it to stun the alligator, wielding it with one of my hands, while I continued to grip the stick with which I had impaled it in the other, until the beast had all but ceased to thrash about. My companion, bolder now, took my place, enabling me to use both my hands, thanks to which I managed to crush the alligator's head and to cut off its tail.

My victory had taken a great deal out of me: I was shattered, and we did not even consider continuing our journey on that day. We used our time to cook a good meal and to preserve the flesh of the alligator as we had that of our black. We cut it up into pieces about the size of a man's hand. That way they would dry out more easily and we should avoid unnecessary delay. I used the hide to make moccasins for Madame La Couture and myself. We contrived leggings for ourselves from other strips of skin. By wrapping them around our legs we protected them from the bites of the insects which had plagued us: naturally their stings could not penetrate alligator hide. Other strips of hide covered our hands and faces. We used it too for makeshift masks. At first we found them awkward, but by preserving us from insect bites they were worthwhile.

Such were the various types of relief which we derived from our alligator. We spent all that day and the following night in these preparations. Wakeful, we put off until the night after that the need to snatch some rest. We did not want to prolong our trip with breaks. It was already made long enough by the unavoidable brevity of our daily marches.

The next day our progress was thwarted after a mere hour by a river which flowed into the sea. Although not very wide, its current was very swift. I reconnoitered. Hoping to find it fordable, I undressed and waded in to test its depth. I met insuperable obstacles: first the water's depth, which made swimming unavoidable, and second, the strength of the current, which was impossible to overcome and would certainly have swept me into the ocean. Alone I might have been able to cope but Madame La Couture could never have done so. Unbearably frustrated, I returned to the riverbank. We had no choice but to walk inland, following the bank until we found either a more peaceful stretch of river or a place where a shallower bed would make fording feasible.

And so we resumed walking. Two whole days elapsed and we found nothing to inspire optimism. The farther we went, the less practicable seemed a river crossing. Our concern and desperation grew. We had already given up hope of ever leaving Florida. We chanced on nothing to eat in those two days and consequently survived on alligator meat, leaving the black's flesh as a last resort. We worried that we would exhaust all our provisions before arriving at an inhabited place where we could replenish them.

Frightened by our past experience, doubtful of the future, and uncertain of how long our run of bad luck would last, we spent our time in hoping, complaining, and then despairing. The sight of the river invariably flowing briskly seemed to increase our weariness. The seeming impossibility of ever crossing it and the consequent need to keep walking upstream, without knowing when we would strike a crossing point, robbed us of courage.

At the end of the second day on which we had followed this river, I saw a turtle, which must have weighed ten pounds, and I turned it onto its back with my stick. This new providential source of food, for a while, quelled our complaints, converting them in fact to prayers of thanksgiving. Previously we had seen a plump turkey hen, which regularly came to drink at the river, each morning and evening. It seemed to have its nest somewhere near but we looked for it in vain. The hope of finding wholesome food had caused us to make the most minute search for its eggs, but we had no luck. It was a frustration which added greatly to our ill humor and made us curse our fate.

Discovering the turtle to some extent reconciled us to our destiny. We thought of cooking it and our hearth was ready. You can imagine what a shock it was when I could not find my gun-flint! I emptied all my pockets and then turned them inside out. I undid all our packets of provisions. I rummaged everywhere with the most scrupulous attention. Madame La Couture helped. We did not find it. Our woe was proportionate to the need we had for the flint and to the help it had afforded us. Never has a loss given more grief to a man. We now thought of the turtle, over which we had gloated, with the utmost indifference. We would have willingly exchanged it for the flint. The loss of half of our provisions would have troubled us less. Without the flint, how could we protect ourselves from the cold and the attacks of wild beasts? How could we cook and preserve our food, or keep ourselves dry?

Madame La Couture's distress equaled mine. I reasoned that we must have lost the flint either in the place where we had slept the previous night or on the path which we had subsequently taken. I felt tired and weak but did not hesitate for a second to retrace my steps to look for it. I suggested to Madame La Couture that she might either come with me or wait for me. She had no real choice. Although she was nervous about staying alone, she lacked the strength to make the journey again. At the same time she longed, no less than I, to recover the treasure we had lost. She made me promise not to abandon her and to return as soon as possible.

It was fortunate that we had covered little ground on the most recent stage of our journey. We had walked for a mere hour and a half, and nightfall was still far off. I retraced our path with the intention of returning before darkness fell, but it proved impossible. I was too feeble to move briskly. Besides, I did not take a single step without looking around for the flint. I hoped that I had lost it on the path and that I would recover it without the need to walk very far, but it proved necessary to go all the way back to the place where we had slept.

I had used up a great deal of time. Night had already fallen when I arrived. I could see almost nothing. I looked about in every place where I could discern footprints. It was a fruitless exercise. I found nothing. I lay on the ground feeling all around with my hands. They had to do duty for my eyes, which darkness had made useless. Tired of wearing myself out without result, I ran to the fire which I had lit the previous night to see if I could find an ember which might enable me to revive it and thus give me the light needed for my search. The fire was utterly dead. I found only cinders without the least glimmer.

Overwhelmed by this latest disappointment, as though I had a right to expect anything else, I remained lying down, giving way to deep depression, despairing of deriving any good from my efforts, unable to rejoin Madame La Couture that night, and not even giving thought to doing so. The notion of going back to her without my flint was unbearable. I decided to wait until morning to resume my search, in the hope that in the end I would find it. I went to throw myself down on the pile of ferns, leaves, and various plants which had been our makeshift bed. I thought that perhaps it was there that I had lost my flint. For a moment I debated with myself whether to wait until the following day before resuming my search. It was clearly the most sensible course. Broad daylight was absolutely necessary. I could not expect to find anything in the dark. My reason was fully persuaded but my mind was too agitated to put up with delay.

I passed my hands repeatedly over every part of the surface of the bed but they encountered nothing. My initial intention had been to stop after doing this and to put off a more thorough search until daylight, but in my impatience I could not resist going on. Fistful by fistful I went through the pile of foliage. After examining each handful I put it down elsewhere. I spent the best part of the night doing this. I was losing hope of recovering my treasure because I had been through and displaced every single plant comprising the bed. I stretched my hands finally onto the earth which the plants had formerly covered. They came to rest on the object of my longing. I snatched it up with a joy equal to the distress which its loss had caused me. Holding it tightly, I took all manner of precautions to avoid losing it in future.

While occupied with these activities I was a little concerned about wild animals. Although they came from far away, I could hear their cries and I worried from time to time both for myself and for my unfortunate companion. She was alone and her fear in the middle of the night must have been acute. I thought of rushing to her side to reassure her, if that was possible, but I admit that fear of a dangerous encounter on the way kept me from doing anything for a long time. It finally struck me that the care we had taken to make fires every night along our route must have persuaded the brutes to keep their distance, causing them to retire to the far corners of the wasteland we were crossing in order to avoid the fires. Actually during this time they had never come near the places where we made camp and we had heard their snarling only from a certain distance—which had done much to minimize our fear. At last I persuaded myself that I was unlikely to meet any beasts and with some qualms set off. Several times I was on the point of stopping to light a fire to give myself reassurance, but did not in fact halt. Fear lent me wings and, despite my weak condition, I got back to Madame La Couture about two hours before daybreak. I could easily have missed her and might have wandered far from the place I had left her, because a combination of darkness and fear prevented me from recognizing the spot. Only a moan, which I heard purely by chance and which made me shudder, told me that I was about to pass her by without her seeing me. She had heard the sound of my footsteps and, in her fright, had thought that a fierce animal was coming toward her. It was she who had moaned. I asked at the top of my voice, "Is that you, Madame?"

"Yes," she replied almost inaudibly. "My God, how you frightened me! With you so far away and so late coming back, you have given me some bad moments! Did you hear that horrible snarling? It's been dinning in my ears. When you didn't return I thought you'd been eaten and it wouldn't be long before I was too!"

"I'm still alive," I shouted, "and now I've found you again! Both of us have been petrified with fear but I've found my flint again! We'll have a fire! We'll be able to rest and have something to eat."

Even while uttering these words I was collecting some bits of dry wood. I struck sparks from my flint. For tinder I used a strip from my shirt, which was quite worn out and almost in rags. For a long time I had been using either it or Madame La Couture's chemise to start fires.

We soon had a great blaze going, on which we cooked part of our turtle. Its flesh was extremely tender and succulent. On cutting it open, we found in its body a quantity of little eggs which we grilled on the embers, thus enjoying a food which was as wholesome as it was refreshing. It did wonders for us. We slept afterwards. This needed rest, which lasted five hours, both comforted and strengthened us.

On waking we discussed the advisability of continuing in the direction we were going. The upper course of the river was visible and quite straight. We looked at it and despaired of finding a suitable crossing point for a long time. We decided to risk a passage where we were, for which I thought of building a raft. Solid materials convenient for the job were at hand. They were six trees, defoliated by time, which had floated downstream. They had come to rest on the riverbank near a gnarled tree, which leaned over the river, but whose roots were still embedded in the shore. I got into the water. Luckily it was shallow at this place and, using creepers, I lashed four of the trees together, making them reasonably fast. As best I could, I attached a long pole to them. It was thicker at one end than at the other and was meant to serve as both oar and rudder.

Once I had finished, we prepared to leave. We stripped off our clothes, making a bundle of them, which we bound with natural materials. We took this precaution so that we could save ourselves more readily if some accident happened. Our clothes would have got in our way if we had fallen in the water. Wrapping all our clothes in one bundle would make it easier to retrieve them if I had to go swimming in search of them. The outcome would show how right we were to take these precautions.

Our conditions made prudish conventions irrelevant. While we traveled together, we were scarcely aware that we were of different sexes. I was conscious of my companion's gender only because, like most women, she lacked muscular strength. She was conscious of mine merely from observing the firmness and courage with which I tried to inspire her, and the help which my superior strength enabled me to give her. We were numb to other feelings. Our exhausted bodies, oblivious of all other considerations, asked only that we supply them with food.

Our fear of possible accidents was insufficient to make us part with our provisions as we had done with our clothes. Losing our garments would have been less calamitous than losing our food. We organized our food packages in such a way as to be able to hang them from our bodies. They would survive with us or we would die with them.

We got onto the raft, which I pushed off from the shore, steering as best I could with the pole. At first the current snatched at us with a speed which made me shiver. In an instant it had borne us more than three hundred yards from the place where we had embarked. I was afraid that it would sweep us down to the sea. With the utmost difficulty I labored to cut across it. Finally I succeeded, but only at the cost of losing way and riding downstream at a monstrous rate so that I expected to reach the opposite shore a mile and a half lower than the place from which we had set out.

With considerable effort, I managed to get more than halfway over the river. The current then slackened and we had almost reached the spot where it was most placid. Suddenly the current took our raft sideways onto a tree which was near to us at water level. The movement which I made to avoid it brought disaster. The strain broke the lashings holding our craft together, loosing the lengths of wood of which it was constituted. We fell in the water and would certainly have drowned, had I not seized a branch of the tree with one hand. With the other I simultaneously gripped Madame La Couture's hair at the very instant when she was already sinking, no doubt never to reemerge. She was still conscious and I shouted for her not to grasp me with her arms and legs, the better to hold her up. Where we were, the water was very deep. I made her clamber onto the trunk of the tree while I swam around it. Its other end touched the bank, enabling me to lead her there. She sat on shore while I detached the packages of food hanging from me and placed them at her side. I went back to the river to see if I could retrieve our clothes and soon glimpsed them. They were caught in the branches of the tree, but the river was stirring them. At the moment when I dived in, the current had begun to carry them away. I swam in pursuit and had the good luck to catch up with them. Pushing them in front of me towards the shore, I landed them safely.

My first concern was to take the bundle to Madame La Couture who untied it, wrung the clothes and then spread them out. Meanwhile I prepared a fire to hasten their drying and to cook such pieces of turtle as we still possessed. We had actually lost nothing by being wrecked, and shed no tears over the raft which, having brought us across the river, had served its purpose. We would have abandoned it, whatever happened.

After eating a restoring meal, we dried our provisions, an occupation which kept us busy all day. We spent the night where we were. The next day, rested and refreshed, we resumed our journey. Taking our bearings as well as we could, we tried to keep in the right direction for St. Mark's, Apalache. We were constantly worried that we had lost our way. On the east side of the river the forests were just as dense, and the briars and canes as unpleasant and dangerous as ever. Our shoes, leggings, and makeshift gloves and masks were unserviceable. Immersion in the river had ruined them. As before, brambles scratched and mosquitoes and flies tormented us: our bodies became enormously swollen from their constant poisonous biting. We found even less food than on the western shore. The remains of our black and our alligator were all we had to eat.

Suffering these hardships, which grew progressively worse, we walked for several days. Our bodies and spirits were both affected. Hope with its consoling fancies no longer lulled us. We were in a deplorable condition and looked more like walking barrels than human beings. We walked laboriously, scarcely able to place one foot before the other and rising only with difficulty after sitting down.

Madame La Couture held out longer than I. As long as I had possessed strength, I had been thrifty with hers, and had taken on all the arduous tasks that arose. Her spirits, moreover, were less depressed than mine, because she had let me do all the worrying. Until then, therefore, I had borne the brunt in all respects, but now came a time when I had to give in to sustained misfortune.

One day I was scarcely able to see because the bites of the insects I have mentioned had caused swelling around my eyes which weakened and almost closed them. Feeling beaten and unable to go on, I threw myself down on the shore under a tree about a hundred yards from the sea. After lying there for an hour, I tried to rise to continue our journey, and found it was beyond my strength to get to my feet.

"It's all over," I said to my companion. "I can't go any farther. This spot will mark the end of my journey, my troubles, and my life. Use your remaining strength to try and reach an inhabited place. Take our provisions with you. Don't squander them by uselessly waiting here for me. I see that God does not want me to survive. My utter exhaustion is a sign of it. The courage and strength which He has allowed you to keep means that He has other plans for you. Enjoy your blessings and think sometimes of the wretch who has shared your troubles for such a long time, who has eased them for you as much as he could, and who would never have deserted you, if he had been allowed to travel with you provided he could be useful. Let's surrender to cruel necessity which is commanding us with its harsh laws. Leave! Try to survive and, when you are enjoying abundance again, and becoming forgetful of the privations we experienced, say sometimes: 'I lost a friend in the wastes of America.' No doubt you will be with Europeans again one of these days. You will hear of ships sailing for France. When you do, please do me a favor, the only one I want and expect from our friendship. Write to my parents describing the fate of their unlucky son. Tell them he is no more and that they can divide among themselves the sorry remains of his estate. They are to do with it what they think fit, without worrying that I shall ever come back to reclaim it. Tell them to pray for and pity me."

Madame La Couture did not reply except with tears. Her emotion touched me: it is a great consolation for the afflicted to see that they have aroused compassion. She took my hands and pressed them tenderly. I tried again to persuade her to leave me and to show her that it was necessary, but failed. "No, my friend," she said. "No, I shan't leave you. I shall give you, as far as I can, the care that I owe you, like that you gave me for such a long time. Be brave! Your strength may return. If that hope proves false I shall still have time enough to be left alone in this vast wasteland, accompanied only by my fears. If I abandoned you, I would feel sure every minute that God was going to send wild beasts to rip me apart as punishment for leaving you at a time when I could have helped you. As to our provisions, we'll try to make do with them. I'll also see what there is on the seashore. Any that I find will help restore your health. From now on I am going to begin to look after you. You can't protect yourself against insects, so take this!"

With these words, she took off one of her two petticoats. Using my knife she split it in two. With one piece she covered my legs: the other she placed over my arms and face. They gave me great relief, providing effective protection against possible stings. My companion then lit a fire and went to the beach, from which she returned with a turtle. I thought that the blood of this creature might prove soothing if rubbed into my wounds. I tried it and advised Madame La Couture to follow my example. She readily did so, for her head, neck, and arms were covered with mosquito bites. We then rested, but my feeling of weakness remained. I felt so ill that I had no doubt that death was near. A large turkey-hen, which we then saw, flew back into a copse only a few yards from us, making us think she had a nest there. Naturally it inspired us to get hold of her eggs. Madame La Couture undertook to look for them. I was in no state to go myself, being totally immobile, and so remained lying by the fire.

I stayed alone like that for about three hours. The sun had just set and I was in a kind of stupid torpor, unmoving and almost without the power to think. I can compare my condition only to that deep calm one experiences between sleeping and waking. A frightening numbness pervaded my heavy limbs. I felt no pain but instead a general malaise throughout my body. At this moment, I heard shouts, which dragged me from my lethargy and aroused my attention. I strained my ears. They seemed to come from the seashore. I thought they must be from a band of Indians following the coastline and getting nearer.

"Great God!" I cried. "Does this clamor portend the end of all my hardships? Have You sent these Indians to my rescue or are they coming to stamp out the last remaining flickering spark of my life? Whatever You want, I am ready. Whether it is to strike or to save me, either will deliver me from my sorrows. I will equally accept whichever it is."

The same shouts were repeated over and over. A ray of hope lightened my heart. I tried to get myself up into a sitting position and succeeded only by dint of atrocious efforts. A doleful thought occurred then to lessen my excitement. Perhaps, I reflected, these men I hear are skirting the coast in a boat. Soon they will have rowed farther on and they won't see me unless they disembark. What will become of me if they don't get out of their boat here? In the predicament I was in, how could I let them know that in this place was a wretch needing rescue?

This idea made me desperate. I tried to shout but my voice was gone. My fear, however, of letting slip the only chance of help which had occurred in a very long while restored a little of my strength. I used it to drag myself on hands and knees as close as possible to the beach. I could distinctly see a large open boat working its way along the coast. It had not yet passed me. Rising to my knees I took my cap in one hand and tried to wave it but was constantly thwarted by my inability to hold myself up. I kept falling on my stomach. I much regretted then that I did not have Madame La Couture with me. She would have been able to go to the beach and run along it shouting for help and would certainly have attracted attention. But she was far away and surely beyond earshot of the shouts of the men in the boat. Otherwise she would have come running.

In her absence I did all that I could to make myself visible. I found a pole nearby. On it I fixed my cap and a scrap of the petticoat which my companion in misfortune had left me. This makeshift flag, wafted in the air, caught the attention of those in charge of the boat. I realized it both from their excited shouts and from an alteration in the course of their craft, which now veered toward the shore. I dug my pole into the sand so that they would not lose sight of my signal and let myself drop onto the sand. I lay at full stretch, worn out with the efforts I had just made, but comforted by the certainty of imminent deliverance. I thanked God for the blessing which He had been pleased to bestow on me.

Looking closely at the boat, I noticed that the men crewing it wore clothes. This observation, which persuaded me that I would be dealing with Europeans, rid my mind of fears which would certainly have troubled me had they been Indians. While awaiting my rescuers I cast my eyes toward the fireside, looking for Madame La Couture. I could not wait to see her so that I could tell her of and share with her our good luck. Without her I could not savor it fully. Her tender concern for me and her determination never to abandon me had confirmed the friendship between us, which had been engendered by our joint experience of misfortune. I could not see her and it took something from the joy of the moment; not much, because her happiness was sure to come. It could be delayed only very briefly. Her return could not be far off because it was getting late: nightfall was very close.

At that moment, the people I had been waiting for arrived. My extreme joy almost killed me. It precipitated a physical reaction so severe that, for several minutes, I could not answer their questions. I could not utter even one word. They gave me a drop of taffia to steady me and I was able to say something of my ordeal. At once they realized the danger of my condition and had the good sense not to make me talk much. I was delighted to see Europeans. I knew from the way they spoke French that it was not their native language, but did not ask their nationality. Actually it was of no importance. It was enough that I was among men who wanted to help me.

I begged them to resume their hailing while searching in the nearby copse, so that Madame La Couture might hear them. Her prolonged absence had begun to worry me but, a moment later, all my fears evaporated. She appeared, running toward me with all her might. She had caught the turkey-hen and had brought its nest too.

from Typee

by Herman Melville

Herman Melville (1819–1891) in 1842 joined a whaling expedition to the Pacific Ocean. After six months at sea the crew put in at the Marquesas Islands in Polynesia. Melville and his shipmate Toby, fed up with the ship's tyrannical captain, deserted. They eventually encountered and befriended the Typees, islanders reputed to be cannibals. Toby disappeared, and an ailing Melville became a captive.

It must have been more than four months since I entered the valley, when one day, about noon, and whilst everything was in profound silence, Mow-Mow, the one-eyed chief, suddenly appeared at the door, and leaning forward towards me as I lay directly facing him, said, in a low tone, "Toby pemi ena," (Toby has arrived here). Gracious heaven! What a tumult of emotions rushed upon me at this startling intelligence! Insensible to the pain that had before distracted me, I leaped to my feet, and called wildly to Kory-Kory, who was reposing by my side. The startled islanders sprang from their mats; the news was quickly communicated to them; and the next moment I was making my way to the Ti on the back of Kory-Kory, and surrounded by the excited savages.

All that I could comprehend of the particulars which Mow-Mow rehearsed to his auditors as we proceeded, was that my long-lost companion had arrived in a boat which had just entered the bay. These tidings made me most anxious to be carried at once to the sea, lest some untoward circumstance should prevent our meeting; but to this they would not consent, and continued their course towards the royal abode. As we approached it, Mehevi and several chiefs showed themselves from the piazza, and called upon us loudly to come to them.

As soon as we had approached, I endeavoured to make them understand that I was going down to the sea to meet Toby. To this the king objected, and motioned Kory-Kory to bring me into the house. It was in vain to resist; and in a few moments I found myself within the Ti, surrounded by a noisy group engaged in discussing the recent intelligence. Toby's name was frequently repeated, coupled with violent exclamations of astonishment. It seemed as if they yet remained in doubt with regard to the fact of his arrival, and at every fresh report that was brought from the shore they betrayed the liveliest emotions.

Almost frenzied at being held in this state of suspense, I passionately besought Mehevi to permit me to proceed. Whether my companion had arrived or not, I felt a presentiment that my own fate was about to be decided. Again and again I renewed my petition to Mehevi. He regarded me with a fixed and serious eye, but at length, yielding to my importunity, reluctantly granted my request.

Accompanied by some fifty of the natives, I now rapidly continued my journey, every few moments being transferred from the back of one to another, and urging my bearer forward all the while with earnest entreaties. As I thus hurried forward, no doubt as to the truth of the information I had received ever crossed my mind. I was alive only to the one overwhelming idea, that a chance of deliverance was now afforded me, if the jealous opposition of the savages could be overcome.

Having been prohibited from approaching the sea during the whole of my stay in the valley, I had always associated with it the idea of escape. Toby, too,—if indeed he had ever voluntarily deserted me,— must have effected his flight by the sea; and now that I was drawing near to it myself, I indulged in hopes which I had never felt before. It was evident that a boat had entered the bay, and I saw little reason to doubt the truth of the report that it had brought my companion. Every time, therefore, that we gained an elevation, I looked eagerly around, hoping to behold him.

In the midst of an excited throng, who by their violent gestures and wild cries appeared to be under the influence of some excitement as strong as my own, I was now borne along at a rapid trot, frequently stooping my head to avoid the branches which crossed the path, and never ceasing to implore those who carried me to accelerate their already swift pace.

In this manner we had proceeded about four or five miles, when we were met by a party of some twenty islanders, between whom and those who accompanied me ensued an animated conference. Impatient of the delay occasioned by this interruption, I was beseeching the man who carried me to proceed without his loitering companions, when Kory-Kory, running to my side, informed me, in three fatal words, that the news had all proved false—that Toby had not arrived. "Toby owlee permi." Heaven only knows how, in the state of mind and body I then was, I ever sustained the agony which this intelligence caused me; not that the news was altogether unexpected, but I had trusted that the fact might not have been made known until we should have arrived upon the beach. As it was, I at once foresaw the course the savages would pursue. They had only yielded thus far to my entreaties, that I might give a joyful welcome to my long-lost comrade; but now that it was known he had not arrived, they would at once oblige me to turn back.

My anticipations were but too correct. In spite of the resistance I made, they carried me into a house which was near the spot, and left me upon the mats. Shortly afterwards, several of those who had accompanied me from the Ti, detaching themselves from the others, proceeded in the direction of the sea. Those who remained—among whom were Marheyo, Mow-Mow, Kory-Kory, and Tinor—gathered about the dwelling, and appeared to be awaiting their return.

This convinced me that strangers—perhaps some of my own countrymen—had for some cause or other entered the bay. Distracted at the idea of their vicinity, and reckless of the pain which I suffered, I heeded not the assurances of the islanders that there were no boats at the beach, but, starting to my feet, endeavoured to gain the door. Instantly the passage was blocked up by several men, who commanded me to resume my seat. The fierce looks of the irritated savages admonished me that I could gain nothing by force, and that it was by entreaty alone that I could hope to compass my object.

Guided by this consideration, I turned to Mow-Mow, the only chief present, whom I had been much in the habit of seeing, and, carefully concealing my real design, tried to make him comprehend that I still believed Toby to have arrived on the shore, and besought him to allow me to go forward to welcome him. To all his repeated assertions that my companion had not been seen, I pretended to turn a deaf ear: while I urged my solicitations with an eloquence of gesture which the one-eyed chief appeared unable to resist. He seemed, indeed, to regard me as a froward child, to whose wishes he had not the heart to oppose force, and whom he must consequently humour. He spoke a few words to the natives, who at once retreated from the door, and I immediately passed out of the house.

Here I looked earnestly round for Kory-Kory; but that hitherto faithful servitor was nowhere to be seen. Unwilling to linger even for a single instant when every moment might be so important, I motioned to a muscular fellow near me to take me upon his back: to my surprise he angrily refused. I turned to another, but with a like result. A third attempt was as unsuccessful, and I immediately perceived what had induced Mow-Mow to grant my request, and why the other natives conducted themselves in so strange a manner. It was evident that the chief had only given me liberty to continue my progress towards the sea, because he supposed that I was deprived of the means of reaching it.

Convinced by this of their determination to retain me a captive, I became desperate; and almost insensible to the pain which I suffered, I seized a spear which was leaning against the projecting eaves of the house, and, supporting myself with it, resumed the path that swept by the dwelling. To my surprise, I was suffered to proceed alone, all the natives remaining in front of the house, and engaging in earnest conversation, which every moment became more loud and vehement; and, to my unspeakable delight, I perceived that some difference of opinion had arisen between them; that two parties, in short, were formed, and consequently that, in their divided counsels, there was some chance of my deliverance.

Before I had proceeded a hundred yards I was again surrounded by the savages, who were still in all the heat of argument, and appeared every moment as if they would come to blows. In the midst of this tumult old Marheyo came to my side, and I shall never forget the benevolent expression of his countenance. He placed his arm upon my shoulder, and emphatically pronounced one expressive English word I had taught him—"Home." I at once understood what he meant, and eagerly expressed my thanks to him. Fayaway and Kory-Kory were by his side, both weeping violently; and it was not until the old man had twice repeated the command that his son could bring himself to obey him, and take me again upon his back. The one-eyed chief opposed his doing so, but he was overruled, and, as it seemed to me, by some of his own party.

We proceeded onwards, and never shall I forget the ecstacy I felt when I first heard the roar of the surf breaking upon the beach. Before long, I saw the flashing billows themselves through the opening between the trees. Oh! glorious sight and sound of ocean! with what rapture did I hail you as familiar friends. By this time the shouts of the crowd upon the beach were distinctly audible, and in the blended confusion of sounds I almost fancied I could distinguish the voices of my own countrymen.

When we reached the open space which lay between the groves and the sea, the first object that met my view was an English whale-boat, lying with her bow pointed from the shore, and only a few fathoms distant from it. It was manned by five islanders, dressed in short tunics of calico. My first impression was that they were in the very act of pulling out from the bay; and that, after all my exertions, I had come too late. My soul sunk within me: but a second glance convinced me that the boat was only hanging off to keep out of the surf; and the next moment I heard my own name shouted out by a voice from the midst of the crowd.

Looking in the direction of the sound, I perceived, to my indescribable joy, the tall figure of Karakoee, an Oahu Kannaka, who had often been aboard the *Dolly* while she lay in Nukuheva. He wore the green shooting-jacket, with gilt buttons, which had been given to him by an officer of the *Reine Blanche*—the French flag-ship—and in which I had always seen him dressed. I now remembered the Kannaka had frequently told me that his person was tabooed in all the valleys of the island, and the sight of him at such a moment as this filled my heart with a tumult of delight.

Karakoee stood near the edge of the water with a large roll of cotton-cloth thrown over one arm, and holding two or three canvas bags of powder, while with the other hand he grasped a musket, which he appeared to be proffering to several of the chiefs around him. But they turned with disgust from his offers, and seemed to be impatient at his presence, with vehement gestures waving him off to his boat, and commanding him to depart.

The Kannaka, however, still maintained his ground, and I at once perceived that he was seeking to purchase my freedom. Animated by the idea, I called upon him loudly to come to me; but he replied, in broken English, that the islanders had threatened to pierce him with their spears, if he stirred a foot towards me. At this time I was still advancing, surrounded by a dense throng of the natives, several of whom had their hands upon me, and more than one javelin was threateningly pointed at me. Still I perceived clearly that many of those least friendly towards me looked irresolute and anxious.

I was still some thirty yards from Karakoee, when my farther progress was prevented by the natives, who compelled me to sit down upon the ground, while they still retained their hold upon my arms. The din and tumult now became tenfold, and I perceived that several of the priests were on the spot, all of whom were evidently urging Mow-Mow and the other chiefs to prevent my departure; and the detestable word—"Roo—ne! Roo—ne!" which I had heard repeated a thousand times during the day, was now shouted on every side of me. Still I saw that the Kannaka continued his exertions in my favour—that he was boldly debating the matter with the savages, and was striving to entice them by displaying his cloth and powder, and snapping the lock of his musket. But all he said or did appeared only to augment the clamours of those around him, who seemed bent upon driving him into the sea.

When I remembered the extravagant value placed by these people upon the articles which were offered to them in exchange for me, and , which were so indignantly rejected, I saw a new proof of the same fixed determination of purpose they had all along manifested with regard to me, and in despair, and reckless of consequences, I exerted all my strength, and, shaking myself free from the grasp of those who held me, I sprang upon my feet and rushed towards Karakoee.

The rash attempt nearly decided my fate; for, fearful that I might slip from them, several of the islanders now raised a simultaneous shout, and pressing upon Karakoee, they menaced him with furious gestures, and actually forced him into the sea. Appalled at their violence, the poor fellow, standing nearly to the waist in the surf, endeavoured to pacify them; but at length, fearful that they would do him some fatal violence, he beckoned to his comrades to pull in at once, and take him into the boat.

It was at this agonizing moment, when I thought all hope was ended, that a new contest arose between the two parties who had accompanied me to the shore; blows were struck, wounds were given, and blood flowed. In the interest excited by the fray, every one had left me except Marheyo, Kory-Kory, and poor dear Fayaway, who clung to me, sobbing convulsively. I saw that now or never was the moment. Clasping my hands together, I looked imploringly at Marheyo, and moved towards the now almost deserted beach. The tears were in the old man's eyes, but neither he nor Kory-Kory attempted to hold me, and I soon reached the Kannaka, who had anxiously watched my movements; the rowers pulled in as near as they dared to the edge of the surf; I gave one parting embrace to Fayaway, who seemed speech-less with sorrow, and the next instant I found myself safe in the boat,

and Karakoee by my side, who told the rowers at once to give way.
Marheyo and Kory-Kory, and a great many of the women, followed me
into the water, and I was determined, as the only mark of gratitude I
could show, to give them the articles which had been brought as my
ransom. I handed the musket to Kory-Kory, in doing which he would
fain have taken hold of me, threw the roll of cotton to old Marheyo,
pointing as I did so to poor Fayaway, who had retired from the edge of
the water, and was sitting down disconsolate on the beach, and tum-
bled the powder-bags out to the nearest young ladies, all of whom were
vastly willing to take them. This distribution did not occupy ten seconds, and before it was over the boat was under full way, the Kannaka
all the while exclaiming loudly against what he considered a useless
throwing away of valuable property.

Although it was clear that my movements had been noticed by several of the natives, still they had not suspended the conflict in which
they were engaged, and it was not until the boat was above fifty yards
from the shore, that Mow-Mow and some six or seven other warriors
rushed into the sea and hurled their javelins at us. Some of the
weapons passed quite as close to us as was desirable, but no one was
wounded, and the men pulled away gallantly. But although soon out
of the reach of the spears, our progress was extremely slow; it blew
strong upon the shore, and the tide was against us; and I saw Karakoee,
who was steering the boat, give many a look towards a jutting point of
the bay round which we had to pass.

For a minute or two after our departure, the savages, who had
formed into different groups, remained perfectly motionless and
silent. All at once the enraged chief showed by his gestures that he had
resolved what course he would take. Shouting loudly to his companions, and pointing with his tomahawk towards the headland, he set off
at full speed in that direction, and was followed by about thirty of the
natives, among whom were several of the priests, all yelling out,
"Roo—ne! Roo—ne!" at the very top of their voices. Their intention
was evidently to swim off from the headland and intercept us in our
course. The wind was freshening every minute, and was right in our

teeth, and it vas one of those chopping, angry seas, in which it is so difficult to row. Still the chances seemed in our favour, but when we came within a hundred yards of the point, the active savages were already dashing into the water, and we all feared that within five minutes' time we should have a score of the infuriated wretches around us. If so our doom was sealed, for these savages, unlike the feeble swimmers of civilized countries, are, if anything, more formidable antagonists in the water than when on the land. It was all a trial of strength; our natives pulled till their oars bent again, and the crowd of swimmers shot through the water, despite its roughness, with fearful rapidity.

By the time we had reached the headland, the savages were spread right across our course. Our rowers got out their knives and held them ready between their teeth, and I seized the boat-hook. We were all aware that if they succeeded in intercepting us, they would practise upon us the manœuvre which proved so fatal to many a boat's crew in these seas. They would grapple the oars, and, seizing hold of the gunwale, capsize the boat, and then we should be entirely at their mercy.

After a few breathless moments I discerned Mow-Mow. The athletic islander, with his tomahawk between his teeth, was dashing the water before him till it foamed again. He was the nearest to us, and in another instant he would have seized one of the oars. Even at the moment I felt horror at the act I was about to commit; but it was no time for pity or compunction, and with true aim, and exerting all my strength, I dashed the boat-hook at him. It struck him just below the throat, and forced him downwards. I had no time to repeat the blow, but I saw him rise to the surface in the wake of the boat, and never shall I forget the ferocious expression of his countenance.

Only one other of the savages reached the boat. He seized the gunwale, but the knives of our rowers so mauled his wrists that he was forced to quit his hold, and the next minute we were past them all, and in safety. The strong excitement which had thus far kept me up, now left me, and I fell back fainting into the arms of Karakoee.

• • •

The circumstances connected with my most unexpected escape may be very briefly stated. The captain of an Australian vessel being in distress for men in these remote seas, had put into Nukuheva in order to recruit his ship's company, but not a single man was to be obtained; and the barque was about to get under weigh, when she was boarded by Karakoee, who informed the disappointed Englishman that an American sailor was detained by the savages in the neighbouring bay of Typee; and he offered, if supplied with suitable articles of traffic, to undertake his release. The Kannaka had gained his intelligence from Marnoo, to whom, after all, I was indebted for my escape. The proposition was acceded to; and Karakoee, taking with him five tabooed natives of Nukuheva, again repaired aboard the barque, which in a few hours sailed to that part of the island, and threw her main-top-sail aback right off the entrance to the Typee bay. The whaleboat, manned by the tabooed crew, pulled towards the head of the inlet, while the ship lay "off and on" awaiting its return.

The events which ensued have already been detailed, and little more remains to be related. On reaching the *Julia,* I was lifted over the side, and my strange appearance, and remarkable adventure, occasioned the liveliest interest. Every attention was bestowed upon me that humanity could suggest; but to such a state was I reduced, that three months elapsed before I recovered my health.

The mystery which hung over the fate of my friend and companion, Toby, has never been cleared up. I still remain ignorant whether he succeeded in leaving the valley, or perished at the hands of the islanders.

from Robinson Crusoe

by Daniel Defoe

Daniel Defoe (1660–1731) based The Life and Strange Surprizing Adventures of Robinson Crusoe on the story of English seaman Alexander Selkirk, a castaway on one of Chile's Juan Fernández islands. Robinson for 20 years believes himself alone, then sees a human foot-print in the sand. Here we meet him soon after he has caught his first glimpse of the "savages" who may have left it.

I t was one of the nights in the rainy season in March, the four and twentieth year of my first setting foot in this island of solitariness. I was lying in my bed, or hammock, awake, very well in health, had no pain, no distemper, no uneasiness of body, no, nor any uneasiness of mind, more than ordinary, but could by no means close my eyes, that is, so as to sleep; no, not a wink all night long, otherwise than as follows.

It is as impossible, as needless, to set down the innumerable crowd of thoughts that whirled through that great thoroughfare of the brain, the memory, in this night's time. I ran over the whole history of my life in miniature, or by abridgment, as I may call it, to my coming to this island, and also of the part of my life since I came to this island. In my reflections upon the state of my case since I came on shore on this island, I was comparing the happy posture of my affairs in the first years of my habitation here compared to the life of anxiety, fear, and care which I had lived ever since I had seen the print of a foot in the sand; not that I did not believe the savages had frequented the island even all the while, and might have been several hundreds of them at times on shore there; but I had never known it, and was incapable of any apprehensions about it. My satisfaction was perfect, though my danger was the same; and I was as happy in not knowing my danger, as if I had never really been exposed to it. This furnished my thoughts with many very profitable reflections, and particularly this one: how infinitely good that Providence is which has provided, in its government of mankind, such narrow bounds to his sight and knowledge of things; and though he walks in the midst of so many thousand dangers, the sight of which, if discovered to him, would distract his mind and sink his spirits, he is kept serene and calm, by having the events of things hid from his eyes, and knowing nothing of the dangers which surround him.

After these thoughts had for some time entertained me, I came to reflect seriously upon the real danger I had been in for so many years in this very island, and how I had walked about in the greatest security, and with all possible tranquillity, even when perhaps nothing but a brow of a hill, a great tree, or the casual approach of night had been between me and the worst kind of destruction, viz., that of falling into the hands of cannibals and savages, who would have seized on me with the same view as I did of a goat or a turtle, and have thought it no more a crime to kill and devour me, than I did of a pigeon or a curlew. I would unjustly slander myself if I should say I was not sincerely thankful to my great Preserver, to whose singular protection I acknowledged, with great humility, that all these unknown deliverances were due, and without which I must inevitably have fallen into their merciless hands.

When these thoughts were over, my head was for some time taken up in considering the nature of these wretched creatures, I mean the savages, and how it came to pass in the world that the wise Governor of all things should give up any of His creatures to such inhumanity; nay, to something so much below even brutality itself, as to devour its own kind. But as this ended in some (at that time fruitless) speculations, it occurred to me to inquire what part of the world these wretches lived in? how far off the coast was from whence they came? what they ventured over so far from home for? what kind of boats they had? and why I might not order myself and my business so, that I might be as able to go over thither, as they were to come to me.

I never so much as troubled myself to consider what I should do with myself when I came thither; what would become of me, if I fell into the hands of the savages; or how I should escape from them, if they attempted me; no, nor so much as how it was possible for me to reach the coast, and not be attempted by some or other of them, without any possibility of delivering myself; and if I should not fall into their hands, what I should do for provision; or whither I should bend my course. None of these thoughts, I say, so much as came in my way; but my mind was wholly bent upon the notion of my passing over in my boat to the mainland. I looked back upon my present condition as the most miserable that could possibly be; that I was not able to throw myself into anything, but death, that could be called worse; that if I reached the shore of the main, I might perhaps meet with relief, or I might coast along, as I did on the shore of Africa, till I came to some inhabited country, and where I might find some relief; and after all, perhaps I might fall in with some Christian ship that might take me in; and if the worse came to the worst, I could but die, which would put an end to all these miseries at once. Pray, note, all this was the fruit of a disturbed mind, an impatient temper, made as it were desperate by the long continuance of my troubles, and the disappointments I had met in the wreck I had been on board of, and where I had been so near the obtaining what I so earnestly longed for, viz., somebody to speak to, and to learn some knowledge from of the place where I was, and of the probable means of my deliverance. I say, I was agitated wholly by these thoughts. All my calm of mind, in my resignation to Providence, and waiting the issue of the dispositions of Heaven, seemed to be suspended; and I had, as it were, no power to turn my thoughts to anything but to the project of a voyage to the main, which came upon me with such force, and such an impetuosity of desire, that it was not to be resisted.

When this had agitated my thoughts for two hours, or more, with such violence that it set my very blood into a ferment, and my pulse beat as high as if I had been in a fever, merely with the extraordinary fervor of my mind about it, Nature, as if I had been fatigued and exhausted with the very thought of it, threw me into a sound sleep. One would have thought I should have dreamed of it, but I did not, nor of anything relating to it; but I dreamed that as I was going out in the morning, as usual, from my castle, I saw upon the shore two canoes and eleven savages coming to land, and that they brought with them another savage, whom they were going to kill in order to eat him; when, on a sudden, the savage that they were going to kill jumped away, and ran for his life. And I thought, in my sleep, that he came running into my little thick grove before my fortification to hide himself; and that I, seeing him alone, and not perceiving that the others sought him that way, showed myself to him, and smiling upon him, encouraged him; that he kneeled down to me, seeming to pray me to assist him; upon which I showed my ladder, made him go up, and carried him into my cave, and he became my servant; and that as soon as I had gotten this man, I said to myself, "Now I may certainly venture to the mainland; for this fellow will serve me as a pilot, and will tell me what to do, and whither to go for provisions, and whither not to go for fear of being devoured; what places to venture into, and what to escape." I waked with this thought, and was under such inexpressible impressions of joy at the prospect of my escape in my dream, that the disappointments which I felt upon coming to myself and finding it was no more than a dream were equally extravagant the other way, and threw me into a very great dejection of spirit.

Upon this, however, I made this conclusion; that my only way to go about an attempt for an escape was, if possible, to get a savage into my possession; and, if possible, it should be one of their prisoners whom they had condemned to be eaten, and should bring thither to kill. But these thoughts still were attended with this difficulty, that it was impossible to effect this without attacking a whole caravan of them, and killing them all; and this was not only a very desperate attempt, and might miscarry, but, on the other hand, I had greatly scrupled the lawfulness of it to me; and my heart trembled at the thoughts of shedding so much blood, though it was for my deliverance. I need not repeat the arguments which occurred to me against this, they being the same mentioned before. But though I had other reasons to offer now, viz., that those men were enemies to my life, and would devour me if they could; that it was self-preservation, in the highest degree, to deliver myself from this death of a life, and was acting in my own defence as much as if they were actually assaulting me, and the like; I say, though these things argued for it, yet the thoughts of shedding human blood for my deliverance were very terrible to me, and such as I could by no means reconcile myself to a great while.

However, at last, after many secret disputes with myself, and after great perplexities about it, for all these arguments, one way and another, struggled in my head a long time, the eager prevailing desire of deliverance at length mastered all the rest, and I resolved, if possible, to get one of those savages into my hands, cost what it would. My next thing then was to contrive how to do it, and this indeed was very difficult to resolve on. But as I could pitch upon no probable means for it, so I resolved to put myself upon the watch, to see them when they came on shore, and leave the rest to the event, taking such measures as the opportunity should present, let be what would be.

With these resolutions in my thoughts, I set myself upon the scout as often as possible, and indeed so often, till I was heartily tired of it; for it was above a year and half that I waited; and for great part of that time went out to the west end, and to the south-west corner of the island, almost every day, to see for canoes, but none appeared. This was very discouraging, and began to trouble me much; though I cannot say that it did in this case, as it had done some time before that, viz., wear off the edge of my desire to the thing. But the longer it seemed to be delayed, the more eager I was for it. In a word, I was not at first so careful to shun the sight of these savages, and avoid being seen by them, as I was now eager to be upon them.

Besides, I fancied myself able to manage one, nay, two or three savages, if I had them, so as to make them entirely slaves to me, to do whatever I should direct them, and to prevent their being able at any time to do me any hurt. It was a great while that I pleased myself with this affair; but nothing still presented. All my fancies and schemes came to nothing, for no savages came near me for a great while.

About a year and half after I had entertained these notions, and by long musing had, as it were, resolved them all into nothing, for want of an occasion to put them in execution, I was surprised, one morning early, with seeing no less than five canoes all on shore together on my side the island, and the people who belonged to them all landed, and out of my sight. The number of them broke all my measures; for seeing so many, and knowing that they always came four, or six, or sometimes more, in a boat, I could not tell what to think of it, or how to take my measures to attack twenty or thirty men single-handed; so I lay still in my castle, perplexed and discomforted. However, I put myself into all the same postures for an attack that I had formerly provided, and was just ready for action if anything had presented. Having waited a good while, listening to hear if they made any noise, at length, being very impatient, I set my guns at the foot of my ladder, and clambered up to the top of the hill, by my two stages, as usual; standing so, however, that my head did not appear above the hill, so that they could not perceive me by any means. Here I observed, by the help of my perspective-glass, that they were no less than thirty in number, that they had a fire kindled, that they had had meat dressed. How they had cooked it, that I knew not, or what it was; but they were all dancing, in I know not how many barbarous gestures and figures, their own way, round the fire.

While I was thus looking on them, I perceived by my perspective two miserable wretches dragged from the boats, where, it seems, they were laid by, and were now brought out for the slaughter. I perceived one of them immediately fell, being knocked down, I suppose, with a club or wooden sword, for that was their way, and two or three others were at work immediately, cutting him open for their cookery, while the other victim was left standing by himself, till they should be ready for him. In that very moment this poor wretch seeing himself a little at liberty, Nature inspired him with hopes of life, and he started away from them, and ran with incredible swiftness along the sands directly towards me, I mean towards that part of the coast where my habitation was.

I was dreadfully frightened (that I must acknowledge) when I perceived him to run my way, and especially when, as I thought, I saw him pursued by the whole body; and now I expected that part of my dream was coming to pass, and that he would certainly take shelter in my grove; but I could not depend, by any means, upon my dream for the rest of it, viz., that the other savages would not pursue him thither, and find him there. However, I kept my station, and my spirits began to recover when I found that there was not above three men that followed him; and still more was I encouraged when I found that he outstripped them exceedingly in running, and gained ground of them; so that if he could but hold it for half an hour, I saw easily he would fairly get away from them all.

There was between them and my castle the creek, which I mentioned often at the first part of my story, when I landed my cargoes out of the ship; and this I saw plainly he must necessarily swim over, or the poor wretch would be taken there. But when the savage escaping came thither he made nothing of it, though the tide was then up; but plunging in, swam through in about thirty strokes or thereabouts, landed, and ran on with exceeding strength and swiftness. When the three persons came to the creek, I found that two of them could swim, but the third could not, and that, standing on the other side, he looked at the other, but went no farther, and soon after went softly back, which, as it happened, was very well for him in the main.

I observed, that the two who swam were yet more than twice as long swimming over the creek as the fellow was that fled from them. It came now very warmly upon my thoughts, and indeed irresistibly, that now was my time to get me a servant, and perhaps a companion or assistant, and that I was called plainly by Providence to save this poor creature's life. I immediately ran down the ladders with all possible expedition, fetched my two guns, for they were both but at the foot of the ladders, as I observed above, and getting up again, with the same haste, to the top of the hill, I crossed toward the sea, and having a very short cut, and all down hill, clapped myself in the way between the pursuers and the pursued, hallooing aloud to him that fled, who, looking back, was at first perhaps as much frightened at me as at them; and I beckoned with my hand to him to come back; and, in the meantime, I slowly advanced towards the two that followed; then rushing at once upon the foremost, I knocked him down with the stock of my piece. I was loth to fire, because I would not have the rest hear; though, at that distance, it would not have been easily heard, and being out of sight of the smoke too, they would not have easily known what to make of it. Having knocked this fellow down, the other who pursued with him stopped, as if he had been frightened, and I advanced apace towards him; but as I came nearer, I perceived presently he had a bow and arrow, and was fitting it to shoot at me; so I was then necessitated to shoot at him first, which I did, and killed him at the first shot.

The poor savage who fled, but had stopped, though he saw both his enemies fallen and killed, as he thought, yet was so frightened with the fire and noise of my piece, that he stood stock-still, and neither came forward nor went backward, though he seemed rather inclined to fly still, than to come on.

I hallooed again to him, and made signs to come forward, which he easily understood, and came a little way, then stopped again, and then a little farther, and stopped again; and I could then perceive that he stood trembling, as if he had been taken prisoner, and had just been to be killed, as his two enemies were. I beckoned him again to come to me, and gave him all the signs of encouragement that I could think of; and he came nearer and nearer, kneeling down every ten or twelve steps, in token of acknowledgment for my saving his life. I smiled at him, and looked pleasantly, and beckoned to him to come still nearer.

At length he came close to me, and then he kneeled down again, kissed the ground, and laid his head upon the ground, and taking me by the foot, set my foot upon his head. This, it seems, was in token of swearing to be my slave for ever. I took him up, and made much of him, and encouraged him all I could. But there was more work to do yet; for I perceived the savage whom I knocked down was not killed, but stunned with the blow, and began to come to himself; so I pointed to him, and showing him the savage, that he was not dead, upon this he spoke some words to me; and though I could not understand them, yet I thought they were pleasant to hear; for they were the first sound of a man's voice that I had heard, my own excepted, for above twenty-five years. But there was no time for such reflections now. The savage who was knocked down recovered himself so far as to sit up upon the ground and I perceived that my savage began to be afraid; but when I saw that, I presented my other piece at the man, as if I would shoot him. Upon this my savage, for so I call him now, made a motion to me to lend him my sword, which hung naked in a belt by my side; so I did. He no sooner had it but he runs to his enemy, and, at one blow, cut off his head as cleverly, no executioner in Germany could have done it sooner or better; which I thought very strange for one who, I had reason to believe, never saw a sword in his life before, except their own wooden swords. However, it seems, as I learned afterwards, they make their wooden swords so sharp, so heavy, and the wood is so hard, that they will cut off heads even with them, ay, and arms, and that at one blow too. When he had done this, he came laughing to me in sign of triumph, and brought me the sword again, and with abundance of gestures, which I did not understand, laid it down, with the head of the savage that he had killed, just before me.

But that which astonished him most was to know how I had killed the other Indian so far off; so pointing to him, he made signs to me to let him go to him; so I bade him go, as well as I could. When he came to him, he stood like one amazed, looking at him, turned him first on one side, then on t'other, looked at the wound the bullet had made, which, it seems, was just in his breast, where it had made a hole, and no great quantity of blood had followed; but he had bled inwardly, for he was quite dead. He took up his bow and arrows, and came back; so I turned to go away, and beckoned to him to follow me making signs to him that more might come after them.

Upon this he signed to me that he should bury them with sand, that they might not be seen by the rest if they followed; and so I made signs again to him to do so. He fell to work, and in an instant he had scraped a hole in the sand with his hands big enough to bury the first in, and then dragged him into it, and covered him, and did so also by the other. I believe he had buried them both in a quarter of an hour. Then calling him away, I carried him, not to my castle, but quite away to my cave, on the farther part of the island; so I did not let my dream come to pass in that part, viz., that he came into my grove for shelter.

Here I gave him bread and a bunch of raisins to eat, and a draught of water, which I found he was indeed in great distress for, by his running; and having refreshed him, I made signs for him to go lie down and sleep, pointing to a place where I had laid a great parcel of rice-straw, and a blanket upon it, which I used to sleep upon myself sometimes; so the poor creature lay down, and went to sleep.

He was a comely, handsome fellow, perfectly well made, with straight strong limbs, not too large, tall, and well-shaped, and, as I reckon, about twenty-six years of age. He had a very good countenance, not a fierce and surly aspect, but seemed to have something very manly in his face; and yet he had all the sweetness and softness of an European in his countenance too, especially when he smiled. His hair was long and black, not curled like wool; his forehead very high and large; and a great vivacity and sparkling sharpness in his eyes. The color of his skin was not quite black, but very tawny; and yet not of an ugly, yellow, nauseous tawny, as the Brazilians and Virginians, and other natives of America are, but of a bright kind of a dun olive color, that had in it something very agreeable, though not very easy to describe. His face was round and plump; his nose small, not flat like the negroes; a very good mouth, thin lips, and his fine teeth well set, and white as ivory.

After he had slumbered, rather than slept, about half an hour, he waked again, and came out of the cave to me, for I had been milking my goats, which I had in the enclosure just by. When he espied me, he came running to me, laying himself down again upon the ground, with all the possible signs of an humble, thankful disposition, making many antic gestures to show it. At last he lays his head flat upon the ground, close to my foot, and sets my other foot upon his head, as he had done before, and after this made all the signs to me of subjection, servitude, and submission imaginable, to let me know how he would serve me as long as he lived. I understood him in many things, and let him know I was very well pleased with him. In a little time I began to speak to him, and teach him to speak to me; and, first, I made him know his name should be Friday, which was the day I saved his life. I called him so for the memory of the time. I likewise taught him to say master, and then let him know that was to be my name. I likewise taught him to say Yes and No, and to know the meaning of them. I gave him some milk in an earthen pot, and let him see me drink it before him, and sop my bread in it; and I gave him a cake of bread to do the like, which he quickly complied with, and made signs that it was very good for him.

I kept there with him all that night; but as soon as it was day, I beckoned to him to come with me, and let him know I would give him some clothes; at which he seemed very glad, for he was stark naked. As we went by the place where he had buried the two men, he pointed exactly to the place, and showed me the marks that he had made to find them again, making signs to me that we should dig them up again, and eat them. At this I appeared very angry, expressed my abhorrence of it, made as if I would vomit at the thoughts of it, and beckoned with my hand to him to come away; which he did immediately, with great submission. I then led him up to the top of the hill, to see if his enemies were gone; and pulling out my glass, I looked, and saw plainly the place where they had been, but no appearance of them or of their canoes; so that it was plain that they were gone, and had left their two comrades behind them, without any search after them.

But I was not content with this discovery; but having now more courage, and consequently more curiosity, I took my man Friday with me, giving him the sword in his hand, with the bow and arrows at his back, which I found he could use very dexterously, making him carry one gun for me, and I two for myself, and away we marched to the place where these creatures had been; for I had a mind now to get some fuller intelligence of them. When I came to the place, my blood ran chill in my veins, and my heart sunk within me, at the horror of the spectacle. Indeed, it was a dreadful sight, at least it was so to me, though Friday made nothing of it. The place was covered with human bones, the ground dyed with their blood, great pieces of flesh left here and there, half-eaten, mangled, and scorched; and, in short, all the tokens of the triumphant feast they had been making there, after a victory over their enemies. I saw three skulls, five hands, and the bones of three or four legs and feet, and abundance of other parts of the bodies; and Friday, by his signs, made me understand that they brought over four prisoners to feast upon; that three of them were eaten up, and that he, pointing to himself, was the fourth; that there had been a great battle between them and their next king, whose subjects it seems he had been one of, and that they had taken a great number of prisoners; all of which were carried to several places by those that had taken them in the fight, in order to feast upon them, as was done here by these wretches upon those they brought hither.

I caused Friday to gather all the skulls, bones, flesh, and whatever remained, and lay them together on a heap, and make a great fire upon it, and burn them all to ashes. I found Friday had still a hankering stomach after some of the flesh, and was still a cannibal in his nature; but I discovered so much abhorrence at the very thoughts of it, and at the least appearance of it, that he durst not discover it; for I had, by some means, let him know that I would kill him if he offered it.

When we had done this we came back to our castle, and there I fell to work for my man Friday; and, first of all, I gave him a pair of linen drawers, which I had out of the poor gunner's chest I mentioned, and which I found in the wreck; and which, with a little alteration, fitted him very well. Then I made him a jerkin of goat's skin, as well as my skill would allow, and I was now grown a tolerable good tailor; and I gave him a cap, which I had made of a hare-skin, very convenient and fashionable enough; and thus he was clothed for the present tolerably well, and was mighty well pleased to see himself almost as well clothed as his master. It is true he went awkwardly in these things at first; wearing the drawers was very awkward to him, and the sleeves of the waistcoat galled his shoulders, and the inside of his arms; but a little easing them where he complained they hurt him, and using himself to them, at length he took to them very well.

The next day after I came home to my hutch with him, I began to consider where I should lodge him. And that I might do well for him, and yet be perfectly easy myself, I made a little tent for him in the vacant place between my two fortifications, in the inside of the last and in the outside of the first; and as there was a door or entrance there into my cave, I made a formal framed door-case, and a door to it of boards, and set it up in the passage, a little within the entrance; and causing the door to open on the inside, I barred it up in the night, taking in my ladders too; so that Friday could in no way come at me in the inside of my innermost wall without making so much noise in getting over, that it must needs waken me; for my first wall had now a complete roof over it of long poles, covering all my tent, and leaning up to the side of the hill, which was again laid cross with smaller sticks instead of laths, and then thatched over a great thickness with the rice-straw, which was strong, like reeds; and at the hole or place which was left to go in or out by the ladder, I had placed a kind of trap-door, which, if it had been attempted on the outside, would not have opened at all, but would have fallen down, and made a great noise; and as to weapons, I took them all into my side every night.

But I needed none of all this precaution; for never man had a more faithful, loving, sincere servant than Friday was to me; without passions, sullenness, or designs, perfectly obliged and engaged; his very affections were tied to me, like those of a child to a father; and I dare say he would have sacrificed his life for the saving mine, upon any occasion whatsoever. The many testimonies he gave me of this put it out of doubt, and soon convinced me that I needed to use no precautions as to my safety on his account.

This frequently gave me occasion to observe, and that with wonder, that however it had pleased God, in His providence, and in the government of the works of His hands, to take from so great a part of the world of His creatures the best uses to which their faculties and the powers of their souls are adapted, yet that He has bestowed upon them the same powers, the same reason, the same affections, the same sentiments of kindness and obligation, the same passions and resentments of wrongs, the same sense of gratitude, sincerity, fidelity, and all the capacities of doing good, and receiving good, that He has given to us; and that when He pleases to offer to them occasions of exerting these, they are as ready, nay, more ready, to apply them to the right uses for which they were bestowed than we are. And this made me very melancholy sometimes, in reflecting, as the several occasions presented, how mean a use we make of all these, even though we have these powers enlightened by the great lamp of instruction, the Spirit of God, and by the knowledge of His Word added to our understanding; and why it has pleased God to hide the like saving knowledge from so many millions of souls, who, if I might judge by this poor savage, would make a much better use of it than we did.

From hence, I sometimes was led too far to invade the sovereignty of Providence, and as it were arraign the justice of so arbitrary a disposition of things, that should hide that light from some, and reveal it to others, and yet expect a like duty from both. But I shut it up, and checked my thoughts with this conclusion: first, that we did not know by what light and law these should be condemned; but that as God was necessarily, and by the nature of His being, infinitely holy and just, so it could not be but that if these creatures were all sentenced to absence from Himself, it was on account of sinning against that light, which, as the Scripture says, was a law to themselves, and by such rules as their consciences would acknowledge to be just, though the foundation was not discovered to us; and, second, that still, as we are all the clay in the hand of the potter, no vessel could say to Him, "Why hast Thou formed me thus?"

But to return to my new companion. I was greatly delighted with him, and made it my business to teach him everything that was proper to make him useful, handy, and helpful; but especially to make him speak, and understand me when I spake. And he was the aptest scholar that ever was; and particularly was so merry, so constantly diligent, and so pleased when he could but understand me, or make me understand him, that it was very pleasant to me to talk to him. And now my life began to be so easy, that I began to say to myself, that could I but have been safe from more savages, I cared not if I was never to remove from the place while I lived.

The Whale Tooth

by Jack London

Jack London (1876–1916) in 1906 began a 27-month voyage in his 43-foot boat Snark, sailing from San Francisco to the Polynesian Islands. His experiences provided material for many of his stories, including this one about a missionary and the people he hopes to convert.

I t was in the early days in Fiji, when John Starhurst arose in the mission house at Rewa Village and announced his intention of carrying the gospel throughout all Viti Levu. Now Viti Levu means the "Great Land," it being the largest island in a group composed of many large islands, to say nothing of hundreds of small ones. Here and there on the coasts, living by most precarious tenure, was a sprinkling of missionaries, traders, bêche-de-mer fishers, and whaleship deserters. The smoke of the hot ovens arose under their windows, and the bodies of the slain were dragged by their doors on the way to the feasting.

The Lotu, or the Worship, was progressing slowly, and, often, in crablike fashion. Chiefs, who announced themselves Christians and were welcomed into the body of the chapel, had a distressing habit of backsliding in order to partake of the flesh of some favorite enemy. Eat or be eaten had been the law of the land; and eat or be eaten promised to remain the law of the land for a long time to come. There were chiefs, such as Tanoa, Tuiveikoso, and Tuikilakila, who had literally eaten hundreds of their fellow men. But among these gluttons Ra Undreundre ranked highest. Ra Undreundre lived at Takiraki. He kept a register of his gustatory exploits. A row of stones outside his house marked the bodies he had eaten. This row was two hundred and thirty paces long, and the stones in it numbered eight hundred and seventy-two. Each stone represented a body. The row of stones might have been longer, had not Ra Undreundre unfortunately received a spear in the small of his back in a bush skirmish on Somo Somo and been served up on the table of Naungavuli, whose mediocre string of stones numbered only forty-eight.

The hard-worked, fever-stricken missionaries stuck doggedly to their task, at times despairing, and looking forward for some special manifestation, some outburst of Pentecostal fire that would bring a glorious harvest of souls. But cannibal Fiji had remained obdurate. The frizzle-headed man-eaters were loath to leave their fleshpots so long as the harvest of human carcases was plentiful. Sometimes, when the harvest was too plentiful, they imposed on the missionaries by letting the word slip out that on such a day there would be a killing and a barbecue. Promptly the missionaries would buy the lives of the victims with stick tobacco, fathoms of calico, and quarts of trade beads. Natheless the chiefs drove a handsome trade in thus disposing of their surplus live meat. Also, they could always go out and catch more.

It was at this juncture that John Starhurst proclaimed that he would carry the Gospel from coast to coast of the Great Land, and that he would begin by penetrating the mountain fastnesses of the headwaters of the Rewa River. His words were received with consternation.

The native teachers wept softly. His two fellow missionaries strove to dissuade him. The King of Rewa warned him that the mountain dwellers would surely kai-kai him—kai-kai meaning "to eat"—and that he, the King of Rewa, having become Lotu, would be put to the necessity of going to war with the mountain dwellers. That he could not conquer them he was perfectly aware. That they might come down the river and sack Rewa Village he was likewise perfectly aware. But what was he to do? If John Starhurst persisted in going out and being eaten, there would be a war that would cost hundreds of lives.

Later in the day a deputation of Rewa chiefs waited upon John Starhurst. He heard them patiently, and argued patiently with them, though he abated not a whit from his purpose. To his fellow missionaries he explained that he was not bent upon martyrdom; that the call had come for him to carry the Gospel into Viti Levu, and that he was merely obeying the Lord's wish.

To the traders who came and objected most strenuously of all, he said: "Your objections are valueless. They consist merely of the damage that may be done your businesses. You are interested in making money, but I am interested in saving souls. The heathen of this dark land must be saved."

John Starhurst was not a fanatic. He would have been the first man to deny the imputation. He was eminently sane and practical.

He was sure that his mission would result in good, and he had private visions of igniting the Pentecostal spark in the souls of the mountaineers and of inaugurating a revival that would sweep down out of the mountains and across the length and breadth of the Great Land from sea to sea and to the isles in the midst of the sea. There were no wild lights in his mild gray eyes, but only calm resolution and an unfaltering trust in the Higher Power that was guiding him.

One man only he found who approved of his project, and that was Ra Vatu, who secretly encouraged him and offered to lend him guides to the first foothills. John Starhurst, in turn, was greatly pleased by Ra Vatu's conduct. From an incorrigible heathen, with a heart as black as his practices, Ra Vatu was beginning to emanate light. He even spoke of becoming Lotu. True, three years before he had expressed a similar intention, and would have entered the church had not John Starhurst entered objection to his bringing his four wives along with him. Ra Vatu had had economic and ethical objections to monogamy. Besides, the missionary's hair-splitting objection had offended him; and, to prove that he was a free agent and a man of honor, he had swung his huge war club over Starhurst's head. Starhurst had escaped by rushing in under the club and holding on to him until help arrived. But all that was now forgiven and forgotten. Ra Vatu was coming into the church, not merely as a converted heathen, but as a converted polygamist as well. He was only waiting, he assured Starhurst, until his oldest wife, who was very sick, should die.

John Starhurst journeyed up the sluggish Rewa in one of Ra Vatu's canoes. This canoe was to carry him for two days, when, the head of navigation reached, it would return. Far in the distance, lifted into the sky, could be seen the great smoky mountains that marked the backbone of the Great Land. All day John Starhurst gazed at them with eager yearning.

Sometimes he prayed silently. At other times he was joined in prayer by Narau, a native teacher, who for seven years had been Lotu, ever since the day he had been saved from the hot oven by Dr. James Ellery Brown at the trifling expense of one hundred sticks of tobacco, two cotton blankets, and a large bottle of painkiller. At the last moment, after twenty hours of solitary supplication and prayer, Narau's ears had heard the call to go forth with John Starhurst on the mission to the mountains.

"Master, I will surely go with thee," he had announced.

John Starhurst had hailed him with sober delight. Truly, the Lord was with him thus to spur on so broken-spirited a creature as Narau.

"I am indeed without spirit, the weakest of the Lord's vessels," Narau explained, the first day in the canoe.

"You should have faith, stronger faith," the missionary chided him.

Another canoe journeyed up the Rewa that day. But it journeyed an hour astern, and it took care not to be seen. This canoe was also the property of Ra Vatu. In it was Erirola, Ra Vatu's first cousin and trusted henchman; and in the small basket that never left his hand was a whale tooth. It was a magnificent tooth, fully six inches long, beautifully proportioned, the ivory turned yellow and purple with age. This tooth was likewise the property of Ra Vatu; and in Fiji, when such a tooth goes forth, things usually happen. For this is the virtue of the whale tooth: Whoever accepts it cannot refuse the request that may accompany it or follow it. The request may be anything from a human life to a tribal alliance, and no Fijian is so dead to honor as to deny the request when once the tooth has been accepted. Sometimes the request hangs fire, or the fulfilment is delayed, with untoward consequences.

High up the Rewa, at the village of a chief, Mongondro by name, John Starhurst rested at the end of the second day of the journey. In the morning, attended by Narau, he expected to start on foot for the smoky mountains that were now green and velvety with nearness. Mongondro was a sweet-tempered, mild-mannered little old chief, short-sighted and afflicted with elephantiasis, and no longer inclined toward the turbulence of war. He received the missionary with warm hospitality, gave him food from his own table, and even discussed religious matters with him. Mongondro was of an inquiring bent of mind, and pleased John Starhurst greatly by asking him to account for the existence and beginning of things. When the missionary had finished his summary of the Creation according to Genesis, he saw that Mongondro was deeply affected. The little old chief smoked silently for some time. Then he took the pipe from his mouth and shook his head sadly.

"It cannot be," he said. "I, Mongondro, in my youth, was a good workman with the adze. Yet three months did it take me to make a canoe—a small canoe, a very small canoe. And you say that all this land and water was made by one man—"

"Nay, was made by one God, the only true God," the missionary interrupted.

"It is the same thing," Mongondro went on, "that all the land and all the water, the trees, the fish, and bush and mountains, the sun, the moon, and the stars, were made in six days! No, no. I tell you that in my youth I was an able man, yet did it require me three months for one small canoe. It is a story to frighten children with; but no man can believe it."

"I am a man," the missionary said.

"True, you are a man. But it is not given to my dark understanding to know what you believe."

"I tell you, I do believe that everything was made in six days."

"So you say, so you say," the old cannibal murmured soothingly.

It was not until after John Starhurst and Narau had gone off to bed that Erirola crept into the chief's house, and, after a diplomatic speech, handed the whale tooth to Mongondro.

The old chief held the tooth in his hands for a long time. It was a beautiful tooth, and he yearned for it. Also, he divined the request that must accompany it. "No, no; whale teeth were beautiful," and his mouth watered for it, but he passed it back to Erirola with many apologies.

In the early dawn John Starhurst was afoot, striding along the bush trail in his big leather boots, at his heels the faithful Narau, himself at the heels of a naked guide lent him by Mongondro to show the way to the next village, which was reached by midday. Here a new guide showed the way. A mile in the rear plodded Erirola, the whale tooth in the basket slung on his shoulder. For two days more he brought up the missionary's rear, offering the tooth to the village chiefs. But village after village refused the tooth. It followed so quickly the missionary's advent that they divined the request that would be made, and would have none of it.

They were getting deep into the mountains, and Erirola took a secret trail, cut in ahead of the missionary, and reached the stronghold of the Buli of Gatoka. Now the Buli was unaware of John Starhurst's imminent arrival. Also, the tooth was beautiful—an extraordinary specimen, while the coloring of it was of the rarest order. The tooth was presented publicly. The Buli of Gatoka, seated on his best mat, surrounded by his chief men, three busy fly-brushers at his back, deigned to receive from the hand of his herald the whale tooth presented by Ra Vatu and carried into the mountains by his cousin, Erirola. A clapping of hands went up at the acceptance of the present, the assembled headman, heralds, and fly-brushers crying aloud in chorus:

"A! woi! woi! woi! A! woi! woi! woi! A tabua levu! woi! woi! A madua, madua, madua!"

"Soon will come a man, a white man," Erirola began, after the proper pause. "He is a missionary man, and he will come today. Ra Vatu is pleased to desire his boots. He wishes to present them to his good friend, Mongondro, and it is in his mind to send them with the feet along in them, for Mongondro is an old man and his teeth are not good. Be sure, O Buli, that the feet go along in the boots. As for the rest of him, it may stop here."

The delight in the whale tooth faded out of the Buli's eyes, and he glanced around him dubiously. Yet had he already accepted the tooth.

"A little thing like a missionary does not matter," Erirola prompted.

"No, a little thing like a missionary does not matter," the Buli answered, himself again. "Mongondro shall have the boots. Go, you young men, some three or four of you, and meet the missionary on the trail. Be sure you bring back the boots as well."

"It is too late," said Erirola. "Listen! He comes now."

Breaking through the thicket of brush, John Starhurst, with Narau close on his heels, strode upon the scene. The famous boots, having filled in wading the stream, squirted fine jets of water at every step. Starhurst looked about him with flashing eyes. Upborne by an unwavering trust, untouched by doubt or fear, he exulted in all he saw. He knew that since the beginning of time he was the first white man ever to tread the mountain stronghold of Gatoka.

The grass houses clung to the steep mountain side or overhung the rushing Rewa. On either side towered a mighty precipice. At the best, three hours of sunlight penetrated that narrow gorge. No cocoanuts nor bananas were to be seen, though dense, tropic vegetation overran everything, dripping in airy festoons from the sheer lips of the precipices and running riot in all the crannied ledges. At the far end of the gorge the Rewa leaped eight hundred feet in a single span, while the atmosphere of the rock fortress pulsed to the rhythmic thunder of the fall.

From the Buli's house, John Starhurst saw emerging the Buli and his followers.

"I bring you good tidings," was the missionary's greeting.

"Who has sent you?" the Buli rejoined quietly.

"God."

"It is a new name in Viti Levu," the Buli grinned. "Of what islands, villages, or passes may he be chief?"

"He is the chief over all islands, all villages, all passes," John Starhurst answered solemnly. "He is the Lord over heaven and earth, and I am come to bring His word to you."

"Has he sent whale teeth?" was the insolent query.

"No, but more precious than whale teeth is the—"

"It is the custom, between chiefs, to send whale teeth," the Buli interrupted. "Your chief is either a niggard, or you are a fool, to come empty-handed into the mountains. Behold, a more generous than you is before you."

So saying, he showed the whale tooth he had received from Erirola. Narau groaned.

"It is the whale tooth of Ra Vatu," he whispered to Starhurst. "I know it well. Now are we undone."

"A gracious thing," the missionary answered, passing his hand through his long beard and adjusting his glasses. "Ra Vatu has arranged that we should be well received."

But Narau groaned again, and backed away from the heels he had dogged so faithfully.

"Ra Vatu is soon to become Lotu," Starhurst explained, "and I have come bringing the Lotu to you."

"I want none of your Lotu," said the Buli, proudly. "And it is in my mind that you will be clubbed this day."

The Buli nodded to one of his big mountaineers, who stepped forward, swinging a club. Narau bolted into the nearest house, seeking to hide among the women and mats; but John Starhurst sprang in under the club and threw his arms around his executioner's neck. From this point of vantage he proceeded to argue. He was arguing for his life, and he knew it; but he was neither excited nor afraid.

"It would be an evil thing for you to kill me," he told the man. "I have done you no wrong, nor have I done the Buli wrong."

So well did he cling to the neck of the one man that they dared not strike with their clubs. And he continued to cling and to dispute for his life with those who clamored for his death.

"I am John Starhurst," he went on calmly. "I have labored in Fiji for three years, and I have done it for no profit. I am here among you for good. Why should any man kill me? To kill me will not profit any man."

The Buli stole a look at the whale tooth. He was well paid for the deed.

The missionary was surrounded by a mass of naked savages, all struggling to get at him. The death song, which is the song of the oven, was raised, and his expostulations could no longer be heard. But so cunningly did he twine and wreathe his body about his captor's that the death blow could not be struck. Erirola smiled, and the Buli grew angry.

"Away with you!" he cried. "A nice story to go back to the coast—a dozen of you and one missionary, without weapons, weak as a woman, overcoming all of you."

"Wait, O Buli," John Starhurst called out from the thick of the scuffle, "and I will overcome even you. For my weapons are Truth and Right, and no man can withstand them."

"Come to me, then," the Buli answered, "for my weapon is only a poor miserable club, and, as you say, it cannot withstand you."

The group separated from him, and John Starhurst stood alone, facing the Buli, who was leaning on an enormous, knotted warclub.

"Come to me, missionary man, and overcome me," the Buli challenged.

"Even so will I come to you and overcome you," John Starhurst made answer, first wiping his spectacles and settling them properly, then beginning his advance.

The Buli raised the club and waited.

"In the first place, my death will profit you nothing," began the argument.

"I leave the answer to my club," was the Buli's reply.

And to every point he made the same reply, at the same time watching the missionary closely in order to forestall that cunning run-in under the lifted club. Then, and for the first time, John Starhurst knew that his death was at hand. He made no attempt to run in. Bareheaded, he stood in the sun and prayed aloud—the mysterious figure of the inevitable white man, who, with Bible, bullet, or rum bottle, has confronted the amazed savage in his every stronghold. Even so stood John Starhurst in the rock fortress of the Buli of Gatoka.

"Forgive them, for they know not what they do," he prayed. "O Lord! Have mercy upon Fiji. Have compasssion for Fiji. O Jehovah, hear us for His sake, Thy Son, whom Thou didst give that through Him all men might also become Thy children. From Thee we came, and our mind is that to Thee we may return. The land is dark, O Lord, the land is dark. But Thou art mighty to save. Reach out Thy hand, O Lord, and save Fiji, poor cannibal Fiji."

The Buli grew impatient.

"Now will I answer thee," he muttered, at the same time swinging his club with both hands.

Narau, hiding among the women and the mats, heard the impact of the blow and shuddered. Then the death song arose, and he knew his beloved missionary's body was being dragged to the oven as he heard the words:

"Drag me gently. Drag me gently."

"For I am the champion of my land."

"Give thanks! Give thanks! Give thanks!"

Next, a single voice arose out of the din, asking:

"Where is the brave man?"

A hundred voices bellowed the answer:

"Gone to be dragged into the oven and cooked."

"Where is the coward?" the single voice demanded.

"Gone to report!" the hundred voices bellowed back. "Gone to report! Gone to report!"

Narau groaned in anguish of spirit. The words of the old song were true. He was the coward, and nothing remained to him but to go and report.

a c k n o w l e d g m e n t s

Many people made this anthology.

At Thunder's Mouth Press and Avalon Publishing Group:
Thanks to Susan Reich, Neil Ortenberg, Dan O'Connor, Ghadah Alrawi, Will Balliett, Maria Fernandez, Simon Sullivan, Paul Paddock, Linda Kosarin, David Riedy, Blanca Olivieri and Tracy Armstead.

At Shawneric.com:
Shawneric Hachey handled permissions and photographs.

At the Writing Company:
Thanks to Clint Willis, Taylor Smith, Mark Klimek, March Truedsson, Nat May, Sean Donahue and John Bishop.

Among friends and family:
Thanks to Elisabeth Thomas, who endured months of dinner-table talk about cannibalism, and my parents, who were supportive despite their distaste for the subject matter.

Finally, I am grateful to the writers whose work appears in this book.

Excerpt from *The Unknown Shore* by Patrick O'Brian. Copyright © 1995 by Patrick O'Brian. Reprinted by permission of W.W. Norton & Company. ❖ Excerpt from *Adrift: Seventy-Six Days Lost at Sea* by Steven Callahan. Copyright © 1996 by Steven Callahan. Reprinted by permission of Houghton Mifflin Company. ❖ Excerpt from *The Rivers Ran East* by Leonard Clark. Copryight © 1953 by Funk & Wagnalls Company, renewed © 1981 by Doris Clark, Mary Clark, and Robert Clark. Reprinted by permission of HarperCollins Publishers, New York. ❖ "Once, in the Jungle" by Daniel Zalewski. Copyright © 2001 by Daniel Zalewski. Reprinted with the permission of the New York Times Agency. ❖ Excerpt from *Keep the River on Your Right* by Tobias Schneebaum. Copyright © 1969 by Tobias Schneebaum. Reprinted by permission of Grove/Atlantic Press. ❖ Excerpt from *The Rage to Survive* by Jacques Vignes. Copyright © 1975 by Jacques Vignes. Translation Copyright © 1975 by Milhalo Voukitchevitch. Reprinted by permission of William Morrow and Company, a division of HarperCollins Publishers, New York. ❖ Excerpt from *Shackleton's Forgotten Men: The Untold Tragedy of the* Endurance *Epic*. Copyright © 2000 by Lennard Bickel. Reprinted courtesy of Avalon Publishing Group. ❖ Excerpt from *Elle Dort Dans la Mer (Let Me Survive)* by Louise Longo. Copyright © 1996 by Editions Fixot. Translation Copyright © 1996 by Sheridan House Inc. ❖ Excerpt from *Shipwreck and Adventures of Monsieur Pierre Viaud* by Pierre Viaud, translated and edited by Robin F.A. Fabel. Copyright © 1990 by Robin F.A. Fabel. Reprinted with permission of the University Press of Florida.

b i b l i o g r a p h y

The selections used in this anthology were taken from the editions listed below. In some cases, other editions may be easier to find. Hard-to-find or out-of-print titles often are available through inter-library loan services or through Internet booksellers.

Bickel, Lennard. *Shackleton's Forgotten Men: The Untold Tragedy of the* Endurance *Epic*. New York: Avalon Publishing Group, 2000.

Callahan, Steven. *Adrift: Seventy-Six Days Lost at Sea*. New York: Houghton Mifflin Company, 1986.

Clark, Leonard. *The Rivers Ran East*. San Francisco: Travelers' Tales, 2001.

Cunningham, Richard. *The Place Where the World Ends*. New York: Universal Press Syndicate/Sheed & Ward Publishers, 1973.

Defoe, Daniel. *Robinson Crusoe*. New York: Scribner's, 1983.

Johnson, Kristin, editor. *Unfortunate Immigrants*. Logan, Utah: Utah State University Press, 1996. (For "Across the Plains in the Donner Party" and "A Dangerous Journey".)

London, Jack. "The Whale Tooth". www.literature.org.

Longo, Louise with Marie-Thérèse Cuny. *Let Me Survive: A True Story*. Dobbs Ferry, NY: Sheridan House, Inc., 1996.

Melville, Herman. *Typee*. New York: Dodd, Mead and Company, 1943.

O'Brian, Patrick. *The Unknown Shore*. New York: W.W. Norton, 1995.

Schneebaum, Tobias. *Keep the River on Your Right*. New York: Grove Press, 1969.

Twain, Mark. "Cannibalism in the Cars". From *New Literary History*, 1998, volume 29.

Viaud, Pierre. *Shipwreck and Adventures of Monsieur Pierre Viaud*, translated and edited by Robin F.A. Fabel. Gainesville, FL: University Presses of Florida, 1990.

Vignes, Jacques. *The Rage to Survive*. New York: William Morrow and Company, 1975.

Zalewski, Daniel. "Once in the Jungle". First appeared in *The New York Times Magazine*, March 25, 2001.

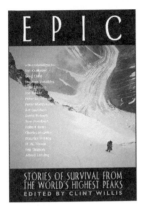

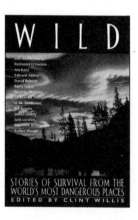

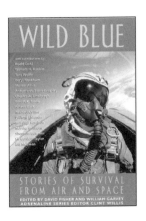
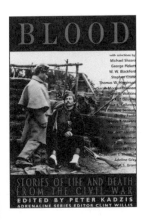
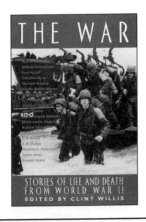

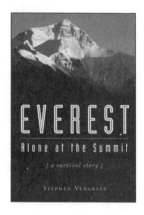
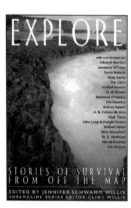
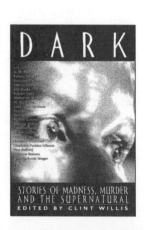